SUCCESSFUL
KEYWORD SEARCHING

SUCCESSFUL
KEYWORD SEARCHING

Initiating Research on Popular Topics Using Electronic Databases

Randall M. MacDonald
and Susan Priest MacDonald

GREENWOOD PRESS
Westport, Connecticut • London

Library of Congress Cataloging-in-Publication Data

MacDonald, Randall M., 1961–
    Successful keyword searching : initiating research on popular topics using electronic
    databases / by Randall M. MacDonald and Susan Priest MacDonald.
        p. cm.
    Includes bibliographical references and index.
    ISBN 0–313–30676–1 (alk. paper)
    1. Database searching. 2. Keyword searching. I. MacDonald, Susan Priest, 1958–
II. Title.
    ZA4460.M33 2001
    025.04—dc21   00–035323

British Library Cataloguing in Publication Data is available.

Library of Congress Catalog Card Number: 00–035323
ISBN: 0–313–30676–1

First published in 2001

Greenwood Press, 88 Post Road West, Westport, CT 06881
An imprint of Greenwood Publishing Group, Inc.
www.greenwood.com

Printed in the United States of America

The paper used in this book complies with the
Permanent Paper Standard issued by the National
Information Standards Organization (Z39.48–1984).

10 9 8 7 6 5 4 3 2

To

Thomas M. Priest
(1926–1999)
and
Odessa Hobby
(1913–1998)

with eternal love and gratitude.

Contents

Health & Wellness

History, Political Science, & Law

Philosophy & Religion

Science & Technology

Social Issues & Sociology

Sports & Recreational Interests

Acknowledgments

This work would not be in your hands without the contributions of a number of media specialists and librarians at all academic levels. We appreciate the assistance of Debby Adams and Barbara Rader at Greenwood Press and the influence of Charles W. Conaway, Gerald Jahoda, and Linda M. Fidler. To our dedicated colleagues at Florida Southern College and Lawton Chiles Middle Academy, we salute your perseverance in bibliographic instruction and education, the results of which are evident in the educational aptitude of your students.

To Malcolm M. MacDonald, Constance Marsh MacDonald, and Betty Jo Priest, thanks for your encouragement and support.

To Sarah Elizabeth MacDonald, we extend our special thanks and a hug for your material assistance and understanding during this project. We love you.

Acknowledgments

Keyword Searching:
An Overview

Electronic databases permeate every facet of modern life. A trip to the bank, grocery store, or driver's license bureau involves some level of interaction with networked electronic storage systems: databases of financial accounts, retail inventories, and government records that support operation and interaction within and between institutions. Most are closed-access databases, accessible only to employees conducting business, although some have a public front end, or interface, which allows access to, and manipulation of, personal account records.

Publicly accessible databases are found in libraries and across the Internet. Online public access catalogs (OPACs), CD-ROMs, and the Internet-accessible World Wide Web provide limitless opportunities for students and researchers to interact with data and to search databases for material of academic or personal interest. Key to retrieving useful information from these databases are a fundamental awareness of how each works and a knowledge of common search techniques and strategies applicable across database types. Searching is also more effective if one knows something about the topic or has access to keywords that help to refine the research process.

CONTROLLED VOCABULARY

OPACs and CD-ROM products are often based on prescribed lists of subject headings that organize databases and speed information retrieval. Subject searching retrieves database records based on terms contained in the subject field of specific records, which may include proper nouns as subjects but not terms found in title, ancillary notes fields, abstracts, or full-text articles. Libraries employ standard subject headings shared across librarianship; the *Sears List of Subject Headings* and *The Library of Congress Subject Headings* (*LCSH*) are used in elementary through university libraries. Although proper nouns are not included in these reference works, they guide researchers to subject terms likely to appear in specific catalogs. They also prescribe current terminology, which affects library cataloging decisions and end-user search success.

Advantages to using controlled vocabularies include internal database consistency, retrieval of precise results, and hierarchical use and display of related and broader search terms. Authority files in OPACs guide users to these additional terms, but authority files are not universally employed or updated to reflect evolving terminologies. In these instances, users must know controlled vocabulary terms prior to searching, an impediment for beginning researchers.

NATURAL LANGUAGE

The use of familiar, informal keywords to search offers an alternative to controlled vocabularies, allowing database searchers to seek information based on natural language or the language of discipline-specific literature. Keyword searching allows the use of terms already known, a clear advantage to beginners. Synonyms for controlled vocabulary terms may be searched with some success, although an important caveat must be observed: various OPACs, CD-ROM indexing programs, and Internet search engines permit searching of dissimilar record fields. What works well in one database will not work as well in every database, and search results may be less precise than when using a controlled vocabulary.

Database features and search techniques are specified in print or electronic documentation, the first place to check for help in formulating a search strategy. Once the parameters of a search process for a unique database have been developed, search terms may be selected from those known or available in a subject guide. OPACs typically permit searching in subject, author, and title fields; many permit searching notes or abstract fields, and most have a keyword search capability that searches every publicly viewable database field. The structure of the database will determine the specific procedure, one that employs single or multiple terms.

SINGLE TERMS

A common beginning search strategy is to type a single word in a catalog text box and perform a keyword search. Depending on the topic, this may provide an acceptable search result, retrieving enough records to satisfy the immediate information need, but not an overwhelming number of records. This may signify the end of a search session, as either a series of call numbers is retrieved, an article is identified, or a series of Web sites is identified for exploration. This process may be repeated often and most effectively if the cumulative results match the research need, but does not take advantage of the search software that most systems utilize, which makes possible simultaneous searching of two or more terms. Search strings of multiple terms are displayed among alphabetical subject or title lists or within blocks of text in articles or Web pages. Often these literal strings are enclosed by a searcher in quotation marks as the search is initiated: "cable television." Results generated through this type of search are more specific than a simple search for *television* and may be made more specific as additional terms are added: "cable television fees."

The rapid proliferation of pages on the World Wide Web and the scope of some OPACs make these searches especially worthwhile. A sample search of this type using the AltaVista search engine (http://www.altavista.com/) during April 2000 retrieved 135,640 matches for "cable television," while the search for "cable television fees" retrieved thirty-six. It would be easier to sort through thirty-six records first to determine whether useful material has been identified and perhaps search using different strings—"fees for cable television" retrieved nine hits—before turning to the insurmountable number of records initially identified.

BOOLEAN SEARCHING

A particular advantage of computer databases over print indexes is the ability to search for information on two or more distinct concepts simultaneously, forming sets of records to satisfy searches. This search technique may be used with controlled vocabulary and natural language terms, although the specifics of searching varies among databases that permit Boolean searching. Central to this search method is the use of "logical operators," which are used to exclude or combine search terms, to narrow or broaden—reduce or increase—the number of records retrieved. Logical operators and their functions include:

and	narrows the search result by eliminating records with only one common term
or	broadens the search result by adding additional term(s)
not	narrows the search result by excluding specific term(s)
with	narrows the search result by eliminating records out of specified ordered proximity to the first term
near	narrows the search result by eliminating records out of specified proximity to the first term

The form of these operators varies somewhat; some databases use *and not* for *not*, use *adj* or *adjacent* for *with*, or use *far* and *before* to specify proximity. The use of parentheses is commonly used to nest search terms to affect the order of operation:

(cable *or* satellite) *and* television

retrieves records on either cable or satellite and then narrows the retrieved results to those with the term television in the record. By comparison, the search:

cable *or* (satellite *and* television)

first retrieves records on satellite and television, and then every record in the database with the term cable is added to search result. The first search is more likely to retrieve relevant records on the topic of cable or satellite television, while the second may include records relating to cable suspension bridges or automotive brake cables, a less specific and less relevant search.

Check the database help file for the best hints on how to apply Boolean or other search techniques and experiment with what provides the most pertinent results. Your proficiency and comfort level will evolve as you search an increasing number of databases, and your willingness to search in various ways will improve the likelihood that retrieved records will be pertinent to your research.

PURPOSE OF THIS BOOK

The keywords in this book constitute a ready-reference guide to research using online public library catalogs (OPACs), CD-ROMs, and the World Wide Web. Keywords and phrases for 144 topics often researched by students in school, public, and college libraries are listed, as are brief selected lists of related organizations, key people in each field of study, and Web sites for additional research. All Web sites and their URLs were current at the time this guide went to press. Covering topics from history and the social sciences to natural sciences and humanities, each topic entry is designed to increase the efficiency of initial research efforts in keyword database searching and help students make effective use of library and Internet resources.

The 144 topics in this volume are divided into nine broad subject areas; Arts and Literature; Business, Communication, and Economics; Culture and Cultural Diversity; Health and Wellness; History, Political Science, and Law; Philosophy and Religion; Science and Technology; Social Issues and Sociology; and Sports and Recreational Interests. The selection of topics was reviewed by school and public librarians to be sure that they reflect the research needs of students and library patrons.

The terms were drawn from hundreds of sources, including reference books and other monographs, journal articles, OPACs and other electronic bibliographic databases, and World Wide Web resources. Chief among initial sources consulted were *The Library of Congress Subject Headings (LCSH), the Sears List of Subject Headings*, and the *Thesaurus of ERIC Descriptors* (both the print version and the electronic search interface, http://ericae.net/scripts/ewiz/amain4.asp). Organizations were identified using the *Encyclopedia of Associations* and Web resources, and contact information can be found therein. Key People were identified using various subject encyclopedias, journal articles, and the Web. This is not a comprehensive list, but these were people that students were most often interested in researching. The Web sites for each topic were selected to present the researcher with additional information about a topic, issue, or event. Where an organization maintains an especially informative Web presence, the organization is not included in the Organizations list but is listed among Web sites.

We have sought to present a balanced view of topics and terminology, although inclusion of terms in this volume does not imply endorsement of their use in the literature or public discourse. While it is not possible to include every term related to a topic, the terms included are common in the dialogue of each topic, are used to define parameters for research, inquiry, and discussion, and will serve as a starting point for your developing research.

ARTS & LITERATURE

Architecture

Keywords may be searched singly or in combination with other words using Boolean operators *and*, *or*, or *not*.

acoustics
Aegean
aesthetics
Americans with Disabilities Act (ADA)
applied arts
arch
architect
architectural
   elements
   history
   programming
   symbolism
arts and crafts movement
atrium
baroque
basilican
Bauhaus
building
   contractor
   design
   plans
   types
buttress
Byzantine
cantilever
cast iron
ceiling
cement
Chicago School
Christian architecture
church
classical
Colonial

column
computer-assisted design (CAD)
construction
   industry
   materials
Corinthian
design requirements
dome
Doric
drafting
engineering drawing
English Baroque architecture
facade
facility planning
federal
flying buttress
French Baroque architecture
gargoyle
Georgian
Gothic
Greece
Greek architecture
Greek Revival
housing
indigenous architecture
interior design
Ionic
Islamic architecture
Italian Baroque architecture
Italian Renaissance architecture
landscape architecture
lighting design
masonry

mass housing
minaret
modern architecture
modernism
modular
monument
neo-classicism
planned communities
post-and-lintel
postmodern

precast concrete
reinforced concrete
Renaissance
rococo
Roman architecture
Romanesque
spatial relationship
symmetry
timber frame
Victorian

ORGANIZATIONS

American Institute of Architects (AIA)
American Institute of Building Design (AIBD)
American Underground-Construction Association (AUA)
Association for Bridge Construction and Design (ABCD)
Association for Computer-Aided Design in Architecture (ACADIA)
Center for Architectural and Design Research
Council on Tall Buildings and Urban Habitat (CTBUH)
Design-Build Institute of America (DBIA)
Design Management Institute (DMI)
École des Beaux-Arts, Paris
Institute for the Human Environment (IHE)
National Organization of Minority Architects (NOMA)
Residential Space Planners International (RSPI)
Society of American Registered Architects (SARA)

KEY PEOPLE

Fifteenth Century
Alberti, Leon Battista
Brunelleschi, Filippo

Sixteenth Century
Michelangelo
Palladio, Andrea

Seventeenth Century
Bernini, Gianlorenzo
Perrault, Claude
Wren, Christopher

Eighteenth Century
Churriguera, José
Jefferson, Thomas

Nineteenth Century
Latrobe, Benjamin Henry

Paxton, Joseph
Richardson, Henry Hobson
Soane, John
Sullivan, Louis Henry

Twentieth Century
Aalto, Alvar
Behrens, Peter
Gaudí, Antonio
Gropius, Walter
Johnson, Philip C.
Kahn, Louis I.
Le Corbusier (Charles Edouard
    Jeanneret)
Mies van der Rohe, Ludwig
Pei, I. M. (Ieoh Ming)
Saarinen, Eero
Wright, Frank Lloyd

WEB SITES

American Architectural Foundation (AAF)
http://www.amerarchfoundation.com/

archINFORM
http://www.archINFORM.de/

Architecture Research Institute
http://www.architect.org/

Cyburbia
http://www.arch.buffalo.edu/pairc/

Frank Lloyd Wright Foundation
http://www.franklloydwright.org/

Society of Architectural Historians
http://www.sah.org/

Dance

Keywords may be searched singly or in combination with other words using Boolean operators *and, or,* or *not.*

aerobic dance
ballet
ballroom
belly dancing
break dancing
cha-cha
Charleston
chassé
choreography
dance therapy
dancers
exotic dancing
folk dancing
fox-trot
hula dancing
hustle
ice dancing
jitterbug
line dancing
macarena
mambo

Maypole dance
meringue
modern dance
music therapy
paso dobla
pointe
polka
popular dance
prom
promenade
rumba
samba
Spanish dance
square dancing
swing
tango
tap dancing
The Twist
Viennese waltz
waltz
western dance
wheelchair dance

ORGANIZATIONS

American Academy of Kinesiology and Physical Education (AAPE)
American Dance Festival (ADF)
Ballet Theatre Foundation (BTF)
Basque Educational Organization (BEO)
British Ballet Organization
Canadian Association for Health, Physical Education, Recreation and Dance (CAHPERD)
Chinese American Arts Council (CAAC)
Hispanic Organization of Latin Actors (HOLA)

International Association for Creative Dance (IACD)
International Council for Traditional Music (ICTM)
International Cultural Centers for Youth (ICCY)
International Dance Council (IDC)
International Theatre Institute of the United States (ITI/US)
National Foundation for Advancement in the Arts (NFAA)
National Square Dance Convention (NSDC)
U.S. Association for Blind Athletes (USABA)

KEY PEOPLE

Ballet
Baryshnikov, Mikhail
Diaghilev, Sergei
Farrell, Suzanne
Kirstein, Lincoln
Nijinsky, Vaslav
Nureyev, Rudolf
Pavlova, Anna
Tallchief, Maria
Ulanova, Galina

Ballroom & Tap Dancing
Astaire, Fred
Castle, Irene
Castle, Vernon
Charisse, Cyd
Hines, Gregory Oliver
Kelly, Gene
Murray, Arthur
Rogers, Ginger

Choreographers
Ailey, Alvin
Balanchine, George
Berkeley, Busby
Cage, John
Cunningham, Merce
de Mille, Agnes

Dunham, Katherine
Fosse, Bob
Graham, Martha
Joffrey, Robert
Robbins, Jerome
St. Denis, Ruth

Modern Dance
Baker, Josephine
Duncan, Isadora
Fuller, Loie
Holm, Hanya
Morris, Mark
Taeuber-Arp, Sophie
Tharp, Twyla
Wigman, Mary

Musicals
Gershwin, George
Hammerstein, Oscar
Lerner, Alan J.
Loewe, Frederick
Martin, Mary
Rogers, Richard
Schlemmer, Oskar
Sondheim, Stephen
Webber, Andrew Lloyd

WEB SITES

Dance Professionals Associates
http://www.dancepro.com/

Imperial Society of Teachers of Dancing (ISTD)
http://www.istd.org/

National Dance Association
http://www.aahperd.org/nda/nda-main.html

WebSurfer's Guide to Ballroom Dance
http://come.to/ballroomdance

Fashion

Keywords may be searched singly or in combination with other words using Boolean operators *and, or,* or *not.*

apparel
attire
belt
bodice
cape
casual
chemise
cloak
clothing
costume
costume design
cotton
design
dress
dress design
fabric
fad
fashion
   designer
   industry
   photography
formal
garment
garment industry
garter
girdle
gown
hat
kilt
loincloth
minimalism
natural fibers

needle trades
New Look
nylon
ornamentation
pattern making
rayon
retail
robe
seamstress
sewing
shirt
shoes
skirt
sleeves
stockings
stole
storage
style
suit
synthetic
tailor
tailoring
textiles
toga
traditional dress
trousers
tunic
uniform
vesture
weave
Western dress
wrap

ORGANIZATIONS

American Apparel Manufacturers Association (AAMA)
American Fashion Association (AFA)
Association of Image Consultants International (AICI)
Association of Total Fashion (ATF)
Chartered Society of Designers (CSD)
Council of Fashion Designers of America (CFDA)
The Fashion Association (TFA)
International Association of Clothing Designers and Executives (IACDE)
National Association of Fashion and Accessory Designers (NAFAD)
National Customers Association (NCA)
National Fashion Accessories Association (NFAA)
Neckwear Association of America (NAA)
Organization for Black Designers (OBD)

KEY PEOPLE

Austria
Carnegie, Hattie

Belgium
Claiborne, Liz
von Fürstenberg, Diane

China
Lee, Ming Cho

France
Chanel, Coco
Dior, Christian
Erté
Givenchy, Hubert de
Lagerfeld, Karl
Picasso, Paloma
St. Laurent, Yves

Italy
Armani, Giorgio
Gigli, Romeo
Versace, Gianni

United Kingdom
Ashley, Laura
Westwood, Vivienne

United States
Abboud, Joseph
Hilfiger, Tommy
Johnson, Betsey
Karan, Donna
Klein, Calvin
Lauren, Ralph
Mackie, Bob

WEB SITES

The Costume Gallery
http://www.costumegallery.com/

Inside Fashion
http://www.insidefashion.com/

Moda Italia Net
http://www.modaitalia.net/

Style Experts
http://www.stylexperts.com/

Language & Languages

Keywords may be searched singly or in combination with other words using Boolean operators *and*, *or*, or *not*.

abstract reasoning
accent
accusative
acoustic phonetics
acquisition
adjectives
adverbs
African languages
Afro-Asiatic
alternative communication
American Indian languages
American sign language
Anatolian
anthropology
applied linguistics
Arabic
argot
articulation
articulatory phonetics
artificial language
artificial speech
assimilation
Athapaskan
audio-lingual
auditory
   perception
   phonetics
   training
augmentative communication
aural language
Australian Aboriginal languages
Austro Asiatic languages
Austronesian

auxiliary language
Baltic
Basque
bidialectalism
bilingual
bilingual education
bilingualism
body language
borrowing
branch
British
Burushaski
business English
case
Caucasian
Caucasian languages
Celtic
Chad languages
child language
classical languages
classification
classification system
clichés
clicks
code
code switching
coherence
cohesion
communication
communication disorder
communicative competence
composition
comprehension

computational linguistics
connected discourse
consonant
construction
context
contrastive linguistics
conversational language
Coptic
Creole
culture
dead language
debate
definition
delayed speech
descriptive linguistics
development
diachronic linguistics
dialect
dialogue
dictation
diction
dictionary
discourse
dramatics
Dravidian languages
Dutch
dyslexia
Ebonics
echolalia
editing
encoding
English
enrichment
error analysis
Eskimo Aleut languages
ESL
Esperanto
etymology
evolution
expression
expressive language
extinct
family
figurative
Finno-Ugric
first-language
fluency
foreign language

formation
French
Gaelic
Gallic
gender bias
genetic classification
German
glottochronology
grammar
grammatic
Great Vowel Shift
Greek
handwriting
hearing impairment
Hebrew
Hindi
Hittite
ideography
idioms
immersion
impairment
indigenous
Indo European languages
Indo-Aryan
Indo-European
Indo-Iranian
inflection
interlanguage
international trade
interpretation
invented spelling
Iranian
Italic
Japanese
jargon
Kartvelian
Khoisan
Korean
language
  acquisition
  classification
  disabilities
  dominance
  family
  levels
  maintenance
  proficiency
  purist

requirements
rhythm
role
skill
skill attrition
styles
test
Latin
learning
  disability
  process
  strategy
lexicology
lexicon
linguistic
  borrowing
  competence
  difficulty
  input
  performance
  reconstruction
  theory
linguistics
listening
listening comprehension
literary device
literature
machine translation
Malayo Polynesian languages
Mandarin Chinese
meaning
metalinguistics
Middle English
modern language
monolingualism
morpheme
morphology
Morse code
multilingualism
mutual intelligibility
Na-Dené
narration
native speaker
native tongue
natural language
neurolinguistics
neurological impairment
Niger-Congo

Nilo-Saharan
nominative
non-English speaking
norm
North American English
noun
obscenity
official language
Old English
onomastics
oral language
origin
Paleo-Siberian languages
paragraph
part of speech
pathology
patterns
perceptual impairment
phonemics
phonetic alphabet
phonetic analysis
phonetics
phonology
phrases
pidgin
poetry
polyglot
Portuguese
pragmatics
prefix
prescriptive linguistics
processing
proficiency
programming language
pronoun
pronunciation
prose
Proto-Indo-European
protolanguage
psycholinguistics
reading
  comprehension
  difficulty
  process
  program
  writing relationship
receptive language
regional dialect

rhetoric
rhythm
role
Romance
root word
Russian
Sanskrit
Scandinavian
second language
second language learning
self-expression
semantics
semiotics
sentence
sentence diagramming
sexism
sibilant
sign language
signaling
Sino Tibetan languages
slang
Slavic languages
social dialect
social group
sociolect
sociolinguistics
sociology
sounds
Spanish
speech
   act
   communication
   compression
   habit
   impairment
   skill
spelling
spoken language
standard spoken usage
standardization
storytelling
structural analysis
structure
style
subfamily
suffix

Swahili
Swedish
symbolism
syntax
tagmemic analysis
technology
thesaurus
thought transfer
tone language
Tourett's Syndrome
tradition
transfer
translation
Tungusic
Turkic
typological classification
typology
understanding
unwritten language
Uralic
Uralic Altaic languages
urban language
usage
Uto-Aztecan
variation
verbal
   ability
   communication
   language
   stimulus
verbs
Vietnamese
visual language learning
visual perception
vocabulary
vocal
vowel
whole language
word
   frequency
   order
   stem
writing
writing processes
writing system
written language

ORGANIZATIONS

College Language Association (CLA)
Conference on English Education (CEE)
Junior Classical League (JCL)
Linguistic Society of America (LSA)
Modern Greek Studies Association (MGSA)
National Committee for Latin and Greek (NCLG)
National Communication Association (NCA)
National Council of State Supervisors of Foreign Languages (NCSSFL)

KEY PEOPLE

Linguists & Authors
Austin, John Langshaw
Bakhtin, Mikhail Mikhailovich
Bloomfield, Leonard
Boas, Franz
Burke, Kenneth
Burritt, Elihu
Carnap, Rudolf
Chomsky, Noam Avram
Chrysippus
Derrida, Jacques

Hobbes, Thomas
Jacobson, Roman
Kroeber, Alfred Louis
Locke, John
Mead, George Herbert
Moore, George Edward
Ricoeur, Paul
Sapir, Edward
Skinner, Burrhus Frederic
Whorf, Benjamin Lee

WEB SITES

American Speech-Language-Hearing Association (ASHA)
http://www.asha.org/

Ethnologue
http://www.sil.org/ethnologue/

European Centre for Modern Languages
http://culture.coe.fr/ecml/

Human-Languages Page (HLP)
http://www.june29.com/HLP/

The LINGUIST List
http://www.linguistlist.org/

Modern Language Association of America (MLA)
http://www.mla.org/

Literature

Keywords may be searched singly or in combination with other words using Boolean operators *and*, *or*, or *not*.

adolescent literature
aesthetics
African American literature
American Indian literature
American literature
anthology
authors
autobiographies
ballads
Baroque literature
Biblical literature
bibliography
bibliometrics
bibliotherapy
biographies
Bloomsbury group
book reviews
characterization
children's literature
classical literature
comedy
coming-of-age
communication
composition
content analysis
creative writing
critical reading
critical response
Dada deconstruction
descriptive writing
dialogue
diary
didacticism

discourse
drama
epic
epilogue
ethnicity
ex-patriot writers
expressionism
fable
feminist interpretation
fiction
figurative language
first person
folktales
foreshadowing
gender
genre
glossary
haiku
Harlem Renaissance
hero
heroine
humanism
humor
interpretation
irony
Italian literature
jazz age
journalism
language
language arts
Latin American literature
Latino literature
letters

literary
- criticism
- device
- history
- style

literature appreciation
medieval literature
metalinguistics
modernism
monologue
mood
motif
multiculturalism
mythology
narration
naturalism
neo-classicism
nonfiction
North American literature
novel
novella
ode
Old English literature
oral interpretation
oral tradition
parallelism
parody
pastoral literature
playwright
poet
poetry
point of view
postmodernism
prose
protagonist
psychological interpretation
queer

reader
reader response
reading
realism
recreational reading
reception
Renaissance literature
rhetoric
rhetorical criticism
romanticism
saga
satire
science fiction
script
serial memoirs
serial novels
setting
short story
skit
slave narrative
sonnet
storytelling
style
stylistic devices
symbolism
tale
theme
third person
tragedy
trope
urban myth
Victorian literature
voice
whole language
world literature
writing
young adult literature

ORGANIZATIONS

Association of Literary Scholars and Critics (ALSC)
Chautauqua Literary and Scientific Circle (CLSC)
International Federation for Modern Languages and Literatures
International Federation of the Societies of Classical Studies (FIEC)
International Institute for Children's Literature and Reading Research (IICLRR)
Modern Language Association of America (MLA)
Society for the Study of Midwestern Literature (SSML)

KEY PEOPLE

Sixteenth Century
Marlowe, Christopher
Shakespeare, William

Seventeenth Century
Bradstreet, Anne
Dryden, John

Eighteenth Century
Goldsmith, Oliver
Wheatley, Phyllis
Wollstonecraft, Mary

Nineteenth Century
Alcott, Louisa May
Austen, Jane
Brontë, Charlotte
Brontë, Emily
Browning, Elizabeth Barrett
Chopin, Kate
Crane, Stephen
Cushing, Eliza Lanesford
Dickens, Charles
Dickinson, Emily
Dostoyevsky, Feodor Mikhailovich
Dumas, Alexandre
Eliot, George
Hardy, Thomas
Hawthorne, Nathaniel
Hugo, Victor
Melville, Herman
Poe, Edgar Allan
Shelley, Mary Wollstonecraft
Stevenson, Robert Louis
Stowe, Harriet Beecher
Tolstoy, Leo
Turgenev, Ivan
Twain, Mark (Samuel L. Clemens)
Wilde, Oscar

Twentieth Century
Albee, Edward
Allen, Paula Gunn
Allende, Isabel
Anaya, Rudolfo
Angelou, Maya
Barrie, James Matthew
Beauvoir, Simone de
Beckett, Samuel
Bishop, Elizabeth

Brecht, Bertolt
Brooks, Gwendolyn
Buck, Pearl S.
Burke, Kenneth
Cather, Willa
Christie, Agatha
Colette
Coward, Noel
Ellison, Ralph
Fitzgerald, F. Scott
Frank, Anne
Genet, Jean
Giraudoux, Jean
Hansberry, Lorraine
Hellman, Lillian
Hemingway, Ernest
Hurston, Zora Neale
Huxley, Aldous
Inge, William
Irving, John
Joyce, James
Kipling, Rudyard
Lawrence, D. H.
Lessing, Doris
Mansfield, Katherine
Marquez, Gabriel Garcia
Maugham, Somerset
Millay, Edna St. Vincent
Miller, Arthur
Montgomery, Lucy Maud
Moore, Marianne
Morrison, Toni
Mourning Dove (Christine
　　Quintasket)
Nabokov, Vladimir
Orwell, George
Potter, Beatrix
Rand, Ayn
Rich, Adrienne
Sartre, Jean-Paul
Shaw, George Bernard
Solzhenitsyn, Alexander Isayevich
Stein, Gertrude
Steinbeck, John
Walker, Alice
Wilder, Laura Ingalls
Wilder, Thornton

Williams, Tennessee   Woolf, Virginia
Wilson, August   Wright, Richard

WEB SITES

American Literature Association
http://humanities.byu.edu/ALA/

Folger Shakespeare Library
http://www.folger.edu/

Great Books Foundation
http://www.greatbooks.org/

Malaspina Great Books Home Page
http://www.mala.bc.ca/~mcneil/

Modern Language Association of America (MLA)
http://www.mla.org/

National Center for Children's Illustrated Literature
http://www.nccil.org/

Motion Pictures/Film

Keywords may be searched singly or in combination with other words using Boolean operators *and*, *or*, or *not*.

acting
action
actuality film
adaptations
additional credits
animation
animatronics
art
   cinema
   form
   house
aspect ratio
audience
auteur theory
auteurism
automated dialogue replacement
   (ADR)
best boy
black and white films
blacklist
blockbuster
body double
bootleg
box office
broadcast industry
cable television
camera
camp
caption
cartoon
casting
casting couch
cell

celluloid
censorship
choreography
chronophotographic camera
cinema
CinemaScope
cinematographer
cinematography
cinema verité
colorization
comedy
coming-of-age
commercial
composers
composition
copyright
costumes
cut
dailies
dialogue
distribution
documentary
Dolby sound
dolly
drawings
dubbing
editing
exhibition
experimentation
expressionism
fantasy
feature film
feature-length film

film
   criticism
   festivals
   industry
   library
   loop
   noir
   production
   stock
   study
   title
filmmaker
filmography
filmstrip
foreign language film
foreign rights
frames per second
free cinema movement
French new wave
gaffe
gaffer
gangster genre
gel
gelatin emulsion
genre
grip
hand-tint
hollow drum
Hollywood studio system
horror
illusion
image
IMAX
independent producer
indie
information industry
instructional film
Kinemacolor
kinescope recording
Kinetograph
Kinetoscope
lead
lens
lighting
literary style
looping
love scene
love story

made for television
makeup
marquee
matinee idol
McCarthyism
melodrama
motion-picture devices
motion-picture studio
movie
movie star
moving-image
multiplex
multiple images
multireel
musicals
musical score
mystery
narrative
narrator
neorealism
newsreel
nickelodeon theater
nonfiction genre
one-reeler
Panavision
perception
perimeter
persistence of vision
photographic equipment
photography
poetic realism
pornography
positive afterimage
positive film
postproduction
preproduction
preservation
print preview
producer
Production Code (1930)
projector
propaganda
pyrotechnics
rating system
raw stock
realism
recording
reel

release date
repetitive film showings
restoration
romance
running time
rushes
scene
score
screening
screenplay
screenwriter
screenwriters guild
sequence
set
shots
shutter
silent film
silent movie
single-concept film
sleeper
slotted disk
slow motion
snuff films
sound film
sound track
special effects
standard reel
star vehicle
still photography
stills
storyboard
story films
storytelling

stunt
stuntperson
subtitles
supporting role
surrealism
surround sound
synchronous sound
synthetic plastic
take
talkies
technical
Technicolor
technology
television
theater
theater arts
Theatre Optique
3-D (three-dimensionality)
transparency
trick photography
union
vaudeville
videocassette recorder (VCR)
videotape
villian
vision concept
visual medium
visual phenomenon
Vitascope
Western
wide screen
zoetrope
zoom
zoopraxiscope

ORGANIZATIONS

Academy of Television Arts and Sciences (ATAS)
Academy of Motion Picture Sciences
Alliance of Motion Picture and Television Producers (AMPTP)
American Cinema Editors (ACE)
American Film Marketing Association (AFMA)
Black Stuntmen's Association (BSA)
Hollywood Radio and Television Society (HRTS)
House Un-American Activities Commission (HUAC)
Motion Picture Association of America (MPAA)
Motion Picture Patents Company (MPPC)
National Cable Television Association (NCTA)
Production Code Administration
Screen Actors Guild

Stuntmen's Association of Motion Pictures (SAMP)
Stuntwomen's Association of Motion Pictures (SWAMP)
Women in Film (WIF)

KEY PEOPLE

Actors
Astaire, Fred
Beatty, Warren
Bogart, Humphrey
Chaplin, Charles Spencer, "Charlie"
Chevalier, Maurice
Cosby, Bill
Eastwood, Clint
Fields, W. C.
Fishburne, Laurence
Freeman, Morgan
Gable, William Clark
Garbo, Greta
Gish, Lillian
Goldberg, Whoopi
Grant, Cary
Hepburn, Audrey
Hepburn, Katherine
Hope, Bob
Jones, James Earl
Keaton, Buster
Kelly, Gene
Laughton, Charles
Lugosi, Bela
McQueen, Butterfly
Monroe, Marilyn
Newman, Paul
Nicholson, Jack
Olivier, Laurence
Pickford, Mary
Poitier, Sidney
Robinson, Edward G.
Sinatra, Francis Albert
Streep, Meryl
Taylor, Elizabeth
Tracy, Spencer
Tyson, Cicely
Wayne, John
Wong, Anna May

**Directors, Producers, &
Choreographers**
Allen, Woody
Altman, Robert

Armstrong, Gillian
Bergman, Ingmar
Berkeley, Busby
Buñuel, Luis
Burton, Tim
Cameron, James
Campion, Jane
Capra, Frank
Coen, Ethan
Coen, Joel
Coppola, Francis Ford
De Mille, Cecil B.
Dickerson, Ernest
Disney, Walt
Eastwood, Clint
Eisenstein, Sergei Mikhailovich
Fassbinder, Rainer Werner
Fellini, Federico
Flaherty, Robert Joseph
Ford, John
Fosse, Bob
Goldwyn, Samuel
Grierson, John
Griffith, D. W.
Hitchcock, Alfred
Houston, John
Howard, Ron
Hughes, Howard Robard
Hughes, John
Jarman, Derek
Kubrick, Stanley
Kurosawa, Akira
Lang, Fritz
Lean, David
Lee, Spike
Lubitsch, Ernst
Lucas, George
Méliès, Georges
Merchant, James
Minelli, Vincent
Minghella, Anthony
Preminger, Otto Ludwig
Redford, Robert

Renoir, Jean
Riefenstahl, Leni
Sanders-Brahms, Helma
Scorsese, Martin
Searles, John
Sennett, Mack
Spielberg, Steven
Stone, Oliver
Truffaut, François
Valdez, Luis
Wang, Wayne
Welles, Orson
Wyler, William

Inventors
Armat, Thomas
De Forest, Lee
Dickson, William Kennedy Laurie
Eastman, George
Edison, Thomas Alva
Jenkins, Charles Francis
Lumière, Auguste
Lumière, Louis
Marey, Étienne-Jules
Muybridge, Eadweard
Paul, Robert W.
Porter, Edwin S.
Reynaud, Émile

WEB SITES

The Academy of Motion Picture Arts and Sciences (AMPAS)
http://www.oscars.org/

American Society of Composers, Authors and Publishers (ASCAP)
http://www.ascap.com/

Celluloid Links
http://www.selfworth.com/

Mandy's International Film and TV Directory
http://www.mandy.com/

Taos Talking Picture Festival
http://www.taosnet.com/ttpix/

Music

Keywords may be searched singly or in combination with other words using Boolean operators *and*, *or*, or *not*.

a cappella
acoustical environment
aerophone
American music
applied music
audience
auditorium
ballads
bands
beat
bel canto
big bands
blues
CD (compact disc)
chant
choral music
chordophone
chords
classical music
communication
composers
composition
concerts
country and western
crooning
dance
disco
discography
electrophone
ensembles
ethnobeat
expressionism
fine arts

folk music
funk
fusion
gangster rap
gospel
Grammys
gramophone
grunge
harmony
hip-hop
honky-tonk
idiophone
improvisation
instrumentation
instruments
interval
jazz
Kodaly method
lyrics
melody
membranophone
meter
minstrel song
MTV
music
    appreciation
    industry
    reading
    therapy
musical
    comedy
    instruments
    score

musician
new wave
opera
orchestra
orchestration
Orff method
performers
pitch
pop music
popular music
punk rock
rap
reggae
rhythm
rhythm and blues
rock and roll
rockabilly
salsa

scales
sheet music
singing
soloist
songs
sound
stage
Suzuki method
swing
synthesizer
tempo
therapy
timbre
tone
vocal music
vocals
western music
worldbeat

ORGANIZATIONS

Academy of Country Music (ACM)
American Disc Jockey Association (ADJA)
American Music Conference (AMC)
Association for Technology in Music Instruction (ATMI)
Country Radio Broadcasters (CRB)
Creative Musicians Coalition (CMC)
Gospel Music Association (GMA)
Independent Music Association (IMA)
International Alliance of Women in Music (IAWM)
International Bluegrass Music Association (IBMA)
International Rock 'n' Roll Music Association (IRMA)
Karaoke International Sing-Along Association (KISA)
Music Women International
National Academy of Television Arts and Sciences (NATAS)
National Music Council (NMC)
National Piano Foundation (NPF)
Recording Industry Association of America (RIAA)
Small Independent Record Manufacturers Association (SIRMA)
Songwriters and Lyricists Club (SLC)

KEY PEOPLE

Classical
Bach, Johann Sebastian
Beethoven, Ludwig van
Chopin Frédéric
Gould, Glenn
Haydn, Franz Joseph
Mahler, Gustav

Mozart, Wolfgang Amadeus
Praetorius, Michael
Schubert, Franz Peter
Schumann, Clara Josephine
Schumann, Robert Alexander
Strauss, Johann, Jr.
Stravinsky, Igor Fedorovich

Country & Western
Cash, Johnny
Cline, Patsy
Lynn, Loretta
Parton, Dolly
Williams, Hank

Folk & Traditional
Baez, Joan
Dylan, Bob
Foster, Stephen Collins
Guthrie, Woodrow Wilson, "Woody"
Joplin, Scott
Ladysmith Black Mambazo
Lomax, Alan
Mitchell, Joni
Seeger, Pete
Simon, Paul
Work, John

Jazz
Adderley, Julian, "Cannonball"
Adderley, Nat
Brubeck, Dave
Calloway, Cab
Coltrane, John
Davis, Miles
Ellington, Edward Kennedy, "Duke"
Fitzgerald, Ella
Gillespie, Dizzy
Monk, Thelonious
Parker, Charlie
Vaughan, Sarah
Waller, Thomas Wright, "Fats"

Opera
Anderson, Marian
Callas, Maria (Maria Anna Sofia Cecilia
    Kalogeropoulos)
Capobianco, Gigi
Caruso, Enrico
Domingo, Placido
Monteverdi, Claudio
Norman, Jessye
Pavarotti, Luciano
Robeson, Paul
Sills, Beverly
Verdi, Giuseppe
Webber, Andrew Lloyd

Orchestral & Big Bands
Babbitt, Milton
Barber, Samuel
Berlin, Irving
Bernstein, Leonard
Cage, John
Carter, Elliott Cook, Jr.
Cole, Nat King
Copland, Aaron
Fiedler, Arthur
Gershwin, George
Gershwin, Ira
Goodman, Benny
Hammerstein, Oscar
Horne, Lena
Porter, Cole Albert
Puente, Tito
Rodgers, Richard
Sessions, Roger Huntington
Sinatra, Frank
Sondheim, Stephen
Sousa, John Philip
Streisand, Barbra
Zander, Benjamin
Ziegfeld, Florenz

Pop
Madonna
Jackson, Michael

Rap & Hip-Hop
Beastie Boys
Dr. Dre
Hill, Lauryn
Kid Rock
Latifah, Queen
Loc, Tone
Puff Daddy
Rhymes, Busta
Shakur, Tupac
Smith, Will
Snoop Doggy Dogg

Rhythm & Blues
Armstrong, Louis Daniel
Charles, Ray
Franklin, Aretha
Gaye, Marvin
Gordy, Berry
Holiday, Billie
Johnson, Robert

Jones, Quincy
King, B. B.
Smith, Bessie
Waters, Muddy

Rock & Roll
The Beatles
Berry, Chuck
Bowie, David
Brown, James
Diddley, Bo
Haley, Bill

Hendrix, Jimi
Holly, Buddy
Jackson, Michael
Joplin, Janis
Led Zeppelin
Little Richard
Madonna
Presley, Elvis Aaron
The Rolling Stones
Santana, Carlos
Turner, Tina
Valens, Ritchie

WEB SITES

American Musicological Society
http://www.sas.upenn.edu/music/ams/

Bate Collection of Musical Instruments
http://www.ashmol.ox.ac.uk/BCMIPage.html

Experience Music Project
http://www.experience.org/hilow.asp

Rock and Roll Hall of Fame and Museum
http://www.rockhall.com

Southern Music Network
http://www.southernmusic.net/

This Day in Rock & Roll History
http://www.arrowfm.com/cgi/history.pl

Whim 'n Rhythm
http://www.yale.edu/whim/

Mythology & Folklore

Keywords may be searched singly or in combination with other words using Boolean operators *and*, *or*, or *not*.

American Indian literature
anecdotes
animism
anthropology
antiquities
archetype
art
ballads
beliefs
Celtic
classical
classical literature
communication
cosmogonic
cosmography
creation
cross-cultural studies
culture
cultural hero
customs
dance
deity
demigod
Doric
drama
end of the world
epic
eschatologic
ethnography
ethnology
expression
fable
fairy tale

fertility
flood
folk
   culture
   drama
   god
   goddess
   heritage
   hero
   heroine
   music
   tale
history
journey
idol
interpretation
language
legend
linguistics
linguists
literature
logic
meaning
medieval literature
memory
metamorphosis
moon
muse
music
mythos
narrative
nature
Norse

oral tradition
original sin
origins
phenomenon
poetry
popular lore
preanimism
proverbs
purification
rebirth
reincarnation
religion
ritual
sacrifice
semantics

spiritual
stars
storytelling
superstition
symbolism
tales
theology
time sequence
tradition
trials
twins
universals
urban legend
witch
world-parent myth

ORGANIZATIONS

American Folklore Society (AFS)
American Hungarian Folklore Centrum (AHFC)
Center for Neo-Hellenic Studies (CNHS)
Center for Southern Folklore (CSF)
English Folklore Society
Folklore Fellows
International Society for Folk-Narrative Research
International Union of Anthropological and Ethnological Sciences (IUAES)
Irish Texts Society (ITS)
Maine Folklife Center (MFC)
National Association of Black Storytellers (NABS)
Popular Culture Association (PCA)
Rural Cultural Heritage Society
Society for the Study of Myth and Tradition (SSMT)
Tennessee Folklore Society (TFS)

KEY PEOPLE

France
Durkheim, Émile
Leenhardt, Maurice
Lévi-Strauss, Claude
Lévy-Bruhl, Lucien
Ricoeur, Paul
Sébillot, Paul

Germany
Dähnhardt, Oskar
Grimm, Jacob
Grimm, Wilhelm
Jung, Carl Gustav
Müller, Friedrich Max
Schmidt, Wilhelm

Italy
Vico, Giovanni Battista

United Kingdom
Aubrey, John
Lang, Andrew
Tylor, Edward Burnett

United States
Boas, Franz
Campbell, Joseph
Eliade, Mircea
Frazer, James
Jakobson, Roman
Thompson, Stith

WEB SITES

Bulfinch's Mythology
http://www.webcom.com/shownet/medea/bulfinch/welcome.html

Encyclopedia Mythica
http://www.pantheon.org/mythica/

Legends
http://www.legends.dm.net/

Myth and Legend from Ancient Times to the Space Age
http://pibweb.it.nwu.edu/~pib/myth.htm

UCLA Folklore and Mythology Archives
http://www.humnet.ucla.edu/humnet/folklore/archives/

Poetry

Keywords may be searched singly or in combination with other words using Boolean operators *and*, *or*, or *not*.

alliteration
anapest
antithesis
avant-garde
ballad
bard
Beat generation
Beowulf
Black Mountain poets
blank verse
choral speaking
chronicles
coffeehouse
composition
couplets
creation
creative writing
dactyl
descriptive writing
drama
elegy
enjamb
epic
epigram
epistle
epitaphs
expression
fiction
folk culture
foot
form
fragment
free voice

genre
haiku
Harlem Renaissance
hexameter
humanism
hymn
iambic
    pentameter
    tetrameter
    trimeter
imagery
imagism
inscription
internal rhyme
irregular form
letters
limerick
lines
lyric poetry
metaphor
meter
metrical writings
minnesinger
modernism
monologue
motif
muse
narrative
New York School
octave
ode
onomatopoeia
open verse

parallelism
pastoral literature
pattern
prose
prosody
psalm
pun
punctuation
quatrain
queer poetics
rebel poets
rhyme scheme
rhythm
riddle
San Francisco Renaissance

short meter
song
sonnet
spontaneous composition
stanza
syllabic
syllable
tale
tanka
terza rima
themes
tragedy
trochee
troubadour
verse
versification

ORGANIZATIONS

Association for Applied Poetry (AAP)
European Association for the Promotion of Poetry (EAPP)
Modern Poetry Association (MPA)
National Association for Poetry Therapy (NAPT)
Science Fiction Poetry Association (SFPA)
Shakespeare Association of America (SAA)

KEY PEOPLE

Seventh Century B.C.
Sappho

Fifth Century B.C.
Pindar

First Century B.C.
Horace (Quintus Horatius Flaccus)
Virgil (Publius Vergilius Maro)

First Century
Martial (Marcus Valerius Martialis)
Ovid (Publius Ovidius Naso)

Fourteenth Century
Chaucer, Geoffrey
Petrarch (Francesco Petrarca)

Sixteenth Century
Spenser, Edmund

Seventeenth Century
Donne, John
Herbert, George
Jonson, Ben
Milton, John
Shakespeare, William

Eighteenth Century
Burns, Robert
Cowper, William
Gay, John
Pope, Alexander

Nineteenth Century
Arnold, Matthew
Blake, William
Browning, Elizabeth Barrett
Browning, Robert
Byron, George Gordon Noel, Lord
Clare, John
Coleridge, Samuel Taylor
Dickinson, Emily
Emerson, Ralph Waldo
Goethe, Johann Wolfgang von
Hardy, Thomas
Heine, Heinrich
Keats, John
Longfellow, Henry Wadsworth
Martí, José Julian
Poe, Edgar Allan

Shelley, Percy Bysshe
Stevenson, Robert Louis
Tennyson, Alfred, Lord
Thoreau, Henry David
Whitman, Walt
Whittier, John Greenleaf
Wordsworth, William

Twentieth Century
Auden, W. H.
Baraka, Amiri (LeRoi Jones)
Bly, Robert
Borges, Jorge Luis
Brooke, Rupert
Brooks, Gwendolyn
Burroughs, William S.
Cocteau, Jean
cummings, e. e.
Dove, Rita Frances
Eliot, T. S.
Ferlinghetti, Lawrence
Frost, Robert
Gibran, Kahlil
Ginsberg, Allen

Guest, Edgar A.
Heaney, Seamus
Hughes, Langston
Kerouac, Jack
Kipling, Rudyard
Lawrence, D. H.
Levertov, Denise
Lowell, Robert
Millay, Edna St. Vincent
Momaday, N. Scott
Nash, Ogden
Neruda, Pablo (Neftali Ricardo Reyes
    y Basoalto)
Parker, Dorothy
Plath, Sylvia
Pound, Ezra Loomis
Rexroth, Kenneth
Rich, Adrienne
Sandburg, Carl
Stein, Gertrude
Stevens, Wallace
Thomas, Dylan
Williams, William Carlos
Yeats, William Butler

WEB SITES

The Academy of American Poets
http://www.poets.org/

International Poetry Hall of Fame
http://www.poets.com/

Introduction to Latin Epic
http://www.sjc.ox.ac.uk/users/gorney/

Poetry Daily
http://www.poems.com/

Snally Gaster's African American Phat Library
http://www.math.buffalo.edu/~sww/Snally_Gaster.html

Theater

Keywords may be searched singly or in combination with other words using Boolean operators *and, or,* or *not.*

acoustical environment
acting
acting styles
action art
actors
actresses
ad-lib
amateur companies
apron
arena stage
art
artistic interpretation
arts centers
audiences
audition
auditorium
avant-garde
back drop
backstage
balcony
blackface
blocking
box office
bridge
Broadway
burlesque
cabaret
cable
callback
cast
catwalk
character analysis
characterization

children's theater
choral speaking
choreography
chorus line
circus acts
collabration
comedy
companies
condenser microphone
costume plot
costumes
creative dramatics
creative expression
cultural activity
curtain call
curtain line
cyclorama
dance
dance drama
designer
deus ex machina
dialogue
director
drama
drama workshop
dramatic play
dramatic presentation
dramatics
dresser
dress rehearsal
electrician
Elizabethan
folk culture

folk drama
footlights
fourth wall
front of house
front row
Globe
Greek tragedy
green room
grip
hero
house
improvisation
ingenue
intermission
interpretation
juvenile lead
kabuki
lead
libretto
lighting
lighting designer
lines
literary devices
live performance
luminaire
mark
mask
matinee
medley
melodrama
mime
mixing desk
monologue
Mr. Sands
multiplexer
music
musical
    comedy
    director
musician
narration
off book
off-Broadway
offstage
on book
one-act
opening night
opera

operetta
oral interpretation
orchestra
pageantry
pantomime
parallel play
performance
performer
performing arts
pit
play
playbill
playwright
playwriting
plot
poetry
potboiler
prepared improvisation
presentation
problem play
producer
production techniques
professional theater
profile
prompt
promptbook
property
props
proscenium
prose
protagonist
puppetry
quick change
radio play
reader's theater
read-through
realism
reenactment
rehearsal
reprise
Restoration drama
review
revival
revolve
revue
rig
role
rostrum

run
run-through
scaffold
scenery
script
self-expression
set
set design
set dressing
shadow plays
sightline
singer
singing
skills
skits
soap operas
soliloquy
sound effects
special effects
speech communication
spontaneity
spotlight
stage
   business
   crew

direction-hand
   manager
standing room
stock
story theater
storyboard
street theater
summer stock
tableau
tension
theater
   arts
   in-the-round
theatrical
thrust stage
ticket
touring company
tragedy
trap
troupe
understudy
vaudeville
villain
voice projection
wardrobe
wings

ORGANIZATIONS

American Alliance for Theatre and Education (AATE)
Americans for the Arts
Association for the Preservation and Presentation of the Arts (APPA)
Association of Speech and Drama
Dance Masters of America (DMA)
Drama League
Institute of Outdoor Drama (IOD)
International Council—National Academy of Television Arts and Sciences
   (IC/NATAS)
Lincoln Center for the Performing Arts (LCPA)
National Association of Performing Arts Managers and Agents (NAPAMA)
National Coalition of Arts Therapy Associations (NCATA)
National Collegiate Players (NCP)
National Foundation for Advancement in the Arts (NFAA)
National Society of Arts and Letters (NSAL)
National Theatre Conference (NTC)
Performing and Visual Arts Society (PAVAS)
Performing Arts Foundation (PAF)
Wolf Trap Foundation for the Performing Arts (WTFPA)
World Modeling Association (WMA)

KEY PEOPLE

Actors
Alexander, Jane
Auberjonois, René
Baranski, Christine
Battle, Hinton
Bedford, Brian
Buckley, Betty
Burton, Richard
Channing, Carol
Cronyn, Hume
Dewhurst, Colleen
Gallagher, Helen
Harris, Julie
Harris, Rosemary
Hines, Gregory
Ivey, Judith
Kelly, Patsy
Kurtz, Swoosie
Lansbury, Angela
Leighton, Margaret
Lopez, Priscilla
Lupone, Patti
Martin, Mary
Merman, Ethel
Nype, Russell
Pleasance, Donald
Price, Jonathan
Rivera, Chita
Robards, Jason, Jr.
Stapleton, Maureen
Sternhagen, Francis
Tandy, Jessica
Verdon, Gwen
Worth, Irene

Directors & Producers
Abbott, George
Anthony, Joseph
Hall, Peter
Kazan, Elia
Mason, Marshall W.
Quintero, José
Richards, Lloyd

Saks, Gene
Schneider, Alan
Stevens, Roger L.

Musical Directors, Composers, & Producers
Bennett, Michael
Champion, Gower
Coleman, Cy
Ebb, Fred
Fosse, Bob
Gershwin, George
Gilbert and Sullivan
Hammerstein, Oscar
Kander, John
MacIntosh, Cameron
Nunn, Trevor
Porter, Cole
Rodgers, Richard
Sondheim, Stephen
Tune, Tommy
Webber, Andrew Lloyd

Playwrights & Authors
Abbott, George
Albee, Edward
Chekhov, Anton
Comden, Betty
Green, Adolph
Hellman, Lillian
Ibsen, Henrik
Lapine, James
Mamet, David
Miller, Arthur
O'Neill, Eugene
Osborne, John
Rabe, David
Shaffer, Peter
Shepard, Sam
Simon, Neil
Stewart, Michael
Wheeler, Hugh
Williams, Tennessee
Wilson, August

WEB SITES

Association of Performing Arts Presenters
http://www.artspresenters.org/

International Society for the Performing Arts (ISPA)
http://ispa.org/

The Livingroom.org
http://livingroom.org/

Playbill On-Line
http://www1.playbill.com/

Shakespeare's Globe Theatre
http://shakespeares-globe.org/

Society of American Fight Directors (SAFD)
http://www.safd.org/

Stomp
http://www.stomponline.com/

Theatre Development Fund
http://www.tdf.org/

United Stage of America
http://unitedstage.com/usa/index.html

Visual Arts

Keywords may be searched singly or in combination with other words using Boolean operators *and, or,* or *not.*

abstract expressionism
acetate
acrylic paint
aesthetics
allegory
architect
architecture
art
    appreciation
    center
    collecting
    criticism
    deco
    exhibitions
    galleries
    history
    nouveau
    products
    schools
    supplies
    theory
    therapy
assemblage
asymmetry
audience response
avant-garde
baroque
bas-relief
bronze
ceramics
classicism
collage
color

color wheel
commercial art
composition
conceptual art
crafts
creative art
creativity
critical viewing
cubism
Dada
decorative arts
drawing
etching
expression
expressionism
fauvism
fine arts
folk art
fresco
futurism
glassblowing
gothic
graphic art
handicrafts
Hellenistic
Hudson River school
iconography
illustration
impressionism
industrial design
landscape architecture
landscape painting
leatherwork

lithography
manuscripts and illumination
maquette
marble
mask
minimalism
mixed media
model
modernism
motif
mural
museum
naturalism
neo-classicism
neo-impressionism
New Deal art
Northern Renaissance
oil paint
painting
pastel
patronage
perspective
photo-realism
photography
pigment
plaster
plastics
point of view
polychrome
pop art
popular culture
portrait
Postimpressionism

prints
realism
rehabilitation
relief
Renaissance
reproductions
restoration
rococo
romanticism
scale
scenography
sculpture
seascape
self-portrait
serigraph
serigraphy
silk screen
still life
Stone Age
storyboard
studio art
study of art
surrealism
symbolism
symmetry
tableau
tempera
textiles
themes in art
therapeutic recreation
trompe-l'oeil
visual literacy
watercolor

ORGANIZATIONS

Allied Artists of America (AAA)
American Abstract Artists (AAA)
Archives of American Art (AAA)
College Art Association (CAA)
National Academy of Design (NAD)
National Academy of Western Art (NAWA)
National Center of Afro-American Artists (NCAAA)
National Oil and Acrylic Painters Society (NOAPS)
National Society of Artists (NSA)
Saving and Preserving Arts and Cultural Environments (SPACES)
Society of American Historical Artists (SAHA)
U.S. Society for Education through Art (USSEA)
Visual Artists and Galleries Association (VAGA)

KEY PEOPLE

Fifteenth Century
Angelico, Fra
Botticelli, Sandro
Donatello (Donato di Niccolò di Betto
    Bardi)
Leonardo da Vinci
Verrocchio, Andrea del

Sixteenth Century
Burgkmair, Hans the Elder
Correggio (Antonio Allegri)
Dürer, Albrecht
Michelangelo
Raphael (Raffaello Sanzio)
Titian (Tiziano Vecellio)

Seventeenth Century
Bernini, Gianlorenzo (Giovanni
    Lorenzo)
Caravaggio (Michelangelo Merisi)
Rembrandt
Rubens, Peter Paul
Vermeer, Jan

Eighteenth Century
Blake, William
Boucher, François
Goya, Francisco

Nineteenth Century
Alma-Tadema, Lawrence
Beardsley, Aubrey
Cassatt, Mary
Cézanne, Paul
Constable, John
Courbet, Gustave
Daumier, Honoré
Degas, Edgar
Gauguin, Paul
Homer, Winslow
Manet, Édouard
Monet, Claude
Moreau, Gustave
Morris, William
Pissarro, Camille
Renoir, Pierre Auguste
Rossetti, Dante Gabriel
Sargent, John Singer
Seurat, Georges
Toulouse-Lautrec, Henri de

van Gogh, Vincent
Whistler, James Abbott McNeill

Twentieth Century
Aalto, Alvar
Adams, Ansel
Andre, Carl
Botero, Fernando
Brancusi, Constantin
Bubley, Esther
Cadmus, Paul
Carr, Emily
Chagall, Marc
Cunningham, Imogen
Dalí, Salvador
De Kooning, Willem
Duchamp, Marcel
Eisenstaedt, Alfred
Finster, Howard
Frankenthaler, Helen
Fuller, Richard Buckminster
Geddes, Anne
Giacometti, Alberto
Guimard, Hector
Harvey, Larry
Hockney, David
Hopper, Edward
Johns, Jasper
Kahlo, Frida
Klee, Paul
Kollwitz, Käthe
Lichtenstein, Roy
Lin, Maya
Luck, Sid
Magritte, René
Mapplethorpe, Robert
Marisol
Marsh, Bruce
Matisse, Henri
Max, Peter
Miró, Joan
Moses, Grandma (Anna Mary Robert-
    son Moses)
Motherwell, Robert
Neel, Alice
Neiman, LeRoy
Noguchi, Isamu
O'Keeffe, Georgia

Owen III, Ben
Owens, Vernon
Parrish, Maxfield
Picasso, Pablo
Pollock, Jackson
Ray, Man
Rivera, Diego
Rockwell, Norman

Rothko, Mark
Rousseau, Henri
Schiele, Egon
Sherman, Cindy
Suddeth, Jimmy Lee
Sudduth, Billie Ruth
Uelsmann, Jerry
Warhol, Andy
Wright, Frank Lloyd

WEB SITES

Americans for the Arts
http://www.artsusa.org/

Metropolitan Museum of Art
http://www.metmuseum.org/

Musée du Louvre
http://www.louvre.fr/

The Museum of Modern Art (MoMA)
http://www.moma.org/

National Endowment for the Arts
http://arts.endow.gov/

National Gallery of Art
http://www.nga.gov/

Smithsonian American Art Museum
http://www.nmaa.si.edu/

The State Hermitage Museum
http://www.hermitagemuseum.org/

Whitney Museum of American Art
http://www.echonyc.com/~whitney/

BUSINESS, COMMUNICATION, & ECONOMICS

Business

Keywords may be searched singly or in combination with other words using Boolean operators *and*, *or*, or *not*.

accounting
administration
agribusiness
banking
board of directors
business
   administration
   cycles
   ethics
   etiquette
   law
   to business
capital investment
chief executive officer (CEO)
chief financial officer (CFO)
Clayton Antitrust Act (1914)
commerce
commercial enterprise
commodity
competition
conglomerate
consumer
consumption
convenience stores
corporation
downsizing
economic
   analysis
   climate
   impact
economics
economy
electronic markets

electronic resources
employee assistance program (EAP)
employee surveillance
employment
employment qualifications
enterprise
entrepreneurship
ethnic entrepreneurship
exports
factory
finance
Fortune 500
franchising
free enterprise system
free market
global marketplace
goods and services
human resource management (HRM)
imports
inflation
international trade
interstate commerce
inventory
inventory control
investments
job skills
job training
just-in-time inventory
labor
   economics
   relations
   statistics
   union

management
manufacturing
market analysis
market share
marketing
mass marketing
merchandising
merchant
merger
migrant worker
monopoly
National Fair Labor Standards Act
      (1938)
nonprofit business
office
   machines
   practice
   space
privatization
production
public administration
public policy

real estate
regulation
research and development (R&D)
retail
self-employment
service company
shopping malls
small business management
sole proprietorship
statistical analysis
statistics
stock market
stocks
strategic planning
supply and demand
Taft-Hartley Act (1947)
target marketing
taxation
trade
unemployment compensation
unemployment insurance
unskilled labor
workers' compensation

ORGANIZATIONS

Association of Home-Based Businesses
Employment and Training Administration (ETA)
Equal Employment Opportunity Commission (EEOC)
Federal Trade Commission (FTC)
Financial Executives Institute (FEI)
Institute of Certified Professional Business Consultants (ICPBC)
Institute of Risk Management (IRM)
International Federation of Business and Professional Women (IFBPW)
Occupational Safety and Health Administration (OSHA)
Society of Research Administrators (SRA)
U.S. Department of Labor

KEY PEOPLE

Seventeenth Century
Sydenham, Thomas
Eighteenth Century
Arkwright, Richard
Cort, Henry
Franklin, Benjamin
Musgrove, Mary (Cousaponokeesa)
Newbery, John
Wedgwood, Josiah
Nineteenth Century
Astor, John Jacob

Benz, Karl
Bessemer, Henry
Catchpole, Margaret
Deere, John
Eastman, George
Goodyear, Charles
Lowell, Francis Cabot
Mason, Bridget, "Biddy"
Morgan, John Pierpont
Prout, Mary
Pullman, George Mortimer

Rhodes, Cecil John
Singer, Isaac M.
Stanford, Amasa Leland
Stanford, Jane Lathrop
Vanderbilt, Cornelius
Ward, Aaron Montgomery
Woolworth, Frank Winfield

Twentieth Century
Arden, Elizabeth
Bartz, Carol
Beach, Sylvia Woodbridge
Bernays, Edward L.
Boeing, William Edward
Buffett, Warren
Carnegie, Andrew
Chanel, Coco
Chrysler, Walter Percy
Citroën, André-Gustave
du Pont, Pierre Samuel
Duke, James Buchanan
Ellison, Lawrence J.
Firestone, Harvey Samuel
Follett, Mary Parker
Forbes, Malcolm
Ford, Henry

Gates, Bill
Goldsmith, James Michael
Greenspan, Alan
Honda, Soichiro
Johnson, John Harold
Lopker, Pamela Meyer
Maxwell, Robert Ian
Mitchell, Wesley
Morgan, Garrett A.
Murdoch, Rupert
Nader, Ralph
Penney, J. C.
Perot, Henry Ross
Rockefeller, John D.
Rodale, Ardath
Sopwith, Thomas Octave Murdoch
Stonesifer, Patty
Toth, Sylvia
Trump, Donald
Walker, Maggie Lena
Walker, Sarah Breedlove McWilliams
Wallington, Patricia
Wells, Mary Georgene
Weston, Elsie V.
Zimmerman, Marie

WEB SITES

Better Business Bureau
http://www.bbb.org/

ComFind Internet Business Directory
http://www.comfind.com/

Hoover's Online
http://www.hoovers.com/

Internet Advertising Resource Guide
http://www.admedia.org/

National Alliance of Business
http://www.nab.com/

U.S. Chamber of Commerce
http://www.uschamber.org/

Communication

Keywords may be searched singly or in combination with other words using Boolean operators *and*, *or*, or *not*.

advertising
advertising campaign
airtime
airwaves
announcement
announcer
article
biography
broadcast industry
broadcast journalism
bulletin
bulletin board
byline
cable broadcasting
caption
censorship
chat room
closed caption
commentary
commercials
Communications Act (1934)
copy
copyright
corporate communication
correspondence
debate
digest
documentary
editor
editorial
electronic communication
electronic mail (e-mail)
fax machine (facsimile)

focus group
forecast
freedom of speech
frequency
hard copy
headline
hyperlink
industry
informant
information management
Internet
interview
investigative reporting
journalism
journals
link
magazine
mass communication
mass media
media research
memoir
moderator
Morse code
multimedia
news media
newsreel
news reporting
nonverbal communication
obituary
op-ed
opinion piece
oral
photo agency

photo-essay
photography
photo journalism
press
   conference
   corps
   kit
print
producer
propaganda
public opinion
public relations
public service announcement
publishing
quotes
radio
retraction
rhetoric
satellite broadcast
search engine
selective dissemination of information
   (SDI)
shortwave
sign language
software
sound

sound bite
speech
spokesperson
sportscaster
synthetic speech
tape
telecast
telecommunications
Telecommunications Act (1996)
telecommunications device for the
   deaf (TDD)
telefacsimile
telegraph
telemarketing
telephone
teletypewriter (TTY)
television
text
video
visual communication
Voce of America
voice mail
voice recognition
wire service
World Wide Web
writing

ORGANIZATIONS

Advanced Research Projects Agency (ARPA)
American Telephone and Telegraph Company (AT&T)
Federal Communications Commission (FCC)
International Advertising Association (IAA)
International Business Machines Company (IBM)
International Radio and Television Society Foundation (IRTSF)
International Television Association (ITVA)
Microsoft
National Cable Television Association (NCTA)
National Federation of Community Broadcasters (NFCB)
National Public Radio (NPR)
Reuters
Satellite Broadcasting and Communications Association (SBCA)

KEY PEOPLE

Communication Device Inventors
Bell, Alexander Graham
Braille, Louis
Cooke, William Fothergill
Farnsworth, Philo T.

Getty, Jean Paul
Gray, Elisha
Gutenberg, Johann
Hearst, William Randolph
Land, Edwin

Marconi, Guglielmo

Maxwell, James Clerk

Morse, Samuel F. B.

Wheatstone, Charles

Zworykin, Vladimir

Berners-Lee, Tim

Case, Steve

Cerf, Vinton

Gates, Bill

Gilster, Paul

Internet

Andreeson, Marc

WEB SITES

Advanced Communications Technology Satellite (ACTS)
http://acts.lerc.nasa.gov/

Center for Information and Communications Technology Research (CICTR)
http://cictr.ee.psu.edu/

Intercultural Research Index
http://www.stephweb.com/forum/index.htm

Internet Communications Corporation (INCC)
http://www.incc.net/

Society for Technical Communication (STC)
http://www.stc-va.org/

Economics

Keywords may be searched singly or in combination with other words using Boolean operators *and*, *or*, or *not*.

accounting
area studies
assets
banking
boomtown
budget
business
   cycles
   finance
   loans
capital
capitalism
change strategy
classical economics
commerce
communism
community change
community development
competition
consumer
consumer economics
consumption
context
cooperative
cost
   -effectiveness
   index
   -of-living index
country studies
credit
currency
debt
deficit

deflation
depression
developed nations
developing nations
diminishing returns
domestic monetary policy
econometrics
economic
   effects
   growth
   impact
   status
employment patterns
enterprise
entrepreneur
entrepreneurship
exchange
expenditures
exports
Federal Reserve Act (1913)
finance
finance reform
financial theory
fiscal capacity
fiscal policy
fluctuations
franchising
free
   enterprise system
   market
   trade
G7
goods

Great Depression
gross national product (GNP)
growth
human capital
imports
income
industrialization
industry studies
inflation
input-output analysis
interest
interest rates
international economics
international trade
investment
investor
Keynesian economics
labor
    economics
    force development
    utilization
laissez-faire
living standards
macroeconomics
market
marketing
Marxism
mathematics
mercantile
microeconomics
monetary policy
monetary systems
money market
money supply
national debt
natural resources
operations research
ownership
physiocracy
population
precious metals
price determination

price theory
private sector
privatization
production
productivity
profit margin
property
prosperity
public sector
purchasing power
quality of life
quantitative economic methods
recession
resources
retail
retrenchment
revenue
rural economics
self-employment
socialism
socioeconomic influences
socioeconomic status (SES)
spending
stagflation
structural unemployment
supply and demand
supply-side economics
surplus
sustainable development
taxation
technological change
technology transfer
trade
trade balance
unemployment
urban and regional economics
urban studies
usury
wages
wealth
welfare programs
welfare state

ORGANIZATIONS

American Association of Enterprise Zones
American Bankers Association (ABA)
American Economic Association (AEA)
American Finance Association (AFA)
Association for Social Economics (ASE)

Brookings Institution (BI)
Committee on the Status of Women in the Economics Profession (CSWEP)
Community Economics, Inc. (CEI)
Council of Professional Associations on Federal Statistics (COPAFS)
Financial Executives Institute (FEI)
National Association of Forensic Economics (NAFE)
Society for Advancement of Management (SAM)
U.S. Federal Reserve Board (FRB)

KEY PEOPLE

Austria
Menger, Karl

France
Bastiat, Frederic
Quesnay, François
Say, Jean Baptiste

Germany
Marx, Karl

United Kingdom
Hayek, Friedrich
Hume, David
Keynes, John Maynard

Malthus, Thomas Robert
Marshall, Alfred
Mill, John Stuart
Pigou, Arthur
Ricardo, David
Smith, Adam

United States
Friedman, Milton
Greenspan, Alan
Lucas, Robert E., Jr.
Merton, Robert C.
Scholes, Myron S.

WEB SITES

Board of Governors of the Federal Reserve System
http://www.bog.frb.fed.us/

Dr. Ed Yardeni's Economics Network
http://www.yardeni.com/

Financial Forecast Center
http://www.neatideas.com/economics/

International Political Economy Network
http://csf.colorado.edu/ipe/

The Public Debt Online
http://www.publicdebt.treas.gov/opd/opd.htm

What Is a Dollar Worth?
http://woodrow.mpls.frb.fed.us/economy/calc/cpihome.html

Employment

Keywords may be searched singly or in combination with other words using Boolean operators *and*, *or*, or *not*.

absenteeism
affirmative action
applicants
application
arbitration
bargaining
benefits
career
   change
   guidance
   ladder
collective bargaining
comparable worth
competitive selection
continuing education
counseling
curriculum vita
demography
dislocated workers
dismissal
early retirement
economic impact
economics
educational background
electronic monitoring
employability
employable skills
employees
employer
employer-employee relationship
employment
   counselors
   forecasts

   potential
   programs
   qualifications
   referral services
entry level
equal opportunities
fringe benefits
full-time equivalency (FTE)
glass ceiling
headhunters
income
interview
job
   analysis
   bank
   experience
   holding patterns
   search
   sharing
   skills
labor
   dispute
   economics
   force
   market
   utilization
layoff
loyalty oath
management
marketable skills
maternity leave
midlife transition
migrant workers

mobility
negotiation
nontraditional occupation
occupational safety and health
occupational tests
occupations
on-the-job training (OJT)
outplacement service
part-time employment
personnel
personnel file
personnel selection
placement
prior experience
probationary period
professional
promotion
qualifications
quality of working life
recruitment
reduction in force
reentry
rehire
representation

résumé
salary wage differentials
seasonal employment
self-employment
seniority
severance pay
supervisors
supply and demand
surveillance
tenure
training
turnover
underemployment
unemployment
uniform
union
vacancy
vocation
work
    -day
    environment
working hours
youth employment

ORGANIZATIONS

Association of Career Management Firms International (AOCMFI)
Employment and Training Service Center (ETSC)
Employment Management Association (EMA)
Equal Rights Advocates (ERA)
Human Resources Development Institute (HRDI)
International City/County Management Association (ICMA)
International Downtown Association (IDA)
National Alliance of Business (NAB)
National Association of Private Industry Councils (NAPIC)
National Child Labor Committee (NCLC)
National Employment and Training Association (NETA)
National Employment Law Project (NELP)
Organization Development Institute
Senior Community Service Employment Program (SCSEP)
Society for Human Resource Management (SHRM)

WEB SITES

Career Paths Online
http://careerpathsonline.com/

CareerWeb
http://www.cweb.com/

Industrial Workers of the World
http://iww.org/

International Salary Calculator
http://www2.homefair.com/calc/salcalc.html

National Jobs for All Coalition
http://www.njfac.org/

Washington Jobs.com
http://www.washingtonpost.com/parachute

Mass Media

Keywords may be searched singly or in combination with other words using Boolean operators *and*, *or*, or *not*.

advertising
affiliates
amplitude modulation (AM)
audience analysis
audience response
audiences
audio signal
audiovisual signal
Big Three
broadcast
    communication
    industry
    journalism
broadcasting
cable television
commercials
communications
communications media
deregulation
documentary
editorial
entertainment
expository writing
fairness doctrine
feature stories
film industry
films
freedom of information
freedom of speech
frequency modulation (FM)
headlines
high-definition television (HDTV)
information

dissemination
industry
sources
utilization
Internet
journalism
mass
    communications
    media effects
    media use
media
media selection
multimedia
narrowcasting
national broadcasting network
network
news
    journalism
    media
    reporting
    -writing
newscast
newscaster
newspaper
nonprint media
pay-per-view
periodicals
photography
photojournalism
press
prime time
printed materials
programming

propaganda
public opinion
publicity
publishing
radio
radio station
radiotelegraph
receivers
regulation
satellites
serials
signal
station
stereo

talk show
technology
Telecommunications Act (1996)
television
   newsmagazine
   viewing
transmission
ultrahigh frequency (UHF)
v-chip
very high frequency (VHF)
videocassette player
videocassette recorder (VCR)
Wireless Act (1910)
World Wide Web

ORGANIZATIONS

Asian American Journalists Association (AAJA)
Association for Education in Journalism and Mass Communication (AEJMC)
Association for Women in Communications
Association of Schools of Journalism and Mass Communication (ASJMC)
Canadian Association of Journalists (CAJ)
Carol Burnett Fund for Responsible Journalism (CBFRJ)
Catholic Media Council (CAMECO)
Center for Communication Programs
College of Wireless and Engineering
Committee on Public Doublespeak (CPD)
Computer Press Association (CPA)
Federal Communications Commission (FCC)
Foreign Press Association (FPA)
Instructional Telecommunications Council (ITC)
International Communication Association (ICA)
International Federation of Journalists (IFJ)
International Organization of Journalists (IOJ)
Media Network (MN)
Media Watch (MW)
National Association of College Broadcasters (NACB)
National Association of Hispanic Journalists (NAHJ)
National Association of Media Women (NAMW)
National Communication Association (NCA)
National Federation of Community Broadcasters (NFCB)
National Newspaper Foundation (NNF)
Newsletter Publishers Association (NPA)
Project Censored (PC)
Public Media Center (PMC)
Religious Speech Communication Association (RSCA)
United Nations Correspondents Association (UNCA)
Westinghouse Electric Corporation
Women's Institute for Freedom of the Press (WIFP)

KEY PEOPLE

Broadcast Journalists & Newscasters
Bradley, Ed
Brokaw, Tom
Couric, Katie
Cronkite, Walter
Imus, Don
Jennings, Peter
Lunden, Joan
Pauley, Jane
Randall, Eunice
Rather, Dan
Russell, Lynne
Sawyer, Diane
Sierens, Gayle
Wallace, Mike
Walters, Barbara
Woodruff, Judy

Inventors
De Forest, Lee
Farnsworth, Philo Taylor
Fessenden, Reginald
Morse, Samuel Finley Breese
Nipkow, Paul Gottlieb

Journalists & Photojournalists
Aker, Dee
Ashmore, Harry Scott
Bennett, James Gordon, Jr.
Bierce, Ambrose Gwinett
Brownmiller, Susan

Buckley, William F., Jr.
Cary, Mary Ann Shadd
Creel, George
Frissell, Toni
Fuller, Margaret
Higgins, Marguerite Hall
Lippmann, Walter
Mencken, Henry Louis
Murrow, Edward R.
Opperman, Pauline Frederick
Pyle, Ernie
Rowan, Carl Thomas
Safire, William
Snow, Edgar
Thompson, Dorothy
Wells, Fay Gillis
Wells-Barnett, Ida Bell

Publishers
Beach, Moses Yale
Bowles, Samuel
Dana, Charles Anderson
Daniels, Josephus
Graham, Katharine Meyer
Greeley, Horace
Hearst, William Randolph
Hobby, Oveta Culp
Murdoch, Rupert
Pulitzer, Joseph
Sulzberger, Arthur Ochs

WEB SITES

AJR NewsLink
http://ajr.newslink.org/

FACSNET
http://www.facsnet.org/

Fairness and Accuracy in Reporting
http://www.fair.org/

FCC V-Chip Page
http://www.fcc.gov/vchip/

International Consortium of Investigative Journalists (ICIJ)
http://www.icij.org/

Library of American Broadcasting
http://www.lib.umd.edu/UMCP/LAB/

Media History Project
http://www.mediahistory.com/

Museum of Television and Radio
http://www.mtr.org/

National Coalition on TV Violence
http://www.nctvv.org/

National Press Photographers Association (NPPA)
http://sunsite.unc.edu/nppa/

Nielsen Media Research
http://www.nielsenmedia.com/

Taxation

Keywords may be searched singly or in combination with other words using Boolean operators *and*, *or*, or *not*.

ad valorem
alternative minimum tax (AMT)
appraisal
assessed valuation
asset
audit
capital
categorical aid
chattel
collection
contribution
corporate welfare
credit
deductible
deduction
delinquency
depreciation
earned income
economic impact
equalization aid
estate planning
exemption
expenditure
filing
finance reform
financial need
fiscal capacity
flat-rate tax
full state funding
gain
gross income
homestead exemption
income

Individual Taxpayer Identification
    Number (ITIN)
interest
levy
liability
lien
loss
millage
ownership
penalty
property
    appraisal
    tax
public policy
qualified
rate
real property
resource allocation
revenue sharing
Social Security Number (SSN)
stadium tax
standard deduction
student financial aid
tax
    allocation
    bracket
    credit
    deduction
    rate
    reform
trust fund
value-added tax (VAT)
withhold

ORGANIZATIONS

American Institute of Certified Public Accountants (AICPA)
American Society of Tax Professionals (ASTP)
CPA Associates International (CPAAI)
Grassroots Against Government-Mandated Entertainment
National Accounting and Finance Council (NAFC)
National Homeowners Association (NHA)
National Society of Public Accountants (NSPA)
Penny Resistance (PR)
Tax Analysts
Tax Council (TC)

KEY PEOPLE

Borah, William Edgar
Bristow, Benjamin Helm
Bryan, William Jennings
Chase, Samuel
Forbes, Steve
George, Henry
Harlan, John Marshall

Hull, Cordell
Johnson, Lyndon Baines
Mellon, Andrew William
Seligman, Edwin Robert Anderson
Taft, William Howard
Warren, Earl

WEB SITES

1040.com: Tax Information for Everyone
http://www.1040.com/

Citizens for an Alternative Tax System
http://www.cats.org/

Internet Law Library Taxation
http://www.lawguru.com/ilawlib/109.htm

Internal Revenue Service
http://www.irs.ustreas.gov/

Stadium Issues
http://www.resonator.com/stad/s_issues.htm

Tax Help Online
http://www.taxhelponline.com/

CULTURE & CULTURAL DIVERSITY

African American Studies

Keywords may be searched singly or in combination with other words using Boolean operators *and*, *or*, or *not*.

Africa
African
   American
   American Vernacular English (AAVE)
   culture
   history
   studies
affirmative action
Afro-American
American blacks
ancestry
apartheid
black
   culture
   dialects
   History Month
   literature
   middle class
   Muslim
   nationalism
   power
Brown v. Board of Education of Topeka (1954)
Caribbean
civil rights
   Act (1965)
   movement
color consciousness
discrimination
Ebonics

Emancipation Proclamation (1863)
equality
ethnic studies
Fifteenth Amendment, Constitution of the United States (1870)
gospel
Gullah
Harlem Renaissance
integration
jazz
Kwanzaa
Martin Luther King Jr. Day
multiculturalism
Negro
nonviolent protest
race relations
racial disparity
racial identification
racism
ragtime
rap
Reconstruction
rhythm and blues
segregation
self-determination
slavery
Thirteenth Amendment, Constitution of the United States (1865)
Underground Railroad
underrepresentation
Voting Rights Act (1965)

ORGANIZATIONS

African Methodist Episcopal Church
Black Panther Party
Congressional Black Caucus
Council for African American Progress (CAAP)
Nation of Islam
National Association for the Advancement of Colored People (NAACP)
National Association of African American Studies (NAAAS)
National Baptist Convention, U.S.A.
National Council for Black Studies (NCBS)
Rainbow Coalition
Tuskegee Airmen
United Negro Improvement Association (UNIA)
Urban League

KEY PEOPLE

The Arts
Angelou, Maya
Baldwin, James Arthur
Bannister, Edward
Baraka, Amiri (LeRoi Jones)
Brown, William Wells
Burleigh, Harry T.
Chesnutt, Charles
Colescott, Robert
Douglas, Aaron
Dove, Rita
Dunbar, Paul Laurence
Ellison, Ralph
Hansberry, Lorraine
Hughes, Langston
Hurston, Zora Neale
Jacobs, Harriet A.
Morrison, Toni
Primus, Pearl
Still, William Grant
Walker, Alice
Wilson, August
Wright, Richard

Civil Rights
Abernathy, Ralph
Cleaver, Eldridge
Farmer, James Leonard
King, Coretta Scott
King, Martin Luther, Jr.
Malcolm X
McKissick, Floyd B.

Newton, Huey
Parks, Rosa Louise
Randolph, A. Philip
Rustin, Bayard

Entertainment
Ailey, Alvin
Anderson, Marian
Baker, Josephine
Belafonte, Harry
Cole, Nat King
Cosby, Bill
Davis, Miles
Gillespie, Dizzy
Fitzgerald, Ella
Freeman, Morgan
Haley, Alex
Holiday, Billie
Jones, James Earl
Lee, Spike
McDaniel, Hattie
Poitier, Sidney
Price, Leontyne
Pryor, Richard
Robeson, Paul

History
Attucks, Crispus
Banneker, Benjamin
Bethune, Mary McLeod
Burns, Anthony
Carver, George Washington
Cinque, Joseph

Coleman, Bessie
Douglass, Frederick
Du Bois, W.E.B. (William Edward
    Burghardt)
Forten, James
Garvey, Marcus
Henson, Josiah
Henson, Matthew
Poor, Salem
Prosser, Gabriel
Purvis, Robert
Scott, Dred
Truth, Sojourner (Isabella van
    Wagener)
Tubman, Harriet
Turner, Nathaniel, "Nat"
Vesey, Denmark
Walker, David
Washington, Booker T.
Wheatley, Phyllis
Woodson, Carter Godwin

Public Service & Business
Arrington, Richard, Jr.
Bolin, Jane
Bradley, Tom
Brown, Ron
Bunche, Ralph Johnson

Chisholm, Shirley
Jackson, Jesse
Jackson, Maynard
Keyes, Alan
Marshall, Thurgood
Moseley-Braun, Carol
Powell, Colin
Thomas, Clarence
Wilder, Douglas

Religion
Allen, Richard
Fard, W. D.
Farrakhan, Louis
Karenga, Maulana
Muhammad, Elijiah (Elijiah Poole)
Turner, Henry McNeal

Sports
Ashe, Arthur
Brown, Jim
Doby, Larry
Gibson, Althea
Jordan, Michael
Louis, Joe
Owens, Jesse
Paige, Satchel
Robinson, Jackie
Rudolph, Wilma
Simpson, O. J.

WEB SITES

The African-American Mosaic
http://lcweb.loc.gov/exhibits/african/intro.html

African American Heritage Preservation Foundation
http://www.preservenet.cornell.edu/aahpf/homepage.htm

African American Resources: American Studies Web
http://www.georgetown.edu/crossroads/asw/afam.html

Black Voices Online
http://www.blackvoices.com/

EverythingBlack.Com
http://www.everythingblack.com/

Asian Studies

Keywords may be searched singly or in combination with other words using Boolean operators *and*, *or*, or *not*.

Afghanistan
agrarian society
ancestor worship
Armenia
Asia Minor
Asian American
Assyrian empire
Australasia
Australia
Azerbaijan
Bahrain
Bangladesh
barbarians
Bhopal, India
Bhutan
Bretton Woods Agreements (1945)
Brunei
Buddha
Buddhism
Burma
Cambodia
caste system
Caucasus
Central Asia
Chechnya
China, People's Republic of (PRC)
Code of Hammurabi
Confucianism
Confucius
Cultural Revolution
demilitarized zone (DMZ)
Dutch East Indies
dynasty

East Asia
East Timor
East Turkistan
Five Dynasties
Five-Year Plans
fung shui
Gang of Four
Georgia
Great Leap Forward
Green Revolution
Hinduism
Hittite empire
Hong Kong
India
Indochina
Indonesia
Iran
Iraq
Israel
Japan
Jordan
Kampuchea
Kashmir
Kashmir Valley
Kazakhstan
Korea
Korean War (1950–1953)
Krishna
Kurdistan
Kuwait
Kyrgyzstan
Laos
Lebanon

Macau
Malaysia
Maldives
Mesopotamia
Middle East
Mongolia
Mongols
most-favored nation (MFN)
Muslim
Myanmar
Nepal
New Zealand
nonresident Indians (NRIs)
North Cyprus
North Korea
North Vietnam
Old Babylonian empire
Oman
one-child policy
the Orient
Pacific Island countries
Pakistan
Palestine
Papua New Guinea
Philippines
protectorate
Qatar
Qur'an (Koran)
Russia
Russian Far East
Saudi Arabia

Shang Dynasty
Shanghai Incident (1932)
Shinto
Shogunate
Siberia
Sikh
Sikhism
silk
Singapore
South Asia
South Korea
South Vietnam
Southeast Asia
Sri Lanka
state-owned enterprise (SOE)
Syria
Taiwan
Tajikistan
Tale of Genji
Taoism
Thailand
Three Kingdoms Era
Tiananmen Square
Tibet
Turkey
Turkmenistan
United Arab Emirates
Uzbekistan
Vietnam
Yemen
Zen Buddhism

ORGANIZATIONS

Asian Development Bank (ADB)
Asia-Pacific Economic Cooperation (APEC)
Association of Southeast Asian Nations (ASEAN)
Chinese Communist Party (CCP)
Chinese People's Political Consultative Congress (CPPCC)
East Asian Economic Grouping (EAEG)
East India Company
Pacific Economic Cooperation Council (PECC)
South Asian Association for Regional Cooperation (SAARC)

KEY PEOPLE

The Arts
Hwang, David Henry
Jang, Jon
Kalidasa

Kingston, Maxine Hong
Sui, Anna
Tan, Amy
Yasunari, Kawabata

Entertainment
Carrere, Tia
Chan, Jackie
Chen, Joan
Cho, Margaret
Chong, Rae Dawn
Lee, Bruce
Morita, Pat
Ono, Yoko
Takei, George
Tomita, Tamlyn
Wang, Wayne
Wong, B. D.
Yan, Martin
Yang, Janet
Yeoh, Michelle
Yun-Fat, Chow

History
Alexander the Great
Chiang Kai-shek
Gandhi, Indira
Gandhi, Mohandas K.
Gandhi, Rajiv
Genghis Khan

Hirohito
Muhammad
Nehru, Jawaharlal
Polo, Marco

Public Service & Business
Chung, Connie
Dalai Lama
Eu, March Fong
Hayakawa, S. J.
Kim Il Sung
Kim Jong Il
Tien, Chang-Lin
Woo, Michael
Woo, S. B.
Yang, Henry

Sports
Chang, Michael
Chung, Eugene
Draves, Vicki Manalo
Kim, Wendall
Nguyen, Dat
Peak, Jim
Sato, Liane
Woods, Tiger
Yamaguchi, Kristi

WEB SITES

Asiadragons
http://www.asiadragons.com/

Asian Studies WWW Virtual Library
http://coombs.anu.edu.au/WWWVL-AsianStudies.html

AsianNet
http://www.asiannet.com/

AsiaSource
http://www.asiasource.org/index.cfm

Orientation Asia
http://as.orientation.com/

United States APEC Index
http://www.apec.org/

Hispanic Studies

Keywords may be searched singly or in combination with other words using Boolean operators *and*, *or*, or *not*.

agringado
barrio
bulto
caló
Caribbean
Catholicism
caudillo
Central America
Chicano
Cinco de Mayo
colonia
Creole
criollo
Cuba
Dominicans
Espinoza v. Farah Manufacturing Company (1973)
Fourteenth Amendment, Constitution of the United States (1868)
Hispanic
Hispanicize
Iberia
immigration
Immigration Reform and Control Act (IRCA, 1986)
indigenismo

Indo-Hispanic
jíbaro
Jones Act (1917)
Latin
Latin America
Latino
lectores
Luso-Hispanic
maquiladora
Marielitos
mestizo
Mexican American
Mexican Farm Labor Supply Program (Bracero Program, 1943–1964)
Mexico
México Lindo
migrant worker
migration
Nuyorican
pachuco
Portugal
Puerto Rico
Raza
santos
South America
Spain
Spanish

ORGANIZATIONS

American G. I. Forum
Labor Council of Latin American Advancement (LCLAA)
League of United Latin American Citizens

National Farm Worker's Association
La Raza Unida
U.S. Immigration and Naturalization Service (INS)

KEY PEOPLE

The Arts
Alarcón, Juan Ruiz de
Aleixandre, Vicente
Allende, Isabel
Alonso, Dámaso
Blasco Ibáñez, Vicente
Bustamante, Javier
Calderón de la Barca, Pedro
Cela, Camilo José
Colón, Mariam
Cortázar, Julio
Dalí, Salvador
De la Cruz, Sor Juana Inés
De la Vega, Garcilaso
De Rojas, Fernando
Echegaray, José
Ferrer, José
García Márquez, Gabriel
Garcilaso de la Vega, El Inca
Gaudí, Antoni
Góngora, Luis de
González, Xavier
Goya, Francisco de
Hayworth, Rita
Jiménez, Juan Ramón
Kahlo, Frida
Lope de Vega, Francisco
Marañón, Gregorio
Marisol
Menéndez Pidal, Ramón
Miró, Joan
Montalbán, Ricardo
Moreno, Rita
Neruda, Pablo
Ortega y Gasset, José
Paz, Octavio
Pérez Galdós, Benito
Picasso, Pablo
Picasso, Paloma
Quevedo, Francisco de
Rivera, Diego
Rojas Zorrilla, Francisco de
Romero, César
Ruiz, Juan

Valdez, Luis
Vargas Llosa, Mario
Velázquez, Diego
Zapata, Carmen
Zorrilla, José

Civil Rights
Chávez, César
García, Héctor Pérez
Hernández, Antonia
Huerta, Dolors
López Tijerina, Reyes
Menchú, Rigoberta
Rodriguez, Arturo S.

Entertainment
Albéniz, Isaac
Baez, Joan
Carreras, José
Carter, Lynda
Daniele, Gracíela
Domingo, Plácido
Estefan, Gloria
Francisco, Don
Iglesias, Julio
Lopez, Jennifer
Martin, Ricky
Perez, Rosie
Puente, Tito
Quinn, Anthony
Rodas, Mary
Rodríguez, Paul
Ronstadt, Linda
Santana, Carlos
Saralegui, Cristina
Selena
Welch, Raquel

History
Bolívar, Simón
Chávez, Dionisio, "Dennis"
Coronado, Pedro Vázquez de
Cortés, Hernán
De Soto, Hernando
Gallegos, José Manuel
Guevara, Ernesto "Ché"

Hernández, Joseph Marion
Martí, José
Perón, Juan Domingo
Pizarro, Francisco
Ponce de León, Juan
Villa, Pancho

Public Service & Business
Bustamante, Albert G.
Bustamante, Anastasio
Carrera, José Rafael
Castro, Fidel
Cavazos, Richard E.
de Lugo, Ron
Escalante, Jaime
Esteves, Luis R.
Franco, Francisco
Fuster, Jaime B.
García Robles, Alfonso
Garrido, Ben Blaz
Gonzalez, Cecilia
Guerra, Stella G.
Hernández, Dora
Juárez, Benito
Marín, Luis Muñoz
Martinez, Elizabeth
Martínez, Matthew G.
Miranda, Francisco de
Ortega, Juan
Ortega, Katherine D.
Ortiz, Solomon P.
Otero-Warren, Nina
Pérez de Cuéllar, Javier
Pérez Esquivel, Adolfo
Quesada, Elwood
Richardson, William B.

Rivero, Horacio
Robinson, Emyré Barrios
Rodriguez, Lina S.
Ros-Lehtinen, Ileana
Salinas, Angela
San Isidoro de Sevilla
San Martín, José de
Santos, Miriam
Serrano, José E.
Torres, Esteban
Zapata, Emiliano

Sciences
De la Cierva, Juan
Finlay, Carlos
Ibarruri, Dolores
Milstein, César
Molina, Mario
Ochoa, Ellen
Ochoa, Severo
Ramón y Cajal, Santiago
Servet, Miguel

Sports
Ballesteros, Severiano
Carew, Rod
Casals, Rosemary
Chávez, Julio César
Clemente, Roberto
Indurain, Miguel
López, Al
Lopez, Nancy
Maradona, Diego
McLish, Rachel
Pelé
Sánchez Vicario, Arantxa
Sosa, Sammy
Trevino, Lee

WEB SITES

Hispanic Americans in Congress
http://lcweb.loc.gov/rr/hispanic/congress/

Hispanic Dot Com
http://www.hispanic.com/

Hispanic Genealogy
http://home.att.net/~Alsosa/

The Hispanic Society of America
http://www.hispanicsociety.org/

LatinWorld
http://www.latinworld.com/

United Farm Workers of America
http://www.ufw.org/

Holidays & Festivals

Keywords may be searched singly or in combination with other words using Boolean operators *and*, *or*, or *not*.

All Saints' Day
All Souls' Day
Annunciation
April Fool's Day
Arbor Day
Armed Forces Day
Ascension
Ash Wednesday
Ashura'
Assumption of the Blessed Virgin Mary
Boxing Day
Butcher's algorithm
Canada Day
Carter's algorithm
celebrations
Chinese New Year
Christmas
Cinco de Mayo
Columbus Day
Corpus Christi
cultural activities
cultural context
Day of Atonement
Days of Awe
Earth Day
Easter Sunday
Eid-al-Fitr
Eighth Day of Assembly
Election Day
Elevation of the Life-Giving Cross
Epiphany
Equinox
Father's Day

Feast of
 Kings
 Lights
 Weeks
federal holiday
Flag Day
Fourth of July
Gates of Repentance
Gauss' algorithm
Good Friday
Groundhog Day
Guy Fawkes Day
Halloween
Hanukkah
Hari Raya Hajj in
Hari Raya Puasa
High Holy Days
Hijra New Year
'Id al Adha
'Id al Fitr
Inauguration Day
Independence Day
Julian calendar
Juneteenth
Kurban Bayram
Kwanzaa
Labor Day
Lailat al Bara'a
Lailat al Kadr
Lailat al Miraj
Leap Day
Lent
Lincoln's Birthday

Lohri
Machzor
Makara Sakrankti
Martin Luther King Jr. Day
Mawlid an Nabi
May Day
Memorial Day
Mother's Day
Nativity of the Virgin Mary
New Year's Day
observance
Orthodox New Calendar
Oudin's algorithm
Passover
Pentecost
Pesach
Pongal
Presentation of Christ in the Temple
Presidents' Day
Purim
Quds Day
Ramadan
Rejoicing of the Law
religious holidays
Rosh Hashanah
Sabbath

Sefer Chayim
Seker Bayram
Shabbat
Shavuot
Shemini Atzeret
shofar
Simchat Torah
social history
St. Patrick's Day
Sukkot
tashlich
Ten Days of Penitence
Teshuvah
Thai Pusam
Thanksgiving Day
tradition
Transfiguration
United Nations Day
Vaisakhi
Valentine's Day
Veterans Day
Vishu/Bahag Bihu
Washington's Birthday
Western Calendar
Yizkor
Yom Kippur
Yugadi

ORGANIZATIONS

Holiday Happenings Ornament Collectors Club (HHOCC)
Holiday Institute of Yonkers (HIY)
Holiday Project
National Father's Day Committee (NFDC)
National Mother's Day Committee

WEB SITES

Holidays on the Net
http://www.holidays.net/

KIDPROJ Multi-Cultural Calendar (MCC)
http://www.kidlink.org/KIDPROJ/MCC/

Worldwide Holiday and Festival Site
http://www.holidayfestival.com

Multiculturalism

Keywords may be searched singly or in combination with other words using Boolean operators *and*, *or*, or *not*.

acculturation
African American
African diaspora
ageism
American-Indian
ancestry
Anglo-American
anthropology
antimiscegenation
Asian American
background
bias
bicultural
bilingual
black
Chicano
citizenship
civil rights
classification
classism
cohesiveness
common culture
cultural
    awareness
    diversity
    isolation
    literacy
    maintenance
    pluralism
culture
    conflict
    contact
    wars

curriculum
diaspora
dictatorship of virtue
differentiation
discrimination
diversity
division
environment
equality
essentialism
ethnic
    diversity
    enclaving
    group
    origins
    relations
ethnicity
ethnocentrism
ethnography
ethnology
Eurocentrism
European American
exploitation
feminism
folk culture
foreign culture
gender
gender-fair
gender-neutral
geographic isolation
glass ceiling
global
group politics

hegemony
heritage
hermeneutics
heterosexism
Hispanic
Hispanoamerican
history
holidays
homeland
hypo-descent
identity
identity politics
immigrant
indigenous
indigenous population
individual differences
indoctrination
institutional cruelty
intellectual history
intercultural communications
intermarriage
international exchange
labeling
language
language role
lateral connectedness
Latino
majority group identifiers
melting pot
Mexican American
middle-class culture
Middle Easterners
minimum competencies
minority
    group identifiers
    group influences
    groups
multicultural education
multicultural textbooks
multiculturalists
multiethnic
multilingual
multiracial
national origin
national unity
nationalism
nationality
Native American

nature-nurture controversy
neocolonialism
non-Western civilization
one-drop rule
oral tradition
Pacific Islanders
Pan-Africanism
pedagogy
people of color
pinnacled learning
political correctness
population
prejudice
race
race relations
racial
    attitudes
    differences
    identification
    quotas
racism
residency
second language acquisition
sexual orientation
social
    characteristics
    construction
    differences
    influences
    isolation
    structure
    values
socialization
society
sociocultural patterns
solidarity
stereotypes
subcultures
subordination
symbolism
Tejano
tolerance
traditionalism
urban culture
victim cult
victimhood
Western civilization
white

ORGANIZATIONS

African Heritage Center for African Dance and Music (AHCADM)
American Indian Institute (AII)
Association for Multicultural Counseling and Development (AMCD)
Before Columbus Foundation (BCF)
Canadian Council of Multicultural and Intercultural Education (CCMIE)
Center for Multicultural Leadership
Common Destiny Alliance (CODA)
Ethnic Materials and Information Exchange Round Table (EMIERT)
European Federation for Intercultural Learning (EFIL)
Folk Alliance
Global Learning (GL)
Multicultural Education, Training, and Advocacy
Multicultural Forum of the American Society for Training and Development
Multicultural Publishers and Education Council
National Association for Bilingual Education (NABE)
National Association for Mediation in Education
National MultiCultural Institute (NMCI)
National Women's Studies Association (NWSA)
Panamerican/PanAfrican Association (PPA)
Women's History Network (WHN)

KEY PEOPLE

Abebe, Zenebe
Dosanjh, Ujjal
Glazer, Nathan

Hirsch, E. D., Jr.
McIntosh, Peggy
Seller, Maxine

WEB SITES

Diversity and Multiculturalism: The New Racism
http://multiculturalism.aynrand.org/

Frederick Douglass Institute
http://www.wcupa.edu/_ACADEMICS/Fdouglass/

Hall of Multiculturalism
http://www.tenet.edu/academia/multi.html

Multicultural Pavilion
http://curry.edschool.Virginia.edu/go/multicultural/

S.E.E.D. Project on Inclusive Curriculum
http://www.wellesley.edu/WCW/projects/seed.html

Web of Culture
http://www.webofculture.com/

Native American Studies

Keywords may be searched singly or in combination with other words using Boolean operators *and*, *or*, or *not*.

Abenaki
Algonquin
Apache
Apalachee
Arapaho
archaeology
Arikara
Attacapa
Bannock
Biloxi
Blackfoot
Brea
buffalo
Caddo Mandan
Calusa
casino gambling
Catawba
Cherokee
Cherokee Nation
Cheyenne
Chickasaw Nation
Chinook
Choctaw Nation
Citizen Potawatomi Nation
Cochimi
Comanche
Conestoga
Cree
Creek
Croatan
Crow
Delaware
Duwamish

Erie
Flathead
forced assimilation
Fox
Great Sioux Nation
Haida
Hopi
Huron
Illinois
Indian Removal Act (1830)
Iowa
Iroquois Nation
Kickapoo
Kiowa Nation
Lagunero
Lakota
Lakota Nation
languages
Lenne Lenape
Makah
Manifest Destiny
Menominee
Meso-American
Miami
Missouri
Mohave
Mohawk Nation
Mohican
Montauk
Narraganset
Natchez
nation
Navajo Nation

Nez Perce
Nisqualli
Nootka
Ojibway
Omaha
Oneida
Osage Nation
Oto
Ottawa
Paiute
Paloos
Papago
Pawnee
Pawtuxet
Pennacook
Pequot
Peyote
Pomo
Potawatomi
Powhatan Confederacy
Pueblo
Quapaw
reburial
repatriation
reservation
Saponi
Sauk
Seneca Nation
Serrano

Shawnee
Shinnecock Indian Nation
Shoshone
Sioux (Dakota)
sun dance
Susquehanna
sweat lodge
Taos
tepee
Tenino
Tillamook
Timucoa
Tlingit
Trail of Tears
tribes
Tsimshian
Tuscarora
Tutelo
Ute
Walapai
Wampanoag
westward expansion
Wichita
Winnebago
Wounded Knee, SD
Wyandot Nation
Yakima
Yuki
Yuma
Zuni

ORGANIZATIONS

All Indian Pueblo Council (AIPC)
American Indian Arts Council (AIAC)
American Indian Culture Research Center (AICRC)
American Indian Graduate Center (AIGC)
American Indian Heritage Foundation (AIHF)
American Indian Higher Education Consortium (AIHEC)
American Indian Institute (AII)
American Indian Liberation Crusade (AILC)
American Indian Lore Association (AILA)
American Indian Research and Development (AIRD)
Association of Community Tribal Schools (ACTS)
Before Columbus Foundation (BCF)
Cherokee National Historical Society (CNHS)
Concerned American Indian Parents (CAIP)
Council for Indian Education (CIE)
Council for Native American Indians (CNAIP)
Crazy Horse Memorial Foundation (CHMF)

Gathering of Nations (GN)
Indian Arts and Crafts Association (IACA)
Indian Heritage Council (IHC)
Indians into Medicine (INMED)
Indigenous Communications Association (ICA)
Institute for American Indian Studies (IAIS)
Institute for the Study of American Cultures (ISAC)
Inter-Tribal Indian Ceremonial Association (ITIC)
National Indian Council on Aging (NICOA)
National Indian Education Association (NIEA)
National Indian Youth Council (NIYC)
Native American Scholarship Fund (NASF)
North American Native American Indian Information and Trade Center
Order of the Indian Wars (OIW)
Society for Advancement of Chicanos and Native Americans in Science
   (SACNAS)
Society for American Archaeology (SAA)
United National Indian Tribal Youth (UNITY)

KEY PEOPLE

Banks, Dennis J.
Bellecourt, Clyde
Billy Bowlegs
Black Elk
Crazy Horse
Mankiller, Wilma P.
Means, Russell
Parker, Quanah
Peltier, Leonard
Pocahontas
Ross, John
Sacajawea
Seqouyah
Sitting Bull (Tatanka Yotanka)
Tecumseh
Tenskwatawa
Tuscaloosa
Wovoka (Jack Wilson)

WEB SITES

Cherokee Nation
http://www.cherokee.org/

Grandmothers' Wisdom Keepers (GWK)
http://www.wisdomkeepers.org/gwk/

Indian World
http://www.indianworld.org/

National Congress of American Indians (NCAI)
http://www.ncai.org/

Sinte Gleska University
http://sinte.indian.com/

Sioux Heritage
http://www.Lakota.com/default.htm

United Indian Nations (UIN)
http://www.uin.net/

HEALTH & WELLNESS

Abortion

Keywords may be searched singly or in combination with other words
using Boolean operators *and*, *or*, or *not*.

abortifacient
abortion
  bill
  clinic
  criminal
  imminent
  incomplete
  induced
  inevitable
  infectious
  justifiable
  late term
  medically induced
  missed
  natural
  partial birth
  pill
  prostaglandin
  selective
  septic
  sex selection
  spontaneous
  therapeutic
  threatened
  tubal
abortion techniques
  dilation and curettage (D&C)
  dilation and evacuation (D&E)
  dilation and extraction (D&X)
  endometrial aspiration
  expulsion
  hysterotomy
  manual vacuum aspiration
  menstrual extraction
  saline injection
  salt poisoning
  suction aspiration
  vacuum aspiration
abortuary
anti-abortion
anti-choice
contraception
contragestion
crisis pregnancy
Cytotec
Doe v. Bolton (1973)
ectopic pregnancy
emergency contraception
family planning
fertility regulation
fetal rights
Freedom of Access to Clinic Entrances
     Act of 1994 (FACE)
gestational age
Harris v. McRae (1980)
Hodgson v. Minnesota (1990)
hysterectomy
infanticide
in-vitro fertilization (IVF)
in-vivo fertilization
live birth
morning-after pill
oligogenics
parental notification and consent
pelvic inflammatory disease (PID)

Planned Parenthood of Southeastern Penn-
      sylvania v. Casey (1992)
postabortion syndrome (PAS)
preborn
pre-embryo
pregnancy reduction
preimplantation genetic diagnosis
pro-abortion
pro-choice
procreative liberty
pro-life
pro-life conflict
prostaglandin

quickening
reproductive rights
right to life
Roe v. Wade (1973)
RU-486
sterilization
stillbirth
termination of pregnancy
tubal pregnancy
unborn
viability
Webster v. Reproductive Health Services
      (1989)

ORGANIZATIONS

Adoption and Family Reunion Center (AFRC)
Advocates for Youth
American College of Obstetrics and Gynecology (ACOG)
Association of Reproductive Health Professionals (ARHP)
Institute for American Values Investing (IAVI)
National Abortion Federation (NAF)
National Organization for Women (NOW)
Operation Rescue (OR)
Planned Parenthood
Pro-Choice Defense League (PCDL)
Right to Life
University Faculty for Life (UFL)
Women for America

KEY PEOPLE

Bensing, Sandra
Goldman, Emma
Hallford, James
Hill, Paul
Lyons, Emily

McCorvey, Norma (Jane Roe)
Salvi, John
Sanger, Margaret
Slepian, Barnett
Wattleton, Faye

WEB SITES

American Life League
http://www.all.org/

Feminist Women's Health Center
http://www.fwhc.org/

Human Life International
http://www.hli.org/

National Abortion Rights Action League (NARAL)
http://www.naral.org/

National Right to Life
http://www.nrlc.org/

Planned Parenthood Federation of America
http://www.plannedparenthood.org/

Pro-Life Action League
http://www.prolifeaction.org/

Republican National Coalition for Life
http://www.rnclife.org/

Adoption

Keywords may be searched singly or in combination with other words using Boolean operators *and*, *or*, or *not*.

adopted children
adoptee rights
adoptees
adoption
  agency
  closed
  designated
  domestic
  familial
  identified
  independent
  infant
  intercountry
  international
  open
  plan
  public agency
  transracial
  unrelated
adoption agencies
Adoption Service Provider (ASP)
Adoption Assistance Programs (AAP)
adoptive
  family
  parent
  parenthood
apostille
authentication
biological family
biological parents
birth
  certificate
  country

family
father
mother
parent
child-placing agency
child welfare
childlessness
closed adoption
closed records
domestic adoption
foster
  care
  child
  children
  family
  parent
home study
infertility
International Soundex Reunion Registry (ISRR)
Interstate Compact on the Placement of Children (ICPC)
liaison agency
natural
  child
  father
  mother
naturalization
open records
orphan
orphanage
parental rights
parent-child relationship

placement
postplacement
postplacement visits
preplacement assessment
relinquishment
social service agency
stepfamily

stepparent
Termination of Parental Rights (TPR)
transracial
Trumanization
Uniform Adoption Act (UAA)
waiting child
waiting period

ORGANIZATIONS

Adoptee-Birthparent Searches (ABC)
Adoptees Liberty Movement Association (ALMA)
Adoption Studies Institute
Adoptive Families of America (AFA)
Child Welfare League of America (CWLA)
Concerned United Birthparents (CUB)
Council for Equal Rights in Adoption (CERA)
Families Adopting Children Everywhere (FACE)
Family Research Council
Independent Search Consultants, Inc. (ISC)
International Concerns for Children (ICC)
National Adoption Information Clearinghouse (NAIC)
National Commission for Creation of Uniform State Laws (NCCUSL)
National Council for Adoption (NCFA)
North American Council for Adoptable Children (NACAC)
Stop the Act Coalition (STAC)
U.S. Immigration and Naturalization Service (INS)

KEY PEOPLE

Adoptees
Audubon, John J.
Berry, Halle
Dickerson, Eric
Ford, Gerald R.
Gilbert, Melissa
Harry, Deborah
Jobs, Steven

Linkletter, Art
Louganis, Greg
Michener, James A.
Monroe, Marilyn
Palmer, Jim
Reagan, Nancy
Thomas, Dave

WEB SITES

AdoptionAgencies.Org
http://www.adoptionagencies.org/

Adoption Crossroads: Council for Equal Rights in Adoption (CERA)
http://www.adoptioncrossroads.org/

Adoption Policy Resource Center
http://www.fpsol.com/adoption/advocates.html

American Adoption Congress
http://www.american-adoption-cong.org/

Joint Council on International Children's Services
http://www.jcics.org/

National Adoption Center
http://nac.adopt.org/nac/nac.html

Wordplay: Adoption Links and Information
http://www.photobooks.com/~poof/adoption/

Aging

Keywords may be searched singly or in combination with other words using Boolean operators *and*, *or*, or *not*.

age discrimination
aged
ageism
Alzheimer's disease (AD)
arthritis
assisted living
atherosclerosis
bone mass
cardiovascular disease
degenerative disease
diet
disability
dysfunctional aging
elder abuse
elderly
geriatrics
gerontology
health care
home health care
independent living
long-term care assessment
longevity
Medicaid
Medicare
memory loss
musculoskeletal disorders
nursing home
older adults
osteoporosis
retirement
retirement community
senescence
Social Security Act of 1935
stroke

ORGANIZATIONS

Association of Jewish Aging Services (AJAS)
Massachusetts Aging Services Association (Mass Aging)
National Association of Nutrition and Aging Services Programs (NANASP)

KEY PEOPLE

Legislators & Public Figures
Burns, George
Connery, Bill
Dill, Clarence
Pepper, Claude
Roosevelt, Franklin Delano
Researchers & Activists
Dobrof, Rose
Flynn, Charlotte

Gatz, Margaret
Hayflick, Leonard
Hodes, Richard J.
Kent, Donald P.
Kuhn, Maggie
Lawton, M. Powell
Metchnikoff, Elie
Salthouse, Timothy A.
Shock, Nathan

WEB SITES

American Association of Retired Persons (AARP)
http://www.aarp.org/

AgeNet
http://www.agenet.com/

American Geriatrics Society
http://www.americangeriatrics.org/

American Society on Aging
http://www.asaging.org/

Gray Panthers
http://www.graypanthers.org/

National Council on the Aging
http://www.ncoa.org/

National Institute on Aging
http://www.nih.gov/nia/

AIDS

Keywords may be searched singly or in combination with other words using Boolean operators *and*, *or*, or *not*.

3TC
Abacavir
abstinence
acquired immunodeficiency syndrome (AIDS)
Active Control Treatment
adenopathy
AIDS
    Clinical Trials Group (ACTG)
    dementia complex
    epidemic
    related complex (ARC)
    test
    vaccination
    vaccine
AIDS/HIV
Amplicor HIV-1 PCR test
Amplicor PCR viral load test
anonymous test
antibody
antibody-dependent cell-mediated cytotoxicity (ADCC)
antiemetic
antigen
anti-HIV treatment
antiretroviral
apoptosis
asymptomatic
Azidothymidine
AZT
B-cell
bDNA test
biological response modifiers (BRMs)

bisexual
blood-borne
blood test
blood-to-blood contact
blood transfusion
bloodstream
B-lymphocytes
casual contact
CD4 count
CD8 cell
CD8 count
CDC AIDS classification system
cell-mediated immunity (CMI)
chemoprophylaxis
clinical trial
cofactor
Combivir
Community Programs for Clinical Research on AIDS (CPCRA)
compassionate use protocol
condom
confidential test
contact tracing
Crixivan
cytomegalovirus (CMV)
d4T
ddC
ddI
delavirdine
didanosine
efavirenz
ELISA (enzyme-linked immunosorbent assay)

encephalopathy
epidemic
epidemiology
Epivir
false-negative
hepatitis
HIVID
homosexual
human immunodeficiency virus (HIV)
human T-cell lymphotropic virus type
    3 (HTLV 3)
immune deficiency
immune system
immunoglobulin
immunosuppression
indinavir
interferons
interleukins
intravenous drug user (IVDU)
Invirase
Kaposi's sarcoma
lamivudine
Lamivudine (3TC)
lentivirus
lesion
lymphadenopathy-associated virus
lymphocyte
monoclonal antibodies
monotherapy
mother-to-child transmission
mycosis
nelfinavir
nevirapine
non-nucleoside reverse transcriptase
    inhibitor (NNRTI)
Norvir
nucleocapsid
nucleoside reverse transcriptase inhibi-
    tor (NRTI)

opportunistic infection
p24 antigen
papillomavirus
partner notification
pathogen
PCR test
person with AIDS (PWA)
pneumocystis carinii pneumonia (PCP)
postexposure prevention (PEP)
Preveon
prophylaxis
Rescriptor
Retrovir
retrovirus
risk
    behavior
    factor
    group
safe sex
saquinavir
sexually transmitted disease (STD)
stavudine
subcutaneous
Sustiva
T4 cell count
T4 cells
T-cell
tests
thymic hormones
T-lymphocytes
Ultra Sensitive Test
vertical transmission
Videx
Viracept
viral load test
Viramune
wasting syndrome
zalcitabine
Zerit
Zidovudine

ORGANIZATIONS

African AIDS Project
AIDS Clinical Trials Group (ACTG)
AIDS Research Consortium of Atlanta (ARCA)
CDC National AIDS Clearinghouse (NAC)
Centers for Disease Control and Prevention
Community AIDS Treatment Information Exchange (CATIE)
Forum for Collaborative AIDS Research

National Institute of Allergy and Infectious Diseases (NIAID)
National Institutes of Health (NIH)
Office of AIDS Research (OAR)
Treatment Action Group (TAG)
U.S. Food and Drug Administration (FDA)

KEY PEOPLE

Researchers
Clements-Mann, Mary Lou
Gallo, Robert
Jekot, Walter F.
Levy, Jay
Mann, Jonathan
Montagnier, Luc

Public Figures
Ashe, Arthur

Glaser, Elizabeth
Hudson, Rock
Johnson, Magic
Louganis, Greg
Mason, Kiki
Santiago, Luis
White, Ryan
Zamora, Pedro

WEB SITES

AEGIS
http://www.aegis.com/

AIDS Memorial Quilt
http://www.aidsquilt.org/

The AIDS Treatment Data Network (The Network)
http://www.aidsinfonyc.org/network/index.html

American Foundation for AIDS Research (AmFAR)
http://www.thebody.com/amfar/amfar.html

The Body: An AIDS and HIV Information Resource
http://www.thebody.com/index.shtml

CDC National Prevention Network
http://www.cdcnpin.org/

Gay Men's Health Crisis
http://www.gmhc.org/

HIV InSite: Gateway to AIDS Knowledge
http://hivinsite.ucsf.edu/

JAMA HIV/AIDS Information Center
http://www.ama-assn.org/special/hiv/hivhome.htm

Project Inform (PI)
http://www.projectinform.org/

Alcoholism

Keywords may be searched singly or in combination with other words using Boolean operators *and*, *or*, or *not*.

abstinence
addiction
alcohol abuse
alcoholic beverage
antisocial behavior
beer
blood alcohol levels
breath alcohol testing
Breathalyzer
cirrhosis
controlled-drinking (CD) treatment
delirium tremens (DTs)

driving under the influence (DUI)
driving while intoxicated (DWI)
drunkenness
fetal alcohol syndrome (FAS)
intoxication
liquor
problem drinking
social drinker
spirits
substance abuse
wine

ORGANIZATIONS

Alcoholics Anonymous (AA)
American Council on Alcoholism (ACA)
Bureau of Alcohol, Tobacco and Firearms (BATF)
Children of Alcoholic Parents (CAPS)
Employee Assistance Professionals Association (EAPA)
International Society for Biomedical Research on Alcoholism (ISBRA)
National Association of Addiction Treatment Providers (NAATP)
National Catholic Council on Alcoholism and Related Drug Problems (NCCA)
National Council on Alcoholism and Drug Dependence
Research Society on Alcoholism (RSA)

KEY PEOPLE

Researchers & Proponents for Treatment
Ford, Betty
Haggard, Howard W.

Jellinek, E. M.
Room, Robin
Smithers, R. Brinkley
Wilson, Bill

WEB SITES

Al-Anon/Alateen
http://www.al-anon.org/

Alcoholics Anonymous World Services
http://www.aa.org/

Another Empty Bottle
http://alcoholismhelp.com/help/index.html

Mothers Against Drunk Driving (MADD)
http://www.madd.org/

National Association for Children of Alcoholics (NACoA)
http://www.health.org/nacoa/

National Black Alcoholism and Addictions Council
http://www.borg.com/~nbac/index.htm

Students Against Destructive Decisions (SADD)
http://www.nat-sadd.org/

Alzheimer's Disease

Keywords may be searched singly or in combination with other words using Boolean operators *and, or,* or *not.*

acetylcholine
Alzheimer's disease and related
    dementias (ADRD)
ampakines
amyloid
    hypothesis
    plaques
    protein precursor (APP)
caregiver
cell death
central nervous system (CNS)
choline acetyltransferase (CAT)
cholinergic hypothesis
cognitive function
cognitive performance
CX-516
dementia
donepezil
dopamine
free radicals
glutamate
mental disorders
monoamine oxidase (MAO)

myelin
neuritic plaques
neurodegeneration
neurofibrillary tangles
neurological disorder
neurologist
neurology
neuron
neurotransmitter
noradrenaline
paranoia
Parkinson's disease
peripheral nervous system (PNS)
positron emission tomography (PET)
    scan
senile dementia
serotonin
sleep disturbance
somatostatin
tacrine
tau detection
vascular dementia
wandering

ORGANIZATIONS

Alzheimer's Family Support Group
Alzheimer's Home Care
American Council on the Treatment of Alzheimer's (ACTA)
Daughters of Scotia (DOS)
Forget Me Not Alzheimer's Support Group
Help and Education for Alzheimer's and Dementia

KEY PEOPLE

Researchers
Alzheimer, Alois
Hardy, John
Jordan, Barry D.
Khachaturian, Zaven
Lee, Virginia
Pericak-Vance, Margaret
Rabins, Peter

Trojanowski, John

Other Figures
Gorman, Bea
Mace, Nancy
Reagan, Ronald W.
Rose, Larry
Shanks, Lela Knox

WEB SITES

The Alzheimer Page
http://www.biostat.wustl.edu/alzheimer/

Alzheimer Society of Canada (ASC)
http://www.alzheimer.ca/

Alzheimer's Association
http://www.alz.org/

Alzheimer's.com
http://www.alzheimers.com/

Alzheimer's Disease Education and Referral (ADEAR) Center
http://www.alzheimers.org/

A Year to Remember . . . with My Mother and Alzheimer's Disease
http://www.zarcrom.com/users/yeartorem/

Anxiety & Panic Attacks

Keywords may be searched singly or in combination with other words using Boolean operators *and, or,* or *not.*

adult respiratory distress syndrome
agoraphobia
Alprazolam
anticipatory anxiety
atrial fibrillation
behavioral therapy
benign positional vertigo
biofeedback
cognitive-behavioral therapy
cyclic antidepressant (CA)
deconditioning
depersonalization
depression
derealization
desensitization
fear
fight or flight
generalized anxiety
heart palpitation
hyperventilation
imipramine
incapacitation
mitral valve prolapse

neurobiological disorders (NBD)
neurochemical dysfunction
obsessive-compulsive disorder
panic disorder (PD)
panic management
paresthesias
phobia
phobic anxiety
phobic avoidance
post-traumatic stress disorder
reactive anxiety
St. John's wort
selective serotonin reuptake inhibitor
    (SSRI)
serotonin reuptake inhibitor (SRI)
somatic
stress
stress management
terror
Tofranil
tricyclic
Valerian
Xanax

ORGANIZATIONS

Agoraphobics Anonymous (AA)
Agoraphobics in Motion (AIM)
Anxiety and Phobia Treatment Center
Child Life Council (CLC)
Council on Anxiety Disorders (CAD)
Depressives Anonymous: Recovery from Depression (DARFD)
Postpartum Support, International (PSI)
Selective Mutism Foundation

Special Interest Group on Phobias and Related Anxiety Disorders (SIGPRAD)
TERRAP Programs

WEB SITES

Anxiety Disorders Association of America (ADAA)
http://www.adaa.org/

CANMAT (Canadian Network for Mood and Anxiety Treatments)
http://www.canmat.org/

National Anxiety Foundation
http://www.lexington-on-line.com/naf.html

Panic Forum
http://www.panic.smithkline-beecham.co.uk/

Stress Less
http://www.stressless.com/

Asthma

Keywords may be searched singly or in combination with other words using Boolean operators *and*, *or*, or *not*.

allergen
allergy
antibody
antigen
antihistamine
anti-inflammatory
asthmatic
atopy
chronic asthmatic bronchitis
controlled hypoventilation
corticosteroid
coughing asthma
dander
emphysema
eosinophil
evidence-based program
extrinsic asthma
FEV1
histamine
hyperventilation
inhalation
interleukin
intrinsic asthma

lung-function monitor
lungs
Metered Dose Inhaler (MDI)
nebulizer
nitric oxide
pathogenic
peak
    expiratory flow (PEF)
    flow
    flow meter
pollen
pollutant
reactive airways disease (RAD)
respiratory
    alkalosis
    system
    tract
severe asthma
status asthmaticus
steroidal deficiency
T lymphocyte
Theophylline
wheezing
work-related asthma

ORGANIZATIONS

American Lung Association Centers for Disease Control (CDC)
Department of Health and Human Services JAMA Asthma Information Center
National Institutes of Health (NIH)

WEB SITES

Allergy, Asthma & Immunology Online
http://allergy.mcg.edu/

alt.support.asthma FAQ: Asthma, General Information
http://www.radix.net/~mwg/asthma-gen.html

American Medical Association Health Insight: Asthma
http://www.ama-assn.org/insight/spec_con/asthma/asthma.htm

Ed's Asthma Track
http://asthmatrack.com/

Global Initiative for Asthma (GINA)
http://www.ginasthma.com/

Attention Deficit Disorder (ADD)

Keywords may be searched singly or in combination with other words using Boolean operators *and*, *or*, or *not*.

Adderall
Americans with Disabilities Act (ADA)
anxiety
attention deficit hyperactivity disorder (ADHD)
attention span
behavior modification
behavioral tool
chemical imbalance
chronic accident repeater
clonidine
concentration
Cylert
Dexedrine
dextroamphetamine
hyperactive-impulsive
hyperactivity
hyperfocus
hyperkinesis
hypoactive
impulsivity
individualized educational program (IEP)
Individuals with Disabilities Education Act (IDEA)
methylphenidate
multimodal intervention
National Rehabilitation Act, Section 504
oppositional defiant disorder
partial syndrome
pervasive developmental disorder
positron emission tomography (PET)
psychotic disorder
Rehabilitation Act (1973)
reticular activating system
Ritalin
Wender Utah Rating Scale

ORGANIZATIONS

ADD—Hope
Attention Deficit Information Network (ADIN)
Attention Disorders Association of Parents and Professionals Together (ADAPPT)
Federation of Behavioral, Psychological and Cognitive Sciences (FBPCS)
Parents Helping Parents (PHP)

WEB SITES

ADD Clinic
http://www.addclinic.com/

Attention-Deficit Hyperactivity Disorder
http://www.mentalhealth.com/dis/p20–ch01.html

C.H.A.D.D. (Children and Adults with Attention Deficit Disorders)
http://www.chadd.org/

National Attention Deficit Disorder Association (ADDA)
http://www.add.org

National Institute of Mental Health (NIMH)
http://www.nimh.nih.gov/

Birth Control

Keywords may be searched singly or in combination with other words using Boolean operators *and*, *or*, or *not*.

abstinence
antiprogesterones
barrier method
birth
   control movement
   control pill
   rate
calendar rhythm
cervical cap
chastity
child spacing
coitus interruptus
condom
contraception
contraceptive failure
Dalkon Shield
Depo-Provera
diaphragm
effectiveness
Eisenstadt v. Baird (1972)
emergency birth control
emergency contraceptive pill (ECP)
failure rate
family planning
female condom
fertility

fertility awareness method (FAM)
foam
Griswold v. Connecticut (1965)
hormonal contraceptive
hormone shot
intrauterine device (IUD)
minipill
morning-after pill
natural family planning (NFP)
nonoxynol-9
Norplant
oral contraceptive
periodic abstinence
postcoital method
prophylactic
rhythm method
RU-486
sexually transmitted disease (STD)
side effects
spermicidal jelly
spermicide
sterilization
sympto-thermal method (STM)
tubal ligation
vasectomy
withdrawal method

ORGANIZATIONS

Advocates for Youth
Catholics for a Free Choice (CFFC)
Couple to Couple League (CCL)
National Latina Health Organization (NLHO)
Ovulation Method Teachers Association (OMTA)

Pharmacists for Life International (PFLI)
Planned Parenthood Federation of America (PPFA)

KEY PEOPLE

Nineteenth Century
Comstock, Anthony
Lease, Mary Elizabeth Clyens
Malthus, Thomas Robert

Twentieth Century
Besant, Annie Wood
Bradlaugh, Charles

Byrne, Ethel
Carr-Saunders, Alexander Morris
Goldman, Emma
Pincus, Gregory Goodwin
Sanger, Margaret
Spellman, Francis Joseph
Stopes, Marie Carmichael

WEB SITES

Contraception
http://lib-sh.lsumc.edu/fammed/grounds/cntrcpt.html

Contraceptive Guide
http://www.mjbovo.com/contracept/index.htm

Family Health International (FHI)
http://www.fhi.org/

Planned Parenthood of America
http://www.plannedparenthood.org/

U.S. Department of Health and Human Services Office of Population Affairs
http://www.hhs.gov/progorg/opa/

Cancer

Keywords may be searched singly or in combination with other words using Boolean operators *and, or,* or *not.*

adenocarcinoma
adjuvant therapy
adjuvant-chemotherapy
alopecia
androgen
anemia
antigen
antimetabolite
apheresis
axillary nodes
basal cell carcinoma
b-cells
biopsy
biotherapy
blood transfusion
bone marrow
bone marrow transplant
brachytherapy
brain scans
breast cancer
breast self-exam (BSE)
Burkitt's lymphoma
cancer
   cells
   detection
   development
   diagnosis
   management
   therapy
carcinogenesis
carcinoma
cervical cancer
chemoprevention

chemotherapy
colon cancer
colonoscopy
combination chemotherapy
computerized axial tomography (CAT Scan)
computerized tomography scan (CT scan)
cryopreservation
cyst
cytology
digital rectal exam
dosimetrist
drug therapy
dysplasia
echocardiogram
endoscopy
Ewing's sarcoma
histopathology
Hodgkin's disease
immunotherapy
interferon
interleukin-2
interstitial implantation
intraoperative radiation
laser therapy
leukemia
leukopheresis
localized cancer
lumpectomy
lung cancer
lymphoma
magnetic resonance imaging (MRI)

malignancy
malignant neoplasms
mammogram
mammography
mastectomy
melanoma
metastasis
myeloma
needle aspiration biopsy
non-Hodgkin's lymphoma
oncogenes
oncology
palliative treatment
Pap smear
polyp
positron emission tomography (PET scan)
prevention
primary therapy
primary tumor
prostate cancer

prostate gland
prosthesis
radiation
radiation therapy
radioactive implant
radiology
radiotherapy
radium
recombinant DNA
recurrence
remission
sarcoma
secondary tumor
skin cancer
survival rate
symptom
t-cell
teletherapy
testicular self-examination (TSE)
tumors
tumor bed

ORGANIZATIONS

Alliance for Cannabis Therapeutics (ACT)
Alliance for Lung Cancer Advocacy, Support and Education (ALCASE)
American Association for Cancer Education (AACE)
American Association for Cancer Research (AACR)
American Brain Tumor Association (ABTA)
American Cancer Society (ACS)
American Joint Committee on Cancer (AJCC)
American Society of Breast Disease (SSBD)
Cancer Biotherapy Research Group
Cancer Care (CC)
Chemotherapy Foundation (CF)
Families Against Cancer Terror (FACT)
National Immunotherapy Cancer Research Foundation
Patient Advocates for Advanced Cancer Treatment (PAACT)
Reach to Recovery
Skin Cancer Foundation (SCF)
We Can Do! (WCD)

KEY PEOPLE

Researchers & Activists
Baltimore, David
Elion, Gertrude B.
Komen, Susan G.
Love, Susan M.
Macdonald, Eleanor Josephine

Mintz, Beatrice
Montagnier, Luc
Papanicolaou, George
Sager, Ruth
Seibert, Florence B.
Singer, Maxine

Slye, Maud   Varmus, Harold Eliot

WEB SITES

American Cancer Society
http://www.cancer.org/

CancerNet: National Cancer Institute (NCI)
http://cancernet.nci.nih.gov/

Gynecologic Oncology Group (GOG)
http://www.gog.org/

Leukemia and Lymphoma Society
http://www.leukemia.org/

National Breast Cancer Coalition
http://www.natlbcc.org/

National Coalition for Cancer Survivorship (NCCS)
http://www.cansearch.org/

National Comprehensive Cancer Network (NCCN)
http://www.NCCN.org/

Susan G. Komen Breast Cancer Foundation
http://www.komen.org/

Depression

Keywords may be searched singly or in combination with other words using Boolean operators *and*, *or*, or *not*.

affective disorder
amitriptyline
antidepressant
bipolar disorder
Celexa
chemical imbalances
clinical depression
cognitive-behavioral therapy
desipramine
dopamine
doxepin
dysthymia
Elavil
electroconvulsive therapy (ECT)
fluoxetine
major depressive disorder
mania
manic-depression
melancholia
monoamine oxidase (MAO) inhibitor
mood disorders
Nardil

nervous breakdown
Norpramin
Paxil
phenelzine
postpartum depression
Prozac
psychodynamic therapy
psychosis
psychotherapy
seasonal affective disorder (SAD)
selective serotonin reuptake inhibitor
    (SSRI)
serotonin
shock treatment
stress
suicide
tyramine
weight gain
weight loss
Wellbutrin
winter blues
Zoloft

ORGANIZATIONS

Depression after Delivery (DAD)
Depression and Related Affective Disorders Association (DRADA)
Depressives Anonymous: Recovery from Depression (DARFD)
Dual Disorders Anonymous
National Alliance for Research on Schizophrenia and Depression (NARSAD)
National Foundation for Depressive Illness (NAFDI)
Project Overcome (PO)
Wellness Center (AWCI)

WEB SITES

Depression
http://www.nimh.nih.gov/publicat/depression.cfm

Depression.com
http://www.depression.com/

Depression Central
http://www.psycom.net/depression.central.html

Harbor of Refuge
http://www.Harbor-of-Refuge.org/

Mental Health Net
http://mentalhelp.nct

National Alliance for the Mentally Ill (NAMI)
http://www.nami.org/

National Depressive and Manic-Depressive Association (NDMDA)
http://www.ndmda.org/

Disabilities

Keywords may be searched singly or in combination with other words using Boolean operators *and*, *or*, or *not*.

accessibility
adaptive behavior
adventitious impairments
Americans with Disabilities Act (ADA, 1990)
assistive devices
attention deficit disorder (ADD)
attention deficit hyperactivity disorder (ADHD)
auditory discrimination
autism
blindness
civil rights
communication disorders
developmental disabilities
dyslexia
employment
group homes
hyperactivity

learning disabilities
learning disabled
long-term disability
mainstreaming
mental disorder
mental retardation
minimal brain dysfunction (MBD)
paralysis
receptive language disorder
rehabilitation
Rehabilitation Act (1973)
short-term disability
Social Security Disability Insurance (SSDI)
special education
specific language disability (SLD)
specific learning disability (SLD)
traumatic brain injury (TBI)
visual impairments

ORGANIZATIONS

Commission on Mental and Physical Disability Law (CMPDL)
Disability Rights Education and Defense Fund (DREDF)
Employment Policy Foundation (EPF)
Family Resource Center on Disabilities (FRCD)
Inclusion International (II)
Mobility International USA (MIUSA)
National Legal Center for the Medically Dependent and Disabled (NLCMDD)
National Mental Health Association (NMHA)
National Organization for Rare Disorders (NORD)
National Organization on Disability (NOD)
Organization for Equal Education of the Sexes (OEES)
Self Help for Hard of Hearing People (SHHH)

Social Security Administration

KEY PEOPLE

Activists & Researchers
Amato, David
Anthony, Milton
Bloch, Nancy
Dart, Justin
Jacobs, Jill
Kemp, John D.
Kerford, George
Montgomery, Sylvester
Roth, Marcie
Salaiz, Emanuel

Walker, Sylvia

People with Disabilities
Abbott, Jim
Hawking, Stephen William
Hearne, Paul
Jordan, I. King
Keller, Helen
Martin, Casey
Matlin, Marlee
Plain, Sharon M.
Reeve, Christopher

WEB SITES

ADA Information Center
http://www.ada-infonet.org/

American Association of People with Disabilities (AAPD)
http://aapd-dc.org/

Americans with Disabilities Act Document Center
http://janweb.icdi.wvu.edu/kinder/

Communicating the Americans with Disabilities Act
http://www.annenberg.nwu.edu/pubs/sears/

Council for Disability Rights
http://www.disabilityrights.org/

The Disability Rights Activist
http://www.disrights.org/

Disability Social History Project
http://www.disabilityhistory.org/

Disabled American Veterans
http://www.dav.org/

Independent Living USA
http://www.ilusa.com/

National Council on Disability
http://www.ncd.gov/

U.S. Department of Justice ADA Page
http://www.usdoj.gov/crt/ada/adahom1.htm

World Association of Persons with Disabilities (WAPD)
http://www.wapd.org/

Drug Abuse

Keywords may be searched singly or in combination with other words using Boolean operators *and*, *or*, or *not*.

addiction
alcohol
alcohol abuse
alcoholism
anabolic steroids
angel dust
antibiotics
antihistamines
atropine
barbiturates
barbituric acid
belladonna
benzedrine
biphetamine
black beauty
brain damage
butyl nitrite
caffeine
cannabis
chemical dependence
chewing tobacco
cigarettes
cocaine
codeine
coke
correction fluid
cough syrup
crack
crack baby
crack cocaine
crank
crystal
deadly nightshade

Demerol
designer drugs
dexedrine
Dilaudid
downers
driving while intoxicated (DWI)
drug abuse
Drug Abuse Treatment Outcome
    Study (DATOS)
drug addiction
drug use
drug use testing
ecstasy
ergot
freebase
ganja
gateway drugs
glue
hash
hashish
hemp
heroin
homicide
hyscocyamine
ice
illegal drug use
illegal substance
illicit drugs
inhalant
jimsonweed
ketamine
Librium
locoweed

LSD (lysergic acid diethlyamide)
ludes
marijuana
mescaline
meth
methadone
methamphetamine
methaqualone
microdot
morning glory
morphine
narcotics
narcotics addiction
nicotine
nitrous oxide
opiate
overdose
paint thinner
PCP (phencyclidine)
pep pill
Percodan
peyote
pharmacology
physical addiction
pot
predator drugs
prescription drugs
psilocybe
psychological addiction
Quaaludes
recreational use
reefer
Rohypnol
rufies
scopolamine
sedatives
sinsemilla
smack
smoking
snow
speed
stimulants
substance abuse
tobacco
tranquilizers
underage drinking
uppers
Valium
warning signs
withdrawal symptoms
workplace testing

ORGANIZATIONS

Alcohol and Drug Problems Association of North America (ADPA)
Alcohol Research Information Service (ARIS)
American Outreach Association (AOA)
Center for Human Services (CHS)
Defense for Children International—United States of America (DCI-USA)
National Black Youth Leadership Council (NBYLC)
National Clearinghouse for Alcohol and Drug Information (NCADI)
National Parents' Resource Institute for Drug Education (PRIDE)
Students Against Destructive Decisions (SADD)
Women's Drug Research Project (WDR)

KEY PEOPLE

Law Enforcement
Bennett, William
Calderoni, Guillermo Gonzalez
Constantine, Tom
McCaffrey, Barry

Public Figures
Barry, Marion
Belushi, John
Downey, Robert, Jr.

Farley, Chris
Fuentes, Amado Carrillo
Garcia, Jerry
Hofmann, Albert
Joplin, Janis
Leary, Timothy
Morrison, Jim
Phoenix, River

WEB SITES

American Society of Addiction Medicine (ASAM)
http://www.asam.org/

The National Center on Addiction and Substance Abuse at Columbia University
http://www.casacolumbia.org/

National Inhalant Prevention Coalition (NIPC)
http://www.inhalants.org/

National Institute on Drug Abuse (NIDA)
http://www.nida.nih.gov/

Mothers Against Drunk Driving (MADD)
http://www.madd.org/default.shtml

Prevline: Prevention Online. The National Clearinghouse for Alcohol and Drug Information
http://www.health.org/

Eating Disorders

Keywords may be searched singly or in combination with other words using Boolean operators *and, or,* or *not.*

amenorrhea
anorexia nervosa
appetite
appetite disorders
arthritis
binge eating
binge eating disorder (BED)
blood pressure
body
   image
   shape
   weight
bulimarexia
bulimia
bulimia nervosa
cholesterol
compulsive and binge eating
compulsive overeating
death
denial
depression
detection
dietetics
dieting
disease
diuretic
eating habits
eating patterns
endocrine disorder
enema
exercise
fasting
fear of weight gain

guilt
heart attack
hunger
ideal body weight
kidney failure
laxatives
malnutrition
menstrual cycle
menstruation
moodiness
nausea
nutrition
obesity
overeating
potassium
psychological disorder
psychological patterns
pulse rate
purging
seizures
self-esteem
self-image
self-induced starvation
self-perception
starvation
teens
thinness
treatment
underweight
vomiting
weight
weight loss

ORGANIZATIONS

American College of Nutrition (ACN)
American Mental Health Counselors Association (AMHCA)
Anorexia Nervosa and Related Eating Disorders (ANRED)
Association for Advancement of Behavior Therapy (AABT)
Association for the Study of Obesity (ASO)
Bulimia Anorexia Nervosa Association (BANA)
Council on Size and Weight Discrimination (CSWD)
International Association of Eating Disorders Professionals (IAEDP)
National Association of Anorexia Nervosa and Associated Disorders (ANAD)
National Eating Disorder Information Centre (NEDIC)
National Eating Disorders Organization (NEDO)
Overeaters Anonymous (OA)
Rational Recovery Systems (RRS)

KEY PEOPLE

Carpenter, Karen   Henrich, Christy
Costin, Carolyn   Hornbacher, Marya
Diana, Princess of Wales   Krasnow, Michael
Gold, Tracey   Stoner, Carolyn

WEB SITES

Academy for Eating Disorders
http://www.acadeatdis.org/

Eating Disorders in a Disordered Culture
http://www.eating.ucdavis.edu/

Eating Disorders: Mirror-Mirror
http://www.mirror-mirror.org/eatdis.htm

Eating Disorders Shared Awareness (EDSA)
http://www.eating-disorder.com/

The Something Fishy Eating Disorders Web Site
http://www.something-fishy.org

Fetal Alcohol Syndrome (FAS)

Keywords may be searched singly or in combination with other words using Boolean operators *and, or,* or *not.*

addiction
alcohol related birth defects (ARBD)
alcohol related neurodevelopmental
    disorder (ARND)
alcoholics
attention deficit disorder (ADD)
behavioral problems
binge drinking
birth defects
bloodstream
brain damage
brain disorder
central nervous system
characteristics
children
clinical evaluation
concentration
detection
developmental disabilities
diagnosis
drugs
embryo
epidemiology
facial deformities
fetal alcohol effects (FAE)
fetal growth
fetus
first trimester
genetics
growth rate

growth retardation
hearing impairment
hyperactivity
intervention
learning disabilities
live birth
low birth weight
memory
mental damage
mental retardation
microcephaly
miscarriages
mother
nervous system
newborn
oxygen shortage
physical damage
postnatal
pregnancy
premature birth
prenatal
prevention
risk
stillbirth
substance abuse
toxicity
unborn
unborn child
uterus
vision problems

ORGANIZATIONS

Native American Community Board (NACB)
Pro-Life Education Association (PLEA)
Running Strong for American Indian Youth (RSAIY)
Society of Special Needs Adoptive Parents (SNAP)

KEY PEOPLE

Researchers & Activists

Andreasen, Nancy C.
Battaglia, Frederick C.
Carroll, Kathleen M.
Charness, Michael
Day, Nancy
Dono, Michael
Goodlett, Charles R.

Howe, Cynthia
Jacobson, Sandra
Lemoine, Paul
Miller, Michael W.
Ritchie, Bruce
Sokol, Robert J.
Stratton, Kathleen

WEB SITES

The Arc's Fetal Alcohol Syndrome Resource and Materials Guide
http://thearc.org/misc/faslist.html

Clean Water International
http://www.shadeslanding.com/clean-water/index.html

Fetal Alcohol Syndrome Consultation, Education and Training Services
http://www.fascets.org/

Fetal Alcohol Syndrome Family Resource Institute
http://www.accessone.com/~delindam/

The National Organization on Fetal Alcohol Syndrome (NOFAS)
http://www.nofas.org/

Health—General

Keywords may be searched singly or in combination with other words using Boolean operators *and, or,* or *not.*

abortion
aging
AIDS (acquired immunodeficiency
    syndrome)
alcoholism
allied health occupations
alternative medicine
anatomy
anesthesiology
audiology
behavioral and mental disorders
biochemistry
bioethics
biological influences
biomedicine
biotechnology
cancer
cardiology
cardiovascular disease
care evaluation
case history
case management
chronic accident repeater
clinic
clinical medicine
communication disorders
death rate
dentistry
diabetes
diagnosis
diet
dietetics
disability

disease
   outcomes
   prevention
   state
drug abuse
drug therapy
electroencephalography
embryology
emergency care
emergency medicine
endocrinology
environment
enzymes
epidemiology
euthanasia
evaluation
exercise
experimental medicine
family practice
fee-for-service
fitness
French paradox
genetic engineering
genetics
geriatrics
germ theory
government
gynecology
handicap
health
   care
      administration
      costs

professional
  center
  department
  education
  facilities
  insurance
  occupations
  professionals
  promotion
  services administration
holistic medicine
hospice
hospitals
human body
human genetics
hygiene
immune system
immunology
infectious disease
internal medicine
intervention
long-term care
managed care
medical
  associations
  care
  care insurance
  research
  services
  specialty
  testing
mental health
microbiology
morbidity
mortality
national health insurance program
national health service
neurology
noninfectious disease
nurse practitioner
nursing home
nutrition
obstetrics
occupational
  health
  medicine
  therapy
oncology

ophthalmology
osteopathy
paramedical professions
pathology
patient
patient rights
pediatric care
pediatrics
personal hygiene
pharmaceutical
pharmacist
pharmacology
pharmacy
physical
  health
  restoration
  therapy
physician
physician-assisted suicide
physician-patient relationship
physiology
podiatry
population and reproductive biology
positive health
prenatal care
preventive medicine
primary health care
prognostic tests
psychiatry
psychology
public assistance
public health
radiation biology
radiology
rehabilitation
respiratory therapy
risk factors
safety
sanitation
severity of illness (SI)
social rehabilitation
social well-being
speech therapy
sports medicine
surgery
terminal care
termination of treatment
therapy

tissue donor
toxicology
treatment
trepanation

vaccine
vitality
vocational rehabilitation
walk-in clinic
wellness

ORGANIZATIONS

Aerobics and Fitness Association of America (AFAA)
American Alliance for Health, Physical Education, Recreation and Dance (AAHPERD)
American Association for Active Lifestyles and Fitness (AAALF)
American Fitness Association (AFA)
American Holistic Medical Association (AHMA)
American Yoga Association (AYA)
Association for Worksite Health Promotion (AWHP)
Association of Physical Fitness Centers (APFC)
Children's Health and Fitness Fund (CHeaFF)
Council on Health Information and Education (CHIE)
National Health Club Association (NHCA)
National Safety Council (NSC)
National Wellness Association (NWA)
World Health Organization (WHO)

KEY PEOPLE

Nineteenth Century
Barton, Clara
Blackwell, Elizabeth
Blackwell, Emily
Darwin, Charles
Dix, Dorothea
Koch, Robert
Mahoney, Mary Eliza
Mendel, Gregor Johann
Nightingale, Florence
Pasteur, Louis
Richards, Linda

Twentieth Century
Abbott, Maude
Apgar, Virginia
Barrett-Conner, Elizabeth
Breckinridge, Mary
Brown, Rachel Fuller
Calderone, Mary S.
Canady, Alexa
Chinn, May Edward
Cormack, Allan MacLeod
Crick, Francis Harry Compton
Dunn, Gladys Ward

Elion, Gertrude Belle
Friend, Charlotte
Grobstein, Ruth
Hamilton, Alice
Hazen, Elizabeth Lee
Horney, Karen
Hounsfield, Godfrey Newbold
Jemison, Mae C.
Kenny, Elizabeth
Koch, Robert
Kubler-Ross, Elisabeth
Novello, Antonia
Platt, Joan Miller
Rozier, Betty M.
Sanger, Margaret
Seddon, Margaret Rhea
Taussig, Helen Brooke
Vallino, Lisa
Wald, Florence
Wald, Lillian D.
Watson, James
Wexler, Nancy
Wilkins, Maurice
Yalow, Rosalyn Sussman

WEB SITES

American Medical Association
http://www.ama-assn.org/

American Physical Therapy Association
http://www.apta.org/

American Red Cross
http://www.redcross.org/

Friends' Health Connection
http://www.48friend.org/

National Library of Medicine
http://www.nlm.nih.gov/

New Jersey State Library Health and Medical Resources
http://www.njstatelib.org/cyberdesk/health.htm

U.S. Consumer Product Safety Commission
http://www.cpsc.gov/

Health Care & Insurance

Keywords may be searched singly or in combination with other words using Boolean operators *and, or,* or *not.*

access
accreditation
administration
Aid to Families with Dependent
    Children (AFDC)
ambulatory care
assessment
attending physician
audit
authorization
auxiliary
beneficiary
benefit package
benefits
capitation
care provider
case management
catastrophic case management
chronic illness
clinician
coinsurance
community health
comparative data
Consolidated Omnibus Budget Recon-
    ciliation Act (COBRA, 1985)
consumer empowerment
contact directory
coordination of benefits (COB)
coordinator of care
copayment
cost-shifting
coverage
death

deductible
dentistry
diagnosis
disability
disease management
dual coverage
elective surgery
emergency care
emergency surgery
enrollment
exercise
family practice
fee-for-service
fees
first aid
fitness
gatekeeping
general practitioner
group health insurance
group medical practice
gynecology
health
    delivery
    maintenance organization (HMO)
    plan
    professional
health care
    contract
    delivery system
    development
    industry
    institution
    provider

status
Hippocratic oath
HMO
home health care
hospice
hospital
hospital services
hospitalization
immunization
indemnity plan
inpatient
insurance
insurance carrier
insurance plan
intensive care unit
long-term care
malpractice
managed care
managed competition
Medicaid
medical
 equipment
 ethics
 personnel
 plan
 treatment
 waste
medically necessary
Medicare
medication
medigap coverage
mental heath
morbidity
mortality
notch group
nurse practitioner
nursing home
obstetrics
open enrollment
optometry
orthopedics
out-of-pocket expense
outpatient
outpatient care
over-the-counter
pathology
patient
patient's bill of rights

pediatrics
pharmaceutical
pharmacy
physical examination
physical therapy
physician-assisted suicide
physician care
podiatry
point of service (POS)
portability
practice
preexisting condition
preferred provider organization (PPO)
premiums
prescription
prescription medication
preventive care
primary care
primary care physician
primary care provider (PCP)
private physician
provider
psychology
quality of health
recidivism
referral
regulation
rehabilitation
Resource Based Relative Value Scale
 (RBRVS)
routine physical examination
self-medication
short-term care
single-payer
skilled nursing facility (SNF)
Social Security Act (1965)
socialized medicine
specialist
standards
sterilization
surgical procedure
surgicenter
terminal-illness
tertiary care
therapy
third-party payer
triage
uninsured

urgent care   wellness
walk-in clinic   workers' compensation

ORGANIZATIONS

American Medical Association
Health Care Financing Administration (HCFA)
Joint Commission on Accreditation of Healthcare Organizations (JCAHO)
Office of Health Maintenance Organizations (OHMO)
U.S. Department of Health and Human Service (HHS)
U.S. Food and Drug Administration
U.S. Veterans Administration

WEB SITES

Health Care Compliance Association (HCCA)
http://www.hcca-info.org/

National Council for Reliable Health Information
http://www.ncrhi.org/

National Hospice and Palliative Care Organization
http://www.nhpco.org/

National Voluntary Health Agencies (NVHA)
http://www.nvha.org/

Holistic Medicine

Keywords may be searched singly or in combination with other words using Boolean operators *and*, *or*, or *not*.

acupuncture
Alexander technique
allopathy
alternative
   healing
   health care
   medicine
aromatherapy
arthritis
ayurvedic medicine
biofeedback
chelation therapy
chiropractic medicine
colchicum autumnale
colon therapy
complementary medicine
dentistry
detoxification
diet
diet therapy
drugs
emotional healing
environmental medicine
fasting
fitness
healing research
herbal medicine
herbalism
herbology
herbs
holism
holistic
   healing

   treatment
homeopath
homeopathic medicine
homeopathic pharmacopeia
homeopathy
hypnosis
hypnotherapy
iridology
kinesiology
lifestyle
light therapy
macrobiotics
massage
medical freedom
meditation
mercurius corrosivus
mind-body medicine
modalities
movement
moxibustion
natural
   childbirth
   healing
   medicine
naturopathy
noninvasive medicine
nutrition
occupational therapy
Oriental medicine
osteopathy
palliative care
pathogens
physiotherapy

podiatry
prevention
psychotherapy
Qi
Qi Gong
reflexology
rehabilitation
Reiki
saunas
self-help

skeletal adjustment
surgery
tai chi
therapy
toxin
traditional Chinese medicine (TCM)
treatment
vegetarianism
wellness
Western medicine
yoga

ORGANIZATIONS

Advocate Health Care (AHC)
Alliance for Alternatives in Healthcare (AAH)
Alternative Age of Healing Association (AAA)
Alternative Medical Association (AMA)
American Association for Holistic Health
American Holistic Medical Association (AHMA)
American Holistic Medical Foundation (AHMF)
Health Optimizing Institute (HOI)
International Association of Holistic Health Practitioners (IAHHP)
International Association of Holistic Medicine
International Laser Acupuncture Society (ILAS)
National Association for Holistic Aromatherapy
Wilbur Hot Springs Health Sanctuary (WHSHS)

KEY PEOPLE

Researchers & Proponents
Anderson, Greg
Berthold-Bond, Annie
Chopra, Deepak
Galland, Leo
Kao, Laurel Skurko
Manahan, William D.
McGarey, Gladys T.

Northrup, Christiane
Null, Gary
Robertson, Dave
Sahelian, Ray
Siegel, Bernard
Strohecker, James
Ullman, Dana
Weil, Andrew

WEB SITES

American Association of Drugless Practitioners (AADP)
http://www.aadp.net/

American Holistic Health Association (AHHA)
http://ahha.org/

American Holistic Nurses' Association (AHNA)
http://www.ahna.org/

Health Medicine Forum
http://www.healthmedicine.org/

Health Pyramid
http://www.healthpyramid.com/

Holistic Healing Web Page
http://www.holisticmed.com/

WholePeople
http://www.wholepeople.com

Mental Health

Keywords may be searched singly or in combination with other words using Boolean operators *and*, *or*, or *not*.

abuse
adaptive behavior
addiction
adjustment
affective disorder
aggression
aging
agoraphobia
alcohol
Alzheimer's disease
amnesia
anger
anomaly
anorexia nervosa
antidepressant
anxiety
Asperger's syndrome
attention deficit disorder (ADD)
autism
behavior disorders
behavior problems
behavioral science
behavioral therapy
behaviorism
bereavement
biomedicine
bipolar affective disorder
bipolar disorder
borderline personality disorder (BPD)
brain injury
bulimia nervosa
child development
child health

clinic
clinical psychology
cognition
cognitive therapy
community care
compulsion
conduct
coping
counseling
counselors
crime
cyclothymic
debilitation
defense mechanism
deficiency
delinquency
delusion
dementia
dependence
depression
depressive disorder
deterioration
developmental disorder
deviant
diagnosis
Diagnostic and Statistical Manual of Mental Disorders (DSM-IV)
disability
disorder
disposition
dissociation
dissociative identity disorder (DID)
drug abuse

drug therapy
dyslexia
dysthymic
eating disorder
emotional abuse
emotional disturbance
emotions
employee assistance programs
employment
enabler
epidemiology
episodes
flashbacks
functional mental illness
generalized anxiety disorder
genetic
Gilles de la Tourette's syndrome
grief
halfway house
hallucination
helplessness
homelessness
hospital
hostility
housing
Human Brain Project
hygiene
incapacitation
institutionalization
intervention
isolation
mania
manic-depression
mental disorders
mental health
    clinics
    programs
    services
mental institution
mental retardation
moderate
mood
morale
multiple personality disorder (MPD)
narcissism
neuroanatomy
neurochemistry
neuroleptic

neurological impairments
neurology
neuropsychology
neuroscience
neurosis
neurotic
obsession
obsessive-compulsive
organic mental illness
panic attack
paranoia
patient
personality disorder
pervasive developmental disorder
    (PDD)
phobia
physical disabilities
post-traumatic stress disorder
prenatal
prevention
primary care
Prozac
psychiatric
    hospital
    services
psychiatrists
psychiatry
psychoanalysis
psychological services
psychologists
psychology
psychopathology
psychopharmacology
psychosis
psychotherapy
rational-emotive therapy
rehabilitation centers
rehabilitation programs
residential programs
schizophrenia
school psychologists
seasonal affective disorder
self-
    actualization
    destructive behavior
    esteem
    injury
serotonin

sexology
sexual abuse
social issues
speech disorder
stigma
stress

substance abuse
suicide
symptoms
therapeutic environment
therapy
trauma
withdrawal

ORGANIZATIONS

Alliance for the Mentally Ill
American Psychiatric Association (APA)
Federation of Families for Children's Mental Health (FFCMH)
International Committee Against Mental Illness (ICAMI)
National Resource Center on Homelessness and Mental Illness (NRCHMI)
Network Against Coercive Psychiatry (NACP)

KEY PEOPLE

Eighteenth Century
Pinel, Philippe

Nineteenth Century
Dix, Dorothea Lynde
Howe, Samuel Gridley
Lloyd, Henry Demarest
Lowell, Josephine Shaw
Rush, Benjamin

Twentieth Century
Adler, Alfred
Carter, Rosalynn Smith

Freud, Sigmund
Horney, Karen
Jung, Carl
Montessori, Maria
Pauling, Linus Carl
Pavlov, Ivan Petrovich
Peck, M. Scott
Sacks, Oliver
Skinner, B. F.
Sullivan, Harry Stack
Watson, John

WEB SITES

The Arc
http://www.thearc.org/

Behavior Online
http://www.behavior.net/

Mental Health InfoSource
http://www.mhsource.com/

National Alliance for the Mentally Ill (NAMI)
http://www.nami.org/

National Institute of Mental Health (NIMH)
http://www.nimh.nih.gov/

Screening for Mental Health (SMH)
http://www.nmisp.org/

World Federation for Mental Health
http://www.wfmh.com/

Physical Fitness

Keywords may be searched singly or in combination with other words using Boolean operators *and, or,* or *not.*

adaptation
aerobics
agility
alcoholism
allergy
anaerobic
anemia
anorexia nervosa
asthma
athletic equipment
athletic training
athletics
body composition
bulimia
calisthenics
cancer
characteristics
child health
coach
communicable diseases
coordination
cycling
dance
diabetes
diet
disability
disease
eating disorders
eating habits
endurance
energy
exercise
   equipment

physiology
   program
fatigue
fitness
flexibility
games
gymnastics
health
health promotion
heart disorder
heart rate
human body
hygiene
hypertension
illness
intercollegiate athletics
jogging
leisure
locker room
medicine
metabolism
midlife transition
movement
muscular strength
nutrition
obesity
pain
parks
performance
physical
   conditioning
   development
   education

examination
recreation
stress
therapy
physiology
playground
psychosomatic disorders
public health
recreation
recreational activities
rehabilitation
running
sanitation
seizures

sickle-cell anemia
smoking
sport psychology
sports
sports medicine
sportsmanship
strength
stress
stretching
substance abuse
swimming
triathlon
venereal disease
ventilation
walking

ORGANIZATIONS

Aerobics and Fitness Association of America (AFAA)
Amateur Athletic Union (AAU)
American Association for Active Lifestyles and Fitness (AAALF)
American Council on Exercise (ACE)
American Fitness Association (AFA)
American Running and Fitness Association (AR&FA)
Aquatic Exercise Association (AEA)
Association of Physical Fitness Centers (APFC)
Athletic Institute (AI)
Children's Health and Fitness Fund (CHeaFF)
Exercise Safety Association (ESA)
Fitness Motivation Institute of America Association (FMIAA)
IDEA, the Health and Fitness Source
International Physical Fitness Association (IPFA)
Medical Fitness Association
National Health Club Association (NHCA)
National Organization of Mall Walkers (NOMW)
President's Council on Physical Fitness and Sports
Sports Foundation (SF)
Weight Watchers

KEY PEOPLE

Fitness & Diet Specialists
Atlas, Charles
Austin, Denise
Everson, Cory
Fonda, Jane
LaLane, Jack

Little, Tony
Ornish, Dean
Powter, Susan
Simmons, Richard
Smith, Kathy
Steinfeld, Jake

WEB SITES

American Alliance for Health, Physical Education, Recreation and Dance
http://www.aahperd.org/

Fitness Online
http://www.fitnessonline.com/

HealthCalc Network
http://www.healthcalc.net/

Shape Up America
http://www.shapeup.org/

Worldguide: Health and Fitness Forum
http://www.worldguide.com/Fitness/hf.html

Post-Traumatic Stress Disorder

Keywords may be searched singly or in combination with other words using Boolean operators *and*, *or*, or *not*.

accident
alcoholism
anxiety
attack
avoidance
battered woman syndrome
child abuse
combat fatigue
concentration
control
crisis
depression
distress
drug abuse
emotion
event
experience
extreme
flashback
guilt
intensity
memory

mental illness
natural disaster
nightmare
outburst
pain
panic
psychology
psychotherapy
rape trauma
reaction
recurrence
response
sensation
sexual assault
shell shock
sleep loss
stress
survival
threat
trauma
violence
warfare
witness

ORGANIZATIONS

AMCHA, the National Israeli Centre for Psychosocial Support of Survivors of the Holocaust

American Psychiatric Association (APA)

Association of Traumatic Stress Specialists (ATSS)

Council on Anxiety Disorders (CAD)

Incest Survivors Resource Network, International (ISRNI)

Institute for the Advancement of Human Behavior (IAHB)

National Association for Black Veterans (NABV)

Veterans of the Vietnam War (VVnW)
Vietnam Veterans Against the War (VVAW)

WEB SITES

American Academy of Experts in Traumatic Stress
http://www.aaets.org/

International Society for Traumatic Stress Studies On-Line
http://www.istss.com/

Internet Mental Health: Post-Traumatic Stress Disorder
http://www.mentalhealth.com/dis/p20–an06.html

Sidran Foundation
http://www.sidran.org/

Pregnancy

Keywords may be searched singly or in combination with other words using Boolean operators *and*, *or*, or *not*.

abortion
adoption
alpha-feto protein (AFP)
amniocentesis
amniotic membrane
amniotomy
anemia
anovulation
artificial insemination (AI)
artificial insemination donor (AID)
assisted reproductive technology (ART)
baby
basal body temperature (BBT)
beta HCG test
biological influences
biology
birth
   assistant
   canal
   center
   defect
   plan
   -rate
   weight
birthing
blood test
bloodstream
bloody show
Bradley method
breach birth
breast-feeding
capacitation
cervical mucus

cervix
cesarean section
Chadwick's sign
childbirth
childbirth class
child health
chorionic villus sampling (CVS)
chromosome
cilia
clinical
coitus
colostrum
community health services
complication
conception
congenital impairment
contraception
contraction
craving
cumulus oophorus
delivery
diet
dilation
disease
donor
doula
Down's syndrome
due date
early parenthood
eclampsia
ectopic pregnancy
egg
embryo

endocrinology
endometriosis
epidural
episiotomy
estrogen
exercise
expectant mother
fallopian tubes
family
family planning
father
fatigue
feeding
fertility
fertility treatment
fertilization
fetal
    alcohol syndrome (FAS)
    care
    development
    distress
    kick
    monitor
    motion
fetus
fitness
folate
folic acid
forceps delivery
gamete
gender
genetic counseling
genetics
gestation
gonad
Goodell's sign
gynecology
health
heredity
home birth
hospital
illegitimate birth
implantation
in utero
induced labor
infant
    care
    mortality

infertility
insemination
intrauterine
in-vitro
in-vivo
Kegel exercises
labor
Lamaze
last menstrual period (LMP)
maternity
maternity leave
medical services
menarche
menstrual cycle
metabolic toxemia of late pregnancy
        (MTLP)
midwife
miscarriage
mitosis
morning sickness
mother
multiple pregnancy
Naegele's rule
natural birth
natural childbirth
nature-nurture controversy
nausea
neonatology
newborn
nurses
nutrition
OB/GYN
obstetrics
oral contraceptives
ovary
ovum
parent
pediatrician
perinatal
perineal massage
period
physical development
physician
placenta
postpartum
pre-eclampsia
pregnancy
    -induced hypertension (PIH)

loss
test
premature birth
premature labor
prenatal
   care
   test
preventive medicine
primary health care
quadruplets
quickening
reproduction
reproductive
   endocrinologist (RE)
   endocrinology
   tract
Rh factors
sciatica
sciatic-nerve pain
semen
sex
sexual intercourse
sonogram
sperm
spider veins
spina bifida
spotting

stillbirth
stretch marks
substance abuse
supertwins
teratogenic period
teratogens
tetracycline
thalidomide
toxemia
toxoplasmosis
trimester
triplets
tubal pregnancy
twins
ultrasound
umbilical cord
unwed mother
uterus
vagina
vaginal birth
vena cava
water birth
weight gain
womb
X chromosome
Y chromosome
zygote

ORGANIZATIONS

Center for Loss in Multiple Birth (CLIMB)
Childbirth without Pain Education Association (CWPEA)
Doulas of North America (DONA)
Heartbeat International
Home Birth Association
International Association of Parents and Professionals for Safe Alternatives in
   Childbirth (NAPSAC)
Midwest Parentcraft Center (MPC)
Miscarriage Association
National Abortion Federation (NAF)
National Adoption Information Clearinghouse (NAIC)
National Association of Childbirth Assistants (NACA)
National Maternal and Child Health Clearinghouse (NMCHC)
National Organization of Adolescent Pregnancy, Parenting and Prevention
   (NOAPP)
Peaceful Beginnings (PB)
Pregnancy and Infant Loss Center (PILC)
Unwed Parents Anonymous (UPA)

WEB SITES

BabyZone: Signs and Symptoms of Pregnancy
http://www.babyzone.com/symptom.htm

Childbirth.Org
http://www.childbirth.org/

InterNational Council on Infertility Information Dissemination
http://www.inciid.org/

Surrogate Mothers Online
http://www.SurromomsOnline.com/

Waiting with Love
http://www.erichad.com/wwl/

Psychology

Keywords may be searched singly or in combination with other words using Boolean operators *and*, *or*, or *not*.

abnormal psychology
abnormality
accommodation
achievement need
acquisition
action
adaptation
Adlerian psychology
adrenaline
affection
affective behavior
affiliation need
aggression
alienation
altruism
American functionalism
amnesia
analysis
anger
animal
animal behavior
anxiety
apathy
applied psychology
archetype
arousal
artificial intelligence (AI)
assertiveness
association
association measures
associative bias
attachment
attention span

attitudes
attribution
attribution theory
autism
autonomy
aversion
backwards conditioning
behavior
    genetics
    modification
    problems
behavioral therapy
behaviorism
behaviorist approach
belief
bell curve
bias
biological approach
biophysics
blocking
brain
burnout
bystander intervention model
Capgras syndrome
case study
category
catharsis
cause
centering
cerebrum
chemical straitjacket
child psychology
childhood

classical conditioning
clinical psychology
closedness
cognition
cognitive
   approach
   development
   dissonance
   map
   perspective
   psychology
   science
   therapy
cohort
collective unconscious
collectivism
communication systems
community psychology
comparative psychology
computation
concept
concrete
condition
conditioned response
conditioned stimulus
conditioning
conformity
congruence
consciousness
consequence
continuity
control
control group
coping
corpus callosum
correlation
counseling
counseling psychology
counselors
creativity
credibility
culture
Darwinian
debriefing
deception
decision
decision making
defense mechanisms

delayed conditioning
delusion
dependence
depression
desire
development
developmental psychology
deviant
diagnosis
diagnostic tests
discrimination
dreams
eating disorders
Eckbom's syndrome
educational psychology
effect
efficacy
ego
egocentrism
emotion
emotional
   abuse
   experience
   quotient
   response
empathy
empiricism
environment
equity theory
ethnicity
ethnocentrism
ethnopsychology
evaluation
evolutionary perspective
excitation
experience
experiment
experimental animal psychology
experimental human psychology
exposure
extinction
extrovert
facilitation
fear
field experiment
fixedness
flashbulb memory
folk psychology

force field analysis
free association
frustration
function
functionalism
fuzzy logic
gavagai
gender
gender schema
generalization
genetics
Gestalt psychology
glossolalia
goal orientation
grammar
gratification
group
group therapy
grouping
guilt
habituation
happiness
helplessness
heterosexuality
heuristics
higher-order conditioning
homosexuality
hormone
human
human behavior
humanistic-phenomenological perspective
humanization
hypnosis
hypothalamus
hypothesis
hysteria
id
idealism
identification
identity
ideology
illusion
improvement
individual
individualism
inductive reasoning
industrial-organizational psychology

influence
inhibition
inkblot
insight
instinct
intellect
intelligence
intelligence quotient (IQ)
intelligence tests
interpersonal attraction
interpretation
intervention
intimacy
introspection
introvert
jealousy
knowledge
Korsakoff's Syndrome
latent
law of contiguity
law of effect
learning
learning plateau
leisure
leucotomy
lobe
locus of control
long-term memory
love
maturity
measurement
measures
mechanism
memory
mental
    health
    illness
    life
meta-analysis
metacognition
midlife transition
mind
misperception
monitoring
mood
morale
motivation
motor

multiple intelligences
multiple personality
need gratification
nervous function
neuroleptic
neurology
neuropsychology
neuroscience
neurosis
neurotransmitter
norm
objective
observation
obsession
operant conditioning
pairing
paranoia
paranoid delusion
paranormal psychology
participant
perception
personality
   assessment
   studies
   traits
perspective
persuasion
phenomenology
philosophy
phobia
physiology
placebo
population
practitioner
praise
preconditioning
prediction
prejudice
prevention
primacy
problem solving
processing
prognosis
psychiatric services
psychiatrists
psychiatry
psychoacoustics
psychoanalysis

psychobiology
psychodynamic perspective
psycholinguistics
psychological
   disorders
   needs
   testing
psychometric psychology
psychometrics
psychopathology
psychophysiology
psychotherapy
psychotic episode
punishment
rape myth
rationalism
rationalization
reality
reason
reciprocity
recovery
reductionism
reference group
rehabilitation
reinforcement
rejection
replication
representation
repression
resentment
resistance
response
responsibility
results
role conflict
Rorschach test
rules of science
sadness
schemata
schizophrenia
school psychology
schools of psychology
science
scientific method
security
self-
   actualization
   concept

congruence
consciousness
destructive behavior
reflection
sensation
sensory
sensory deprivation
sex
sexual identity
sexual orientation
sharing behavior
short-term memory
similarity
simultaneous conditioning
sleep
social
    behavior
    processes
    psychology
    role
    science
sociobiology
split personality
sports psychology
state of mind
statistical sample
statistics
status need
stereotype
Sternberg task
stimulus
stimulus-response
stress
structuralism
structure

study
subculture
subject
subliminal
subordinate
superego
superordinate
survey
survival
symbol
system
taboo
temporal
theory
threat
trace conditioning
training
trait
transition
trauma
triangulation
trust
truth
Turing test
type A behavior
type B behavior
unconditioned response
unconditioned stimulus
understanding
values
variables
verbal
verbal operant conditioning
well-being
will
withdrawal

ORGANIZATIONS

American Academy of Forensic Psychology (AAFP)
American Association for Correctional Psychology (AACP)
American Association for the Advancement of Science (AAAS)
American Counseling Association (ACA)
American Evaluation Association (AEA)
American Psychological Association (APA)
American Psychological Practitioners Association (APPA)
Association for Advancement of Behavior Therapy (AABT)
Association for Advancement of Psychology (AAP)
Association for Transpersonal Psychology (ATP)

Association for Women in Psychology (AWP)
Bulgarian Psychological Association
Center for Applications of Psychological Type (CAPT)
Foundation for International Human Relations (FIHR)
North American Society of Adlerian Psychology (NASAP)
Psi Chi

KEY PEOPLE

Nineteenth Century
Beneke, Friedrich Eduard
Dix, Dorothea Lynde
Ebbinghaus, Hermann
Herbart, Johann F.
Huxley, Thomas Henry
James, William
Kierkegaard, Søren Aaby
Lotze, Rudolph Hermann
Mendel, Gregor Johann
Mesmer, Franz Anton
Müller, Johannes Peter
Weber, Ernst Heinrich
Wundt, Wilhelm

Twentieth Century
Adler, Alfred
Angell, James Rowland
Bandura, Albert
Binet, Alfred
Calkins, Mary Whiton
Dewey, John
Erikson, Erik
Freud, Anna

Freud, Sigmund
Fromm, Erich
Gardner, Howard
Hall, G. Stanley
Horney, Karen
Jung, Carl Gustav
Kimura, Doreen
Kristeva, Julia
Lewin, Kurt
Loftus, Elizabeth
Lorenz, Konrad Z.
Maslow, Abraham H.
Pavlov, Ivan Petrovich
Peck, M. Scott
Piaget, Jean
Rogers, Carl R.
Sacks, Oliver
Skinner, B. F.
Thorndike, Edward Lee
Tolman, Edward C.
Vygotsky, Lev Semenovich
Watson, John B.
Westheimer, Ruth

WEB SITES

American Psychological Association (APA)
http://www.apa.org/

AmoebaWeb: Psychology Web Resources
http://www.sccu.edu/psychology/amoebaweb.html

Behavior OnLine
http://www.behavior.net/

HyperStat Online
http:/davidmlane.com/hyperstat/

PsychSite
http://stange.simplenet.com/psycsite/

Psych Web
http://www.psywww.com/

Tobacco

Keywords may be searched singly or in combination with other words using Boolean operators *and*, *or*, or *not*.

addiction
adenocarcinoma
adrenaline
alkaloid
alveoli
angina pectoris
antenatal
asthma
autonomic nervous system
blend
bloodstream
bronchial
burley
burn
calabash
cancer
carbon dioxide (CO_2)
carbon monoxide (CO)
carboxyhemoglobin (COHb)
carcinogen
cardiac dysrhythmia
cardiovascular system
central nervous system
chewing tobacco
cigar
cigarette
cigarette smoking
combustion
coronary
cotinine
crop
cultivation
cure

curing
cutting
Cyprian
Djebel
drying
Dubek
environmental tobacco smoke
epidemiology
fatigue
field crops
fumes
glucose
health education
heart attack
heart disease
hydrocarbon vapor
hypersensitivity
illness
industry
leaves
lung cancer
lymphoma
maduro
medical effects
meerschaum
neoplasia
nerve
Nicotiana rustica
Nicotiana tabacum
nicotine
nicotine gum
nicotinic acid
nightshade

oiling
oncology
Oriental
ova
oxygen
passive smoking
peripheral vascular disease
physical health
pipe
   maker
   tobacco
plant
respiratory
risk group
Samsun
scaffold wagon
secondhand smoke
smog
smoke
smoke-free
smokeless tobacco
smoking
Smyrna
snuff
solanaceae
spit tobacco

stem
substance abuse
tar
tobacco
   blend
   fly
   horn worm
   mosaic virus
   sticks
tobacco-free policy
top casings
top flavorings
toxic gas
toxin
Trebizond
tumor
Turkish
Virginia
water pipe
white burley
wilting
wrapper
Xanthi
Yaka
Yeniji

ORGANIZATIONS

Action on Smoking and Health (ASH)
Americans for Nonsmokers' Rights (ANR)
Citizens for a Tobacco-Free Society (CATS)
Commodity Credit Corporation
Council for Tobacco Research—U.S.A. (CTR-USA)
Freedom Organisation for the Right to Enjoy Smoking Tobacco (FOREST)
Group Against Smokers' Pollution (GASP)
INFACT
Stop Teen-Age Addiction to Tobacco (STAT)
Tobacco Industry Labor/Management Committee (TILMC)
Tobacco Institute (TI)
Tobacco Merchants Association (TMA)
Tobacco Pipe Makers' and Tobacco Blenders' Company
Tobacco Products Liability Project (TPLP)
The Universal Coterie of Pipe Smokers (TUCOPS)

KEY PEOPLE

Dewey, Melvil
Drake, Francis
Duke, James Buchanan
Gálvez, José de

Hatch, William Henry
Nicot, Jean
Northrop, John Howard
Raleigh, Walter

Reynolds, R. J.

Rolfe, John
Sandys, Edwin

WEB SITES

American Cancer Society
http://www.cancer.org/

CDC's TIPS: Tobacco Information and Prevention Source
http://www.cdc.gov/tobacco/

Friends of Tobacco
http://www.fujipub.com/fot/

National Center for Tobacco-Free Kids
http://www.tobaccofreekids.org/

HISTORY, POLITICAL
SCIENCE, & LAW

Ancient Civilizations

Keywords may be searched singly or in combination with other words using Boolean operators *and*, *or*, or *not*.

Africa
Amerindian
archaeology
Aroi Sun Kingdom
Assyrian
Atlantis
Aztec
Babylonian
Bimini Wall
Bronze Age
Central America
Chimu
China
Copper Age
Cush
Cuzco
Easter Island
Egypt
Ethiopia
excavation
Gobi Desert
Greeks
Han China
Harappa
Inca
Iron Age
Israel
Lemuria
lost civilization
Malta
Maya
megalithic
Mesopotamia
Mohenjo Daro
Mu
mythology
Nubian
Osirian civilization
Pacific
Peru
Poseid
Puma Punku
pyramids
Rama empire
Romans
ruins
Sukuh
Sumerian
temple
Thera
Tiahuanaco
Uiger
Yucatan Peninsula

ORGANIZATIONS

Ancient Astronaut Society (AAS)
Association for the Study of Classical African Civilizations (ASCAC)
Foundation for Latin American Anthropological Research (FLAAR)
Junior Classical League (JCL)

Mycenaean Commission (MC)
Vergilian Society (VS)

WEB SITES

Aegyptiaca: A Study of Ancient Egypt
http://members.xoom.com/edpa/egypt/egypt.htm

Ancient Civilizations Seen through CG
http://www.taisei.co.jp/cg_e/ancient_world/ancient.html

Ancient Northwest Europe
http://www.brown.edu/Departments/English/people/russom/ancient/index.html

Ancient World Web
http://www.julen.netancient

Atlantis Rising
http://atlantisrising.com/

Exploring Ancient World Cultures
http://eawc.evansville.edu/index.htm

Maecenas: Images of Ancient Greece and Rome
http://wings.buffalo.edu/AandL/Maecenas/index.html

Civil War, United States
(1861–1865)

Keywords may be searched singly or in combination with other words using Boolean operators *and*, *or*, or *not*.

abolition
Anaconda Plan
Andersonville Prison, GA
Appomattox Court House, VA
Army of Northern Virginia
Army of the Cumberland
Battle of
    Antietam (1862)
    Cedar Mountain (1862)
    Chancellorsville (1863)
    Cold Harbor (1864)
    Five Forks (1865)
    Fredericksburg (1862)
    Gettysburg (1863)
    Shiloh (1862)
    Stones River (1862–1863)
    the Wilderness (1864)
burning of Atlanta
Camp Douglas, IL
Campaign of Vicksburg (1863)
casualties
causes
Compromise Measures (1850)
Confederacy
Confederate States of America
Copperheads
Democratic Party
desertion
Dixie
Emancipation Proclamation (1863)
First Battle of Bull Run (1861)
Fort Fisher, NC
Fort Jefferson, FL

Fort Pickens, FL
Fort Sumter, SC
Fort Taylor, FL
Fourteenth Amendment (1868)
Freedman's Village
Gettysburg Address (1863)
Gettysburg, PA
ironclad
Kansas-Nebraska Act (1854)
King Cotton
Louisiana Territory
Manassas, VA
March to the Sea (1864)
Mason-Dixon Line
Merrimack
Missouri Compromise
Monitor
North
Northwest Territory
Perryville, KY
Petersburg, VA
Pickett's Charge
plantations
Reconstruction
Republican Party
Richmond, VA
Scott v. Sandford (1857)
secession
Seven Days' Battle (1862)
slavery
soldiers
South
states' rights

Sultana Disaster
Thirteenth Amendment (1865)
Trent Affair (1861)
Uncle Tom's Cabin
Union
U.S.
   Congress

Navy
   of America
   USS Kearsarge
War
   between the States
   for Southern Independence
   of Rebellion
Western Theater

ORGANIZATIONS

Children of the Confederacy (CofC)
Civil War Society (CWS)
Confederate Memorial Association (CMA)
Daughters of Union Veterans of the Civil War, 1861–1865 (DUV)
Grand Army of the Republic (GAR)
Institute of Civil War Studies (ICWS)
Military Order of the Loyal Legion of the United States (MOLLUS)
Military Order of the Stars and Bars (MOSB)
National Archives and Records Administration(NARA)
North-South Skirmish Association (N-SSA)
Robert E. Lee Memorial Association (RELMA)
Save the Battlefield Coalition (SBC)
Society of Civil War Historians
Sons of Confederate Veterans (SCV)
Ulysses S. Grant Association (USGA)
United Confederate Veterans
United Daughters of the Confederacy (UDC)
U.S. Christian Commission
U.S. Colored Troops

KEY PEOPLE

Confederacy
Beauregard, Pierre G. T.
Bragg, Braxton
Davis, Jefferson
Early, Jubal A.
Forrest, Nathan Bedford
Gist, William Henry
Greenhow, Rose O'Neal
Jackson, Thomas J., "Stonewall"
Johnston, Joseph E.
Kirkland, Richard, "Angel of Marye's
   Heights"
Lee, Robert Edward
Longstreet, James
Pickett, George Edward
Salling, John
Semmes, Raphael
Stephens, Alexander H.

Stuart, J.E.B.
Wilcox, Cadmus Marcellus
Union
Adams, Charles Francis
Buchanan, James
Burnside, Ambrose E.
Butler, Benjamin F.
Chamberlain, Joshua Lawrence
Farragut, David G.
Grant, Ulysses S.
Halleck, Henry W.
Hancock, Winfield Scott
Hooker, Joseph
Johnson, Andrew
Lincoln, Abraham
McClellan, George B.
Meade, George Gordon
Rawlins, John Aaron

Rosecrans, William S.
Sheridan, Philip H.
Sherman, William Tecumseh
Stanton, Edwin
Thomas, George H., "Rock of
    Chickamauga"
Winslow, John A.

Other Figures
Barton, Clara

Booth, John Wilkes
Brady, Matthew
Brown, John
Douglas, Stephen A.
Grimké, Angelina
Grimké, Sarah
McLean, Wilbur
Scott, Dred
Stowe, Harriet Beecher
Whitman, Walt

WEB SITES

American Civil War Association (ACWA)
http://acwa.org/

Gettysburg's First Hours: A Shockwave Movie
http://www.icorps.com/gshock.htm

The Museum of the Confederacy
http://www.moc.org/

Selected Civil War Photographs, Library of Congress
http://rs6.loc.gov/ammem/cwphome.html

Sons of Union Veterans of the Civil War (SUVCW)
http://suvcw.org/

U.S. Civil War Center
http://www.cwc.lsu.edu/

Cold War (1945–1991)

Keywords may be searched singly or in combination with other words using Boolean operators *and*, *or*, or *not*.

Afghanistan
antiballistic missile (ABM)
arms race
atomic bomb
Baghdad Pact (1955)
Bay of Pigs (1961)
Berlin airlift (1948–1949)
Berlin Wall
bomber gap
broken arrow
Checkpoint Charlie
China
cold warriors
communism
containment
Conventional Forces in Europe Treaty (CFE, 1990)
Cuban Missile Crisis (1962)
Cultural Revolution
DEFCON
demilitarized zone (DMZ)
detente
disarmament
East Germany
Eisenhower Doctrine
fallout shelter
first strike
Geneva Agreement (1988)
Geneva Conference
German Democratic Republic (GDR)
glasnost
Great Leap Forward
Helsinki Accords (1975)

Hungarian Revolution (1956)
hydrogen bomb
ideology
INF Treaty (1987)
intercontinental ballistic missile (ICBM)
Intermediate-Range Nuclear Forces Treaty (1987)
Iran hostage crisis (1979)
Iron Curtain
Kitchen Debate (1959)
Korean War (1950–1953)
Limited Test Ban Treaty (1963)
Malta
Manhattan Project
Marshall Plan
McCarthyism
missile gap
mutual assured destruction (MAD)
National Defense Education Act (NDEA, 1958)
North American Air Defense Command (NORAD)
North Korea
North Vietnam
nuclear arms race
nuclear attack survival kit (NASK)
nuclear missiles
Nuclear Non-Proliferation Treaty (1972)
nuclear winter
Ostpolitik
perestroika
Russian revolution

satellites
second-strike capability
Solidarity
South Korea
South Vietnam
Soviet bloc
Soviet Union
space race
spies
Strategic Arms Limitation Talks (SALT)
Strategic Arms Reductions Talks (START)
Strategic Defense Initiative (SDI, Star Wars, 1983)

Suez Crisis (1956)
Tet Offensive (1968)
thermonuclear device
Truman Doctrine
U-2 incident (1960)
Union of Soviet Socialist Republics (USSR)
Velvet Revolution (1989)
Venona
Warsaw Pact (1955)
West Germany
Westpolitik
Yalta (1945)

ORGANIZATIONS

Central Intelligence Agency (CIA)
Commonwealth of Independent States (CIS)
Council for Mutual and Economic Cooperation (COMECON)
Southeast Asia Treaty Organization (SEATO)

KEY PEOPLE

Europe
Adenauer, Konrad
Brandt, Willy
Ceausescu, Nicolae
Churchill, Winston
Havel, Vaclav
Kohl, Helmut
Thatcher, Margaret
Walesa, Lech

Soviet Union
Andropov, Yuri
Brezhnev, Leonid
Gorbachev, Mikhail Sergeyvich
Khrushchev, Nikita
Stalin, Joseph
Yeltsin, Boris Nikolayevich

United States
Acheson, Dean
Bush, George

Carter, James Earl, "Jimmy"
Dulles, John Foster
Eisenhower, Dwight David
Ford, Gerald R.
Johnson, Lyndon Baines
Kennedy, John Fitzgerald
Kissinger, Henry Alfred
Marshall, George, Jr.
McCarthy, Joseph
McNamara, Robert
Nixon, Richard M.
Powers, Francis Gary
Reagan, Ronald W.
Roosevelt, Franklin Delano
Truman, Harry S

Other Figures
Castro, Fidel
Ho Chi Minh
Khomeini, Ayatollah Ruhollah
Mao Tse-tung (Mao Zedong)

WEB SITES

Berlin Wall
http://www.wall-berlin.org/

CNN: Cold War
http://www.cnn.com/SPECIALS/cold.war/

Cold War International History Project (CWIHP)
http://cwihp.si.edu/default.htm

The Cold War Museum
http://www.coldwar.org/

North Atlantic Treaty Organization (NATO)
http://www.nato.int/

Government, U.S.

Keywords may be searched singly or in combination with other words using Boolean operators *and*, *or*, or *not*.

agencies
armed forces
Articles of Confederation
Bill of Rights
bureau
cabinet
Capitol
checks and balances
civil liberties
commission
Constitution of the United States
constitutional
   amendment
   history
   law
Declaration of Independence
District of Columbia
election
executive branch
federal courts
federalism
higher courts
House of Representatives

impeachment
income tax
judicial branch
judicial system
legislative branch
Legislative Reorganization Act (1946)
National Guard
national security
policy making
political parties
president
public policy
public trust
representative
Senate
senator
separation of powers
Speaker of the House
special courts
succession
Supreme Court
term of office
vice-president

ORGANIZATIONS

Administrative Assistants Association of the U.S. House of Representatives
American Council of Young Political Leaders (ACYPL)
American Studies Association (ASA)
Center for the Study of States (CSS)
Chamber of Commerce of the United States—U.S. Chamber
Committee on Justice and the Constitution (COJAC)
Institute of Public Administration (IPA)
League of Women Voters of the United States (LWVUS)

U.S. Congressional Advisory Board (USCAB)
U.S. Senate Press Photographers Gallery (USSPPG)

WEB SITES

American Foreign Service Association
http://www.afsa.org/

CapWeb: The Citizen's Guide to Congress
http://www.capweb.net/

Council of State Governments (CSG)
http://www.statesnews.org/

The Federal Judiciary
http://www.uscourts.gov/

FedWorld Information Network
http://www.fedworld.gov/

Library of Congress
http://lcweb.loc.gov/

National Governors Association (NGA)
http://www.nga.org/

National Security Council
http://www.whitehouse.gov/WH/EOP/NSC/html/nschome.html

Roll Call
http://www.rollcall.com/

THOMAS: Legislative Information on the Internet
http://thomas.loc.gov/

U.S. House of Representatives
http://www.house.gov/

U.S. Senate
http://www.senate.gov/

White House
http://www.whitehouse.gov/

Historical Documents

Keywords may be searched singly or in combination with other words using Boolean operators *and*, *or*, or *not*.

Albany Plan (1754)
Alien and Sedition Acts (1798)
Articles of Confederation (1777)
Atlantic Charter (1941)
Augsburg Confession (1530)
Balfour Declaration (1917)
Bill of Rights (1791)
Cambridge Agreement (1629)
Clayton Anti-Trust Act (1914)
Connecticut Colony Charter (1662)
Constitution of the Confederate States of America (1861)
Constitution of the United States of America (1787)
Contract with America (1994)
Dawes Act (1887)
Declaration of Independence (1776)
Declaration of the Rights of Man and of the Citizen (1789)
Emancipation Proclamation (1863)
Espionage Act (1917)
Fair Labor Standards Act (1938)
Federal Trade Commission Act (1914)
Federalist Papers
Fugitive Slave Act (1850)
Fugitive Slave Law (1793)
Gettysburg Address (1863)
Hatch Act (1939)
Hay-Pauncefote Treaty (1901)
Homestead Act (1862)

Jay's Treaty (1794)
Kansas-Nebraska Act (1854)
Kellogg-Briand Pact (1928)
Lend-Lease Act (1941)
Magna Carta (1215)
Mayflower Compact (1620)
Missouri Compromise (1820)
Monroe Doctrine (1823)
Morrill Act (1862)
Ninety-Five Theses (1517)
North Atlantic Treaty (1949)
Nuclear Nonproliferation Treaty (1968)
Oregon Treaty (1846)
Panama Canal Treaty (1977)
Paris Peace Pact (1928)
Petition of Right (1628)
Platt Amendment (1901)
Quartering Act (1765)
Rush-Bagot Convention (1817)
Self-Reliance (1841)
Sherman Antitrust Act (1890)
Social Security Act (1935)
Stamp Act (1765)
Tenure of Office Act (1867)
Townshend Acts (1767)
Treaty of Ghent (1814)
Treaty of Guadeloupe Hidalgo (1848)
Truman Doctrine (1947)
Walsh-Healey Act (1936)
Zimmerman Note (1917)

ORGANIZATIONS

British Records Association (BRA)
National Archives and Records Administration Volunteer Association (NARA)
New England Antiquities Research Association (NEARA)
New York Cipher Society (NYCS)
Organization of American Historians (OAH)

WEB SITES

A Chronology of U.S. Historical Documents, The University of Oklahoma Law Center
http://www.law.ou.edu/hist/

EuroDocs
http://library.byu.edu/~rdh/eurodocs/

National Archives and Records Administration
http://www.nara.gov/

Texts and Documents: The United States
http://history.hanover.edu/usa.htm

U.S. Government Hypertexts
http://metalab.unc.edu/govdocs.html

U.S. Government Printing Office (GPO)
http://www.gpo.gov/

U.S. Historical Documents Archive
http://w3.one.net/~mweiler/ushda/ushda.htm

Holocaust, Jewish (1939–1945)

Keywords may be searched singly or in combination with other words using Boolean operators *and*, *or*, or *not*.

aktion
Allied Powers
anti-semitism
Aryan race
assimilation
Auschwitz
Auschwitz-Birkenau
Axis Powers
Babi Yar massacre
Belgium
Belzec
Bergen-Belsen
Birkenau
Brown Shirts
Buchenwald
Buna
Bund
Catholics
cattle cars
Chelmno
concentration camp
contra fact
cremation
Dachau
death camp
death march
demonstration
deportation
Die Juden sind under Ungluck
diseases
displaced person (DP)
displacement
Einsatzgruppen

Enabling Act (1933)
European Jewry
euthanasia
Evian Conference (1938)
extermination
extermination camp
fascism
Final Solution
forced labor
France
Free French
führer
Fuhrerstaat
gas chamber
General Government
genocide
German race
Germany
gestapo (Geheime Staatspolizei)
Great Britain
Greater German Reich
Gypsy
homosexuals
Hungary
hydrogen cyanide
imprisonment
incarceration
intermarriage
International Military Tribunal
Italy
Japan
Jehovah's Witness
Jew hunt

Jewish
  badge
  Quarter
  resistance
  Socialist Party
Jew-pure
Jews
Judaism
Judenfrei
Judenrat (Jewish Council)
kapo
killing center
krematoria
labor camp
Law for the Protection of German
    Blood and Honor
liberation
Lidice
Lodz Ghetto
Madagascar Plan
Majdanek
Marrano
massacre
master race
Mauthausen
medical experiments
Mein Kampf (My Struggle)
Mischlinge
Monowitz
Mother's Cross
murder
Muselmann
Nazi Germany
Nazi Party (National Socialist German
    Workers' Party, NASDAP)
Nazi Youth
Nazis
Netherlands
Night and Fog Decree (1941)
Night of the Broken Glass
    (Kristallnacht)
Nuremberg Laws (1935)
Nuremberg Trial
Operation Reinhard (Aktion Reinhard)
partisans
persecution
pogrom
Poland

political prisoner
prisoner of war (POW)
propaganda
protectorate
Protocols of the Elders of Zion
race treason
racial hygiene
racial purity
rallies
Reich Citizenship Law
Reich Representation of German Jews
Reichstag
resettlement
resistance
revisionists
righteous Gentiles
Romania
SA (Sturmabteilung)
Sachsenhausen
Shoah
Sinti
Sobibór
Soviet Union
special treatment
SS (Schutzstaffel)
SS St. Louis
Star of David
starvation
Struma
survivors
swastika
synagogue
Terezin
Third Reich
Torah
torture
trains
Treblinka
Umschlagplatz
underground
United States of America
Wannsee Conference (1942)
war criminals
Warsaw Ghetto
Warsaw Ghetto Uprising
Wehrmacht
World War II (1939–1945)

Yad Vashem Holocaust Memorial, Jerusalem, Israel

Yom ha-Shoah
Zionism
Zyklon-B

ORGANIZATIONS

American Gathering of Jewish Holocaust Survivors (AGJHS)
Anne Frank Center U.S.A. (AFAFC)
Anti-Defamation League (ADL)
Association of Holocaust Organizations (AHO)
Congress for Jewish Culture (CJC)
Facing History and Ourselves National Foundation (FHAO)
Federation of Former Jewish Fighters (FFJF)
Friends of Jerusalem (American Neturei Karta) (FJ)
The Generation After (TGA)
Holocaust Survivors and Friends in Pursuit of Justice (HSFPJ)
Holocaust Survivors of Auschwitz (HSA)
National Association for Holocaust Education (NAHE)
Society for the Philosophical Study of Genocide and the Holocaust (SPSGH)
Thanks to Scandinavia (TTS)

KEY PEOPLE

Bukovina
Applefeld, Aharon

Germany—Nazi Party Members & German Soldiers
Barbie, Klaus
Brunner, Alois
Eichmann, Adolf
Göring, Herman
Grynspan, Herschel
Grynszpan, Herschel
Hess, Walter Richard Rudolf
Heydrich, Reinhard
Himmler, Heinrich
Hitler, Adolf
Mengele, Josef
Stroop, Jürgen

Germany—Other Figures
Arendt, Hannah
Baeck, Leo
Baum, Herbert
Fackenheim, Emil Ludwig
Feuchtwanger, Lion
Frank, Anne
Riefenstahl, Leni

Salomon, Charlotte
Schindler, Oskar
Sennesh, Hannah
Stein, Edith

Italy
Levi, Primo

Poland
Anielewicz, Mordecai
Korczak, Janusz
Wiesenthal, Simon

Romania
Wiesel, Elie

Slovakia
Fleischmann, Gisi

Sweden
Wallenberg, Raoul

United Kingdom
Chamberlain, Neville
Churchill, Winston

United States
Eisenhower, Dwight D.
Freed, James Ingo

WEB SITES

Federation of Jewish Child Survivors of the Holocaust
http://www.fjcsh.org/

Holocaust Memorial Center
http://holocaustcenter.org/

Holocaust Teacher Resource Center (TRC)
http://www.Holocaust-trc.org/

The Simon Wiesenthal Center
http://www.wiesenthal.com/

Survivors of the Shoah Visual History Foundation
http://www.vhf.org/

A Teacher's Guide to the Holocaust
http://fcit.coedu.usf.edu/holocaust/default.htm

U.S. Holocaust Memorial Museum
http://www.ushmm.org/index.html

Yad Vashem
http://www.yad-vashem.org.il/

Industrial Revolution

Keywords may be searched singly or in combination with other words using Boolean operators *and*, *or*, or *not*.

agrarian
airplanes
American Federation of Labor
American Industrial Revolution
artisans
Black Codes
British Industrial Revolution
Central Pacific
child labor
Chimney Sweepers' Regulation Bill
civil service
coal mines
commerce
communications
construction
cotton
   engine
   gin
   industry
   mill
craft union
crop-lien
Darwinism
disease
economic conditions
electricity
empire
employment
engineering
entrepreneurs
epidemic
expansionism
factories

factory owner
factory system
fundamentalism
gilded age
Grangers
Great Expectations
Haymarket Riot Affair (1886)
health
hours of labor
hurrier
illness
industrial class
industrial union
injury
interchangeable parts
internal combustion engine
interstate commerce
Interstate Commerce Act
invention
Jim Crow
The Jungle
Knights of Labor
labor supply
legislation
loom
loss of life
low wages
machines
machinery
Luddites
Manifest Destiny
Mann Act (1910)
manufacturing

market
mass production
mechanization
mine
modernization
monopoly
mortality
Northern Pacific
orphanage
overwork
patent
Pendleton Act (1883)
physical deterioration
political machine
politics
production
profession
protective legislation
public health
Pure Food and Drug Act (1906)
quality
quantity
Radical Republicans
railroad
Reconstruction
regulation
Sadler Committee
sanitation
scientific discovery

sharecropper
sickness
skilled labor
slavery
social Darwinism
speed
spinning jenny
steam engine
steamboat
steel
strikes
survival of the fittest
tariff
technology
telegraph
telephone
tenement
textile mill
theory of evolution
trade
transcontinental railroad
transportation
transportation industry
uniformity-system
Union Pacific
unskilled labor
workforce
working class
working day
Yankee ingenuity

ORGANIZATIONS

Early American Industries Association (EAIA)
Industrial Workers of the World
Knights of Labor
Mugwumps
Populist Party
Society for the Promotion of Science and Scholarship (SPOSS)

KEY PEOPLE

Authors & Publishers
Carlyle, Thomas
Dickens, Charles
Du Bois, W.E.B. (William Edward
    Burghardt)
Nast, Thomas

Business Leaders
Carnegie, Andrew
Fielden, John

Ford, Henry
Gompers, Samuel
Lowell, Francis Cabot
Phyfe, Duncan
Rockefeller, John D.
Slater, Samuel
Stanford, Leland

Inventors & Scientists
Arkwright, Richard

Blanchard, Thomas
Cartwright, Edmund
Cort, Henry
Darwin, Charles Robert
Deere, John
Edison, Thomas
Fulton, Robert
Goodyear, Charles
Howe, Elias
Jacquard, Joseph Marie
McCormick, Cyrus

Nasmyth, James
Newcomen, Thomas
Spencer, Herbert
Watt, James
Whitney, Eli

Social Reformers
Addams, Jane
Chadwick, Edwin
Cobbett, William
Dewey, John
Sinclair, Upton

WEB SITES

Important Historical Inventions and Inventors
http://www.lib.lsu.edu/sci/chem/patent/srs136.html

Industrial Revolution: A Trip to the Past
http://members.aol.com/mhirotsu/kevin/trip2.html

IRWeb: The Industrial Revolution
http://tqjunior.advanced.org/4132/index.htm

Life of the Industrial Worker in 19th-Century England
http://applebutter.freeservers.com/worker/

A Short History of Machine Tools
http://www.darex.com/indurevo.htm

Steam Engine Library
http://www.history.rochester.edu/steam/

International Relations

Keywords may be searched singly or in combination with other words using Boolean operators *and, or,* or *not.*

agricultural research
area studies
arms control
artificial languages
ballistic missile defense
boundary disputes
chemical weapons convention
civil liberties
colonialism
comparative analysis
conflict resolution
consulate
country study
cross-cultural studies
cross-cultural training
cultural exchange
defense budget
developed nations
developing nations
diplomacy
diplomat
diplomatic history
disarmament
disaster assistance
disaster assistance response team
economic
   development
   growth
   sanctions
ethnocentrism
exchange programs
exports
foreign

assistance program
countries
culture
diplomats
nationals
policy
policy objectives
relations
fundamental freedoms
global
   community
   economy
   impact
human rights
humanitarian assistance
immigration
imperialism
imports
institutional cooperation
intercultural communication
intercultural programs
intergovernmental organizations
international
   behavior
   communication
   cooperation
   crime
   educational exchange
   law
   organizations
   policy
   programs
   relations

studies
trade
law of nations
monetary systems
multilingualism
national organizations
national security
nationalism
natural resources
nonproliferation
nuclear terrorism
Olympic Games
overseas mission
peacekeeping
political system
private voluntary organization (PVO)

professional associations
self-determination
standard of living
student exchange programs
study abroad
supply and demand
technical assistance
technology
terrorism
Third World nations
trade
treaties
violent conflict
war
war crimes
world affairs

ORGANIZATIONS

American Academy of Diplomacy (AAD)
Arms Control and Foreign Policy Caucus (ACFPC)
Association of Third World Affairs (ATWA)
Center for International Policy (CIP)
Coalition for Women in International Development (CWID)
Commission on U.S.-Asian Relations
Council on Competitiveness (CoC)
Council on Foreign Relations (CFR)
Foreign Bases Project (FBP)
Foreign Policy Association (FPA)
Human Rights Political Action Committee (HRPAC)
National Advisory Council for South Asian Affairs (NACSAA)
National Association of Pro America (NAPA)
National Committee on American Foreign Policy (NCAFP)
National Committee on United States–China Relations (NCUSCR)
Office of the Americas (OOA)
U.S.–Asia Institute (USAI)
U.S. Defense Committee (USDC)
United States Global Strategy Council (USGSC)
World Policy Institute (WPI)

WEB SITES

Access: An International Affairs Information Service
http://www.4access.org/

DefenseLINK
http://www.defenselink.mil/

Electronic Embassy
http://www.embassy.org/

House Committee on Armed Services
http://www.house.gov/hasc/

International Studies Association Network
http://csf.Colorado.EDU/isa/

North Atlantic Treaty Organisation (NATO)
http://www.nato.int/

Senate Committee on Foreign Relations
http://www.senate.gov/~foreign/

U.S. Department of State
http://www.state.gov/

Korean War (1950–1953)

Keywords may be searched singly or in combination with other words using Boolean operators *and*, *or*, or *not*.

armed aggression
armistice conference
battle
    fatigue
    of Chipyong-ni (1951)
    of Unsan (1950)
    of Yechon (1950)
Big Switch
brainwashing
British Commonwealth Division
campaigns
    UN Defensive (1950)
    UN Offensive (1950)
    CCF Intervention (1950–1951)
    CCF Spring Offensive (1951)
    First UN Counteroffensive (1951)
    UN Summer-Fall Offensive (1951)
    Second Korean Winter (1951–1952)
    Korea Summer-Fall (1952)
    Third Korean Winter (1952–1953)
    Korea Summer-Fall (1953)
China
Chinese Communist Forces (CCF)
Chosin Reservoir
Cold War
communism
counteroffensive
demilitarized zone (DMZ)
Eighth Army
Far East Air Forces (FEAF)
Far East Command (FECOM)
germ warfare
Heartbreak Ridge

Inchon invasion
invasion
Joint Chiefs of Staff
Korean Peninsula
line of demarcation
Manchuria
Military Armistice Commission
mobile army surgical hospital
    (MASH)
Mutual Defense Assistance Program
Neutral Nations Repatriation Com-
    mission
Neutral Nations Supervisory Com-
    mission
North Korea
North Korea People's Army
occupation
Operation Chromite
Operation Killer
Panmunjom
police action
psychological warfare
Pusan Perimeter
repatriation
Republic of Korea (ROK)
Seabees
Seoul, South Korea
sorties
South Korea
task force
Task Force Smith
thermonuclear device
38th Parallel

Union of Soviet Socialist Republics
(USSR)
United Nations Command (UNC)

Western bloc
World War II (1939–1945)
X Corps
Zone of Occupation

ORGANIZATIONS

Korean War Veterans Association
North Atlantic Treaty Organization (NATO)
United Nations (UN)
United Nations Security Council

KEY PEOPLE

United States
Acheson, Dean G.
Almond, Edward M.
Bradley, Omar Nelson
Briscoe, Robert Pearce
Clark, Mark W.
Collins, Joseph Lawton
Dean, William F.
Eisenhower, Dwight David
MacArthur, Douglas
Marshall, George Catlett
Mize, Ola L.
Ridgway, Matthew B.

Shepherd, LeManuel C., Jr.
Taylor, Maxwell D.
Truman, Harry S
Van Fleet, James Alword
Vandenberg, Hoyt Sanford
Walker, Walton H.
Weyland, Otto Paul

Other Figures
Chiang-Kai-shek
Kim Il Sung
Malik, Jacob
Mao Tse-tung (Mao Zedong)
Rhee, Syngman

WEB SITES

Korea: The Land of Morning Calm
http://www.defenselink.mil/specials/korea/

Korean War 50th Anniversary Home Page
http://korea50.army.mil/

Korean War Veterans National Museum & Library
http://www.theforgottenvictory.org/

Korean War Project
http://www.koreanwar.org/

KoreanWar.net
http://www.koreanwar.net/

Remembering the Korean War
http://www.army.mil/cmh-pg/online/kw-remem.htm

U.S.–Korea 2000 Foundation, Inc.
http://www.uskorea2000.org/

Law

Keywords may be searched singly or in combination with other words using Boolean operators *and, or,* or *not.*

accountability
acquittal
adjudication
advocate
affidavit
agricultural law
allegation
appeal
appellant
appellate court
arraignment
arrest
attorney
attorney-client privilege
bail
bankruptcy
barrister
bench trial
brief
capital offense
case
case law
chambers
charge
charge to the jury
chief judge
chief justice
child advocacy
child support
circumstantial evidence
citation
citizenship
civil

case
   law
   liberty
    rights
claim
clerk of court
codification
common law
compensation
complaint
compliance
computer law
conflict of interest
constitutional law
contract
conviction
copyright
counsel
counterclaim
court
court reporter
court supervision
courts of appeals
covenant
crime
crime prevention
criminal
   defendant
  law
criminology
custody
damages
decree

defendant
delinquency
deposition
discriminatory legislation
district attorney (DA)
docket
due process
en banc
entertainment law
environmental law
equal protection
eyewitness
federal court system
felony
forensic science
freedom of information
full court
grand jury
habeas corpus
hearing
hearsay
impeachment
imprisonment
in forma pauperis
in loco parentis
indemnity
indictment
injunction
injury
intellectual property
international crime
international law
interrogatory
judge
judiciary
jurisdiction
jurisprudence
jurist
jus cogens
justice
juvenile justice
labor relations
law clerk
law enforcement
lawsuit
lawyer
legal
  aid

assistant
custody
responsibility
services
system
legislation
liability
libel
litigant
litigation
lower court
magistrate
malpractice
maritime law
miscarriage of justice
misdemeanor
mistrial
negligence
no contest
nolo contendere
oath
offender
offense
officer
opinion
patent
petit jury
petitioner
plaintiff
plea
police
police action
postconviction appeal
practice
precedent
pretrial
prisoner
pro se
probable cause
probation
proceeding
property
prosecutor
protection
public administration
public defender
real property
reasonable doubt

remand
render
respondent
reversal
sentence
sentencing guidelines
sequester
settlement
sidebar
solicitor
staff attorney
statement
statute
subpoena
suit

summons
temporary restraining order
testimony
tort
transcript
treaty
trial
trial jury
tribunal
verdict
voir dire
warrant
witness
writ
writ of certiorari

ORGANIZATIONS

American Association of Police Polygraphists (AAPP)
American Bar Association Center for Professional Responsibility (ABACPR)
American Corporate Counsel Association (ACCA)
American Federation of Police and Concerned Citizens
American Intellectual Property Law Association (AIPLA)
American Police Academy (APA)
American Tort Reform Association (ATRA)
Americans for Effective Law Enforcement (AELE)
Association of Certified Fraud Examiners (ACFE)
Association of Former Agents of the U.S. Secret Service (AFAUSSS)
Association of Professional Police Investigators (APPI)
Evidence Photographers International Council (EPIC)
Federal Bar Association (FBA)
Federal Investigators Association (FIA)
Federal Law Enforcement Officers Association (FLEOA)
International Association of Arson Investigators (IAAI)
International Association of Chiefs of Police (IACP)
International Association of Personal Protection Agents (IAPPA)
National Association for Public Interest Law (NAPIL)
National Association of Bar Executives (NABE)
National Association of Criminal Defense Lawyers (NACDL)
National Association of Women Lawyers (NAWL)
National Center for Computer Crime Data (NCCCD)
Society of Professional Investigators (SPI)
World Association of Document Examiners (WADE)

KEY PEOPLE

Attorneys & Justices
Bailey, F. Lee
Blackstone, William
Brandeis, Louis

Bryan, William Jennings
Burger Warren
Cochran, Johnnie
Coke, Edward

Darrow, Clarence Seward
Douglas, William O.
Frankfurter, Felix
Ginsburg, Ruth Bader
Kunstler, William
Laughlin, Gail

Lincoln, Abraham
Marshall, John
O'Connor, Sandra Day
Reno, Janet
Rehnquist, William
Warren, Earl

WEB SITES

American Bar Association (ABA)
http://www.abanet.org/

Association of American Law Schools
http://www.aals.org/

FindLaw: Internet Legal Resources
http://www.findlaw.com/

Legal Recourse
http://www.legal.com/index.htm

National Association of Attorneys General
http://www.naag.org/

Mediation

Keywords may be searched singly or in combination with other words using Boolean operators *and*, *or*, or *not*.

agreement
alternative dispute resolution
antitrust law
arbitrator
award
binding decision
boundary dispute
claim
collective bargaining agreements
commerce
commercial dispute
compulsory
conciliation
contested situation
contract
discharge
disputant
dispute
distribution
employee discipline
evidence
fact-finding
Federal Arbitration Act (1925)
grievance
grievance arbitration
impasse
infringement
insurance
international arbitration
international commercial arbitration

interpretation
interruption
labor
  dispute
  union
Labor–Management Relations Act
  (1947)
lease agreements
lockout
management
negotiation
neutral
parties
patent law
production
propitiation
public law disputes
reconciliation
resolution
securities law
settlement
strike
Taft-Hartley Act (1947)
terms
trade
Treaty of Washington (1871)
United Nations Convention on the
  Recognition of Foreign Arbitral
  Awards
validity

ORGANIZATIONS

Academy of Experts
Chartered Institute of Arbitrators
Colorado Council of Mediators and Mediation Organizations
Commission for Conciliation, Mediation and Arbitration (CCMA)
CPR Institute for Dispute Resolution
Federal Mediation and Conciliation Service
International Academy of Mediators
International Court of Arbitration
Massachusetts Council on Family Mediation
Ontario Labour–Management Arbitrators Association
Prevention and Early Resolution of Conflict (PERC)

WEB SITES

American Arbitration Association
http://adr.org/

Common Bond Institute (CBI)
http://www.ahpweb.org/cbi/home.html

INCORE
http://www.incore.ulst.ac.uk/

National Association for Community Mediation
http://www.nafcm.org/

Peace Net
http://www.igc.org/igc/gateway/pnindex.html

Military

Keywords may be searched singly or in combination with other words using Boolean operators *and*, *or*, or *not*.

active duty
admiral
air base
air force base
air traffic control
airborne
airport
armed forces
armor
armory
army
artillery
assembly
attack
battalion
brigade
cavalry
charge
chauvinism
citizen-soldier
civil defense
colonial militia
combat
command
commandant
commander
commando
conscription
cryptology
defense systems
deployment
desertion
disarmament

division
draft
draft dodger
drill
enlist
enlisted personnel
equipment
federal government
fleet
flight training
foot soldier
force
formation
fortification
general
guerrilla warfare
hitch
ideology
infantry
installation
intelligence
intercontinental ballistic missile
    (ICBM)
joint ventures
judge advocate general
knight
leathernecks
legion
maneuvers
marksmanship
mercenary
militarism
military

aid
air facilities
base
contracts
organizations
personnel
science
service
training
missile
muster
national defense
national militia
National Security Act (1947)
National Security Act Amendments
　　(1949)
nationalism
navy
negotiations
nuclear warfare
officer personnel
peace
phalanx
political science
production
ranks
reconnaissance
regular army
reserve
Reserve Forces Act (1955)
satellites
seafarers
selective service
siege
standing army
stealth technology
strategy
supply
Tacit Blue
technology
telecommunications
troops
Uniform Militia Law (1792)
unit
veterans
veterans education
volunteer
war
warfare
weaponry
weapons

ORGANIZATIONS

Air National Guard
American Military Society (AMS)
Armed Forces Broadcasters Association (AFBA)
Armed Forces Communications and Electronics Association (AFCEA)
Army Air Force
Army Corps of Engineers
Central Committee for Conscientious Objectors
Citizen Soldier (CS)
Coast Guard Auxiliary
Continental Army
Department of the Air Force
Department of the Army
Department of the Navy
French Foreign Legion
International Military Community Executives Association (IMCEA)
Joint Chiefs of Staff
Marine Corps Reserve
National Defense Industrial Association
National Defense Transportation Association (NDTA)
National Guard Association of the United States (NGAUS)
National Guard of the United States

National Security Council
Naval Reserve
Non Commissioned Officers Association of the United States of America
    (NCOA)
North American Air Defense Command (NORAD)
Tactical Air Command
U.S. Air Force Academy
U.S. Coast Guard
U.S. Department of Defense
U.S. Marine Corps
U.S. Military Academy
U.S. Naval Academy
Valley Forge Historical Society (VFHS)
War Department
Women's Army Corps (WAC)

KEY PEOPLE

Sixth Century B.C.
Sun Tzu

Third Century B.C.
Hannibal

First Century
Boudicca

Thirteenth Century
Khan, Genghis

Fourteenth Century
Edward the Black Prince of Wales

Fifteenth Century
Joan of Arc

Sixteenth Century
Hawkins, John

Seventeenth Century
Cromwell, Oliver
Gorges, Ferdinando
Monck, George
Smith, John
Standish, Miles

Eighteenth Century
Allen, Ethan
Amherst, Jeffrey
Arnold, Benedict
Bonny, Anne
Burgoyne, John
Braddock, Edward
Carleton, Guy
Clinton, Henry

Clive, Robert
Corbin, Margaret Cochran
Forbes, John
Gage, Thomas
Greene, Nathanael
Howe, Richard
Knox, Henry
Lincoln, Benjamin
Marion, Francis
Molly Pitcher
Montgomery, Richard
Morgan, Daniel
Murray, James
Phillip, Arthur
Read, Mary
Rush, Benjamin
Sampson, Deborah
Schuyler, Philip John
Shays, Daniel
Spotswood, Alexander
Washington, George
Wayne, Anthony
Wolfe, James

Nineteenth Century
Brock, Isaac
Davis, Jefferson
Decatur, Stephen
Dewey, George
Farragut, David Glasgow
Gadsden, James
Gordon, Charles George

Hobson, William
Houston, Samuel
Hull, William
Kearny, Stephen Watts
Lawrence, James
Maury, Matthew Fontaine
Nelson, Horatio
Perry, Matthew Calbraith
Perry, Oliver Hazard
Pike, Zebulon
Scott, Winfield
Semmes, Raphael
Travis, William Barrett
Wilkes, Charles

Twentieth Century
Abrams, Creighton W.
Arnold, Henry Harley
Bradley, Omar Nelson
Doolittle, James Harold
Haig, Douglas

Halsey, William Frederick
Hire, Kathryn P., "Kay"
Holm, Jeanne M.
Hopper, Grace Murray
James, Daniel, Jr.
Jellicoe, John Rushworth
King, Ernest Joseph
Kitchener, Horatio Herbert
Lawrence, Thomas Edward
LeMay, Curtis Emerson
Montgomery, Bernard Law
Nimitz, Chester William
Powell, Colin Luther
Rickover, Hyman George
Schwarzkopf, Norman
Shalikashvili, John Malchase David
Taylor, Maxwell Davenport
Wavell, Archibald Percival
Westmoreland, William Childs
Wood, Leonard
Zumwalt, Elmo Russell, Jr.

WEB SITES

Black Military History
http://www.fatherryan.org/blackmilitary/

Imperial War Museum
http://www.iwm.org.uk/

Jane's Internet Defence Glossary
http://www.janes.com/defence/resources/defres_gloss.html

U.S. Central Command
http://www.centcom.mil/

U. S. Commission on Military History
http://www.uscmh.org/

U. S. Department of Defense: DefenseLINK
http://www.defenselink.mil/

Militia Groups

Keywords may be searched singly or in combination with other words using Boolean operators *and*, *or*, or *not*.

American identity
antigovernment
antitax movement
assault
bogus check
common-law court
counterfeit money order
domestic extremist
domestic terrorist groups
extremist
false lien
fraudulent lien
gun control
hidden amendments
ideology
insurrection
left wing
military force
military maneuvers
militia
paper terrorism

paramilitary
patriot movement
philosophical agenda
politics
raid
religion
right wing
right-wing extremists
Ruby Ridge, ID
secession
sect
separatism
sovereignty
standoff
sympathizer
tax protest
township movement
Uniform Militia Law (1792)
Waco, TX
warfare
weapons

ORGANIZATIONS

Anti-Defamation League (ADL)
Aryan Nations
Branch Davidians
Bureau of Alcohol, Tobacco, and Firearms (BATF)
Christian Front
Christian Identity
Committee to Restore the Constitution
Federal Bureau of Investigation (FBI)
Internal Revenue Service (IRS)
Ku Klux Klan

Michigan Militia Corps
Montana Freemen
National Association of Attorneys General
Netware International Bank
Phineas Priests
Republic of Texas
Silver Shirts
Texas Constitutional Militia
Zionist Occupation Government (ZOG)

KEY PEOPLE

Barney, John

Beach, Henry L.

Frankle, Nena

Greenup, Calvin

Gritz, Bo

Holland, Joe

Polk, Charles Ray

Schweitzer, Leroy

Skurdal, Rodney Owen

Thrall, Edwin G.

Trochmann, John

Weaver, Randall

WEB SITES

Kurt Saxon's Self-Sufficiency Pages
http://www.kurtsaxon.com/

Militia of Montana
http://www.nidlink.com/~bobhard/mom.html

Militia Watchdog
http://www.militia-watchdog.org/

Southern Poverty Law Center Intelligence Project
http://www.splcenter.org/intelligenceproject/ip-index.html

Vigilance Society of America
http://www.ez-surf.net/~vigilance/

Peace & Conflict Studies

Keywords may be searched singly or in combination with other words using Boolean operators *and*, *or*, or *not*.

absolute pacifism
amnesty
anthropology
antiwar
arbitration
armed conflict
arms exports
arms race
ban
best alternative to a negotiated agreement (BATNA)
citizen diplomacy
Cold War
conflict
   of interest
   resolution
   transformation
criminal justice
dehumanization
diplomacy
disarmament
economics
extremists
foreign policy
global conflict
gradual reduction in tension (GRIT)
history
human needs
identity
identity conflict
ideology
integrative system
interest groups
international
   law
   relations
   security
interpersonal communication
laws of war
legislation
legitimacy
mediation
morality
national defense
negotiation
neutrality
nonviolence
nonviolent struggle
pacifism
passive resistance
peace movement
peacekeeping
peacemaking
persuasion
philosophy
polarization
political psychology
political science
prevention
principled negotiation
problem solving
relative pacifism
restorative justice
revolution
settlement
social

cognition
context
control
sociology
stalemate
theology
treaty

values
violence
war
women's studies
world
　affairs
　peace
　-view

ORGANIZATIONS

Academy for Peace Research (APR)
Academy of Family Mediators (AFM)
America–Israel Council for Israeli–Palestinian Peace (AICIPP)
American Peace Society
Center for Attitudinal Healing (CAH)
Center for Peace Studies (CPS)
Center for War/Peace Studies (CW/PS)
Center on War and the Child (CWC)
Commission on the Study of Peace (CSP)
Consortium on Peace Research, Education and Development (COPRED)
Foundation for Middle East Peace (FMEP)
Foundation for P.E.A.C.E. (FFP)
Friends Peace Committee (FPC)
Global Issues Resource Center (GIRC)
Global Learning (GL)
Ground Zero (GZ)
Institute of World Affairs (IWA)
International Peace Academy (IPA)
International Peace Bureau
Jane Addams Peace Association (JAPA)
Jewish Peace Lobby (JPL)
League of Nations
League of Universal Brotherhood
Mennonite Central Committee Overseas Peace Office (MCCOPO)
National Peace Foundation (NPF)
Office of the Americas (OOA)
Peace Studies Association
Quakers
United Nations (UN)
WAR/WATCH Foundation (WWF)

KEY PEOPLE

Argentina
Pérez Esquivel, Adolfo
Saavedra Lamas, Carlos

Austria
Suttner, Bertha von
Zweig, Stefan

Canada
Pearson, Lester Bowles

Costa Rica
Arias Sánchez, Oscar

France
Bourgeois, Léon

Briand, Aristide

Germany
Schweitzer, Albert
Stresemann, Gustav

Greece
Aristophanes

Guatemala
Menchú, Rigoberta

Israel
Begin, Menachem

Myanmar
Aung San Suu Kyi, Daw

Norway
Nansen, Fridtjof

Poland
Walesa, Lech

South Africa
Luthuli, Albert John
Tutu, Desmond

Soviet Union
Gorbachev, Mikhail Sergeyvich
Sakharov, Andrei

Spain
Altamira y Crevea, Rafaél

Sweden
Hammarskjöld, Dag
Söderblom, Nathan

Switzerland
Dunant, Jean Henri

United Kingdom
Boyd Orr, John
Chamberlain, Arthur Neville
Coward, Noel

Henderson, Arthur
Russell, Bertrand
Vaughan, Henry
Worcester, Noah

United States
Abzug, Bella
Addams, Jane
Andrews, Fannie Fern Phillips
Balch, Emily Greene
Beard, Charles A.
Berrigan, Daniel J.
Borlaug, Norman Ernest
Buchman, Frank
Bunche, Ralph Johnson
Burritt, Elihu
Butler, Nicholas Murray
Cousins, Norman
Debs, Eugene Victor
Dodge, David Low
Goldman, Emma
Hull, Cordell
Kellogg, Frank Billings
King, Martin Luther, Jr.
Kissinger, Henry Alfred
Ladd, William
Marshall, George Catlett
Mott, John Raleigh
Pauling, Linus Carl
Penn, William
Rankin, Jeannette Pickering
Roosevelt, Theodore
Root, Elihu
Rustin, Bayard
Sherwood, Robert E.
Waters, Maxine
Zinn, Howard

WEB SITES

Center for Security Studies and Conflict Research
http://www.fsk.ethz.ch/

Department of Peace and Conflict Research, Uppsala University
http://www.peace.uu.se/

International Institute for Applied Systems Analysis (IIASA)
http://www.iiasa.ac.at/

Nonviolence Web
http://www.nonviolence.org/

PeaceNet
http://www.igc.org/igc/peacenet/

Royal Institute of International Affairs
http://www.riia.org/

Stockholm International Peace Research Institute
http://www.sipri.se/

Persian Gulf War (1990–1991)

Keywords may be searched singly or in combination with other words using Boolean operators *and*, *or*, or *not*.

AH-64 Apache helicopter
airbase
airpower
air strikes
air supremacy
Baghdad, Iraq
battlefield preparation
biological weapons
bombing
cease-fire
chemical or biological warfare (CBW)
chemical warfare
depleted uranium
economic embargo
economic sanctions
Egypt
embargo
emir
F-16 Fighting Falcon
F-117 Stealth Fighter
forces
France
Great Britain
ground forces
ground offensive campaign
Gulf War syndrome
high mobility multi-purpose wheeled vehicle (HMMWV)
Humvee
inspectors
Instant Thunder
invasion
Iran

Iran-Iraq War (1980–1988)
Iraq
Israel
Kurds
Kuwait
Kuwaiti Theater of Operations
land claim
liberation
military strike
missile
mobilization
National Security Directive 54
nerve gas
no-fly zone
occupation
oil
Operation
    Desert Shield
    Desert Storm
    Provide Comfort
Patriot missile
Persian Gulf
petroleum oil
post-traumatic stress disorder
radar cross-section (RCS)
rebels
reparations
Sabah monarchy
sanctions
sarin
Saudi Arabia
Scud missiles
Shiite Muslims

Shiites
smart bomb
sovereignty
strategic air campaign
trade
UN Resolution 678

unconditional withdrawal
Union of Soviet Socialist Republics
    (USSR)
United Arab Emirates
war crimes
withdrawal

ORGANIZATIONS

Arab League
Citizen Soldier (CS)
Middle East Research and Information Project (MERIP)
National Vietnam and Gulf War Veterans Coalition (NV&GWVC)
Organization of Petroleum Exporting Countries (OPEC)
Republican Guards
United Arab Emirates
United Nations (UN)
United Nations Security Council
Veterans of Foreign Wars of the United States (VFW)

KEY PEOPLE

Iraq
Aziz, Tariq
Hussein, Saddam

Kuwait
Sabah, Jaber al-Ahmad al-Jaber al-

United States
Baker, James
Bush, George

Deptula, David
Glosson, Buster C.
Horner, Charles
Powell, Colin Luther
Schwarzkopf, Norman
Shalikashvili, John Malchase David
Warden III, John A.

WEB SITES

Desert-Storm.com
http://www.desert-storm.com/

Fog of War: The 1991 Air Battle for Baghdad
http://www.washingtonpost.com/wp-srv/inatl/longterm/fogofwar/fogofwar.htm

Frontline: The Gulf War
http://www.pbs.org/wgbh/pages/frontline/gulf/index.html

Gulf War Syndrome Chronology
http://www.biofact.com/gulf/index.html

GulfLINK: Office of the Special Assistant for Gulf War Illnesses
http://www.gulflink.osd.mil/

Hoskinson's Gulf War Photo Gallery
http://www.gulfwar.net/gulfwar/

Political Science

Keywords may be searched singly or in combination with other words using Boolean operators *and*, *or*, or *not*.

activism
administration
advertising
affairs of state
agenda setting
area studies
aristocracy
authoritarianism
authority
ballot
bloodless coup
blue-ribbon commission
bond issues
bureaucracy
business
campaign
candidate
capitalism
citizen participation
citizenship
civic belief
civil rights
colonialism
communism
community
community leaders
comparative politics
conservatism
constitutional history
constitutional law
controversial issues
court decisions
credibility

debate
democracy
Democrat
democratic values
demography
diplomatic history
dissent
economics
elections
electoral college
elitism
executive branch
executive power
fascism
federalism
finance
foreign policy
freedom
fund-raising
general election
gerrymandering
governance
government
history
humanitarianism
ideology
imperialism
independent
institution
international
    law
    relations
    studies

trade
judicial branch
law
legislation
legislative branch
legislative process
liberalism
lobbying
local issues
Marxism
mass media
military science
monarchy
Motor-Voter Act (1993)
national government
nationalism
new federalism
nominee
nongovernmental organization (NGO)
ochlocracy
oligarchy
party system
patriotism
persuasive discourse
plurality
policy analysis
political
   affiliation
   campaigns
   economy
   influence
   party
   philosophy
   power
   regime

politics
polling
power structure
primary election
proportional representation
public
   administration
   affairs
   official
   opinion
   policy
redistricting
referendum
representative government
Republican
revolution
runoff election
social
   change
   influence
   science
socialism
socialization
socioeconomics
statistics
surveys
terrorism
think tank
totalitarianism
two-party system
tyranny
voting
voting rights
woman suffrage

ORGANIZATIONS

Academy of Political Science (APS)
American Academy of Political and Social Science (AAPSS)
American Association of Political Consultants (AAPC)
American Society for Legal History (ASLH)
American Society for Political and Legal Philosophy (ASPLP)
American Studies Association (ASA)
Association for Politics and the Life Sciences (APLS)
Association of Social and Behavioral Scientists (ASBS)
Brookings Institution (BI)
Canadian Political Science Association (CPSA)
Caucus for a New Political Science (CNPS)
Conference for the Study of Political Thought (CSPT)

European Consortium for Political Research (ECPR)
Institute for the Study of International Politics
Institute on Pluralism and Group Identity (IPGI)
International Political Science Association (IPSA)
International Society for Human Ethology (ISHE)
Joint Center for Political and Economic Studies (JCPES)
Policy Studies Organization (PSO)
Society for Cross-Cultural Research (SCCR)
Women's Caucus for Political Science (WCPS)
World League for Freedom and Democracy (WLFD)

KEY PEOPLE

Fourth Century B.C.
Aristotle
Plato

Sixteenth Century
Machiavelli, Niccolò

Seventeenth Century
Filmer, Robert
Hobbes, Thomas
Locke, John

Eighteenth Century
Burke, Edmund
Hamilton, Alexander
Kant, Immanuel
Rousseau, Jean Jacques

Nineteenth Century

Madison, James
Marx, Karl
Reed, Thomas Brackett
Tilden, Samuel Jones
Tillman, Benjamin Ryan
Tweed, William Marcy

Twentieth Century
Curley, James Michael
Daley, Richard J.
Holden, Matthew, Jr.
Keohane, Robert O.
La Guardia, Fiorello Henry
Laski, Harold Joseph
Long, Huey Pierce
Lowell, Abbott Lawrence

WEB SITES

American Political Science Association (APSA)
http://www.apsanet.org/

Electronic Policy Network
http://www.epn.org/

Institute for American Liberty
http://www.liberty1.org/

Political Science Manuscripts
http://www.trenton.edu/~psm/

U.S. Department of State
http://www.state.gov/

U.S. Department of State International Information Programs
http://usinfo.state.gov/

Supreme Court

Keywords may be searched singly or in combination with other words using Boolean operators *and, or,* or *not.*

appointments
bankruptcy court
bench
capital offense
case law
chambers
chief judge
chief justice of the United States
circuit court
common law
constitutional issue
court of appeals
criminal defendants
decisions
defendant
deposition
district attorney (DA)
district court
en banc
evidence
federal
   court system
   judge
   judicial system
felony
full court
habeas corpus
indictment
interjudicial
judge
judgment
judicial
   administration

branch
council
education
judiciary
jurisprudence
justices
law clerk
litigants
litigation
lower court
misconduct
nonjudicial court personnel
oath
opinion
   majority
   minority
overturn
panel
plaintiff
postconviction appeal
precedent
procedures
proceeding
record
respondents
reversal
review
sentencing
sentencing guidelines
session
staff attorney
statement
statute

suit
testimony
tort
transcript
trial
tribunal

U.S.
    Bankruptcy Court
    Constitution
    Court of Appeals
    District Court
verdict
writ

ORGANIZATIONS

Administrative Office of the U.S. Courts
American Bar Association (ABA)
Americans for Effective Law Enforcement (AELE)
John Marshall Foundation (JMF)
Judicial Conference of the United States
National Association of Attorneys General (NAAG)
National Center for State Courts
State Justice Institute
U.S. Congress
U.S. Sentencing Commission

KEY PEOPLE

Blackmun, Harry
Brandeis, Louis
Breyer, Stephen
Burger, Warren E.
Chase, Salmon P.
Douglas, William O.
Ellsworth, Oliver
Frankfurter, Felix
Ginsburg, Ruth Bader
Holmes, Oliver Wendell
Hughes, Charles Evans
Jay, John
Kennedy, Anthony
Marshall, John

Marshall, Thurgood
O'Connor, Sandra Day
Rehnquist, William
Rutledge, John
Scalia, Antonin
Souter, David
Stevens, John Paul
Stone, Harlan F.
Taft, William Howard
Taney, Roger B.
Thomas, Clarence
Vinson, Fred M.
Warren, Earl
White, Byron

WEB SITES

Federal Judicial Center
http://www.fjc.gov/

FindLaw: Internet Legal Resources
http://www.findlaw.com/

Legal Information Institute: Supreme Court Collection
http://supct.law.cornell.edu/supct/

The Oyez Project
http://oyez.nwu.edu/

Supreme Court Historical Society (SCHS)
http://www.supremecourthistory.org/

Third World Countries

Keywords may be searched singly or in combination with other words using Boolean operators *and*, *or*, or *not*.

Africa
agrarian
agriculture
aid
area studies
Asia
assistance
businesses
capitalism
Caribbean
Cold War
colonialism
communism
community development
culture
culture lag
developed nations
developing nations
development
disaster relief
economic
   assistance
   development
   growth
   Support Fund (ESF)
economics
economy
education
elections
emerging nations
environment
food assistance
foreign

aid
Assistance Act (1961)
   national
   policy
Fourth World
governance
health care
human resources
human rights
humanitarian assistance
hunger
ideology
immunization
independence
industrialization
international
   affairs
   development
   program
   relations
   trade
investment
labor economics
Latin America
living standard
manufacturing
market
Middle East
military aid
military assistance
modernization
moral imperative
national programs

national security
nationalism
New Economic Order
nonindustrialized
nutrition
peace
politics
population
population control
power bloc
productivity
quality of life
race
religion
resources

revolution
rural
security
social growth
social services
sustainable development
technical assistance
technological advancement
technology
trade
underdeveloped nations
United States of America
vaccination
world food supply
world problems

ORGANIZATIONS

Action for Corporate Accountability (ACTION)
Association of Third World Affairs (ATWA)
Association of Third World Studies (ATWS)
Bread for the World (BFW)
CARE
Food for the Hungry, Inc. (FHI)
Friends of the Third World (FTW)
The International Foundation (TIF)
International Monetary Fund (IMF)
International Red Cross
International Third World Legal Studies Association (INTWORLSA)
International Women's Health Coalition (IWHC)
Overseas Development Network (ODN)
Peace Corps
Third World Conference Foundation (TWCF)
Trees for Life (TFL)
United Nations (UN)
United Nations Children's Fund (UNICEF)
U.S. Agency for International Development (USAID)
U.S. International Development Cooperation Agency (IDCA)
World Export Processing Zones Association (WEPZA)

KEY PEOPLE

Political Leaders
Boumediene, Houari
Fanon, Frantz
Kennedy, John Fitzgerald

Nasser, Gamal Abdel
Nehru, Jawaharlal
Nkrumah, Kwame
Shriver, Sargent
Touré, Sékou

WEB SITES

GOAL
http://www.goal.ie/

Group of 77
http://www.g77.org/

Shared Interest
http://www.shared-interest.com/

TWAS: Third World Academy of Sciences
http://www.ictp.trieste.it/TWAS/TWAS.html

Women's Issues: 3rd World
http://women3rdworld.miningco.com/

United Nations (UN)

Keywords may be searched singly or in combination with other words using Boolean operators *and*, *or*, or *not*.

Afghanistan
agency
agriculture
Angola
apartheid
Arab-Israeli
armistice
arms race
assistance
Atlantic Charter
bacteriological weapons
Cambodia
cease-fire
Charter of the United Nations
chemical weapons
children's rights
China
colonial rule
Conference on Disarmament
conflict resolution
Convention
    Against Illicit Traffic in Narcotic
        Drugs on the Elimination of
        All Forms of Discrimination
        Against Women on the Law of
        the Sea
Declaration on the Granting of Inde-
        pendence to Colonial Countries
        and Peoples
decolonization
deliberative body
developing countries
diplomacy

disarmament
Dumbarton Oaks Conference (1944)
Earth Summit
Economic
    and Social Council
    development
    growth
    reform
education
El Salvador
empowerment
environmental protection
envoy
epidemic
famine
finance
food aid
food production
France
Gaza
General Assembly
Geneva
global trade
Golan Heights
governance
Guatemala
The Hague
Haiti
health
human rights
Human Rights Day
humanitarian assistance
immunization

independence
Inter-Allied Declaration (1941)
International
  Bill of Human Rights
  community
  Convention on the Elimination of
    All Forms of Racial Discrimi-
    nation
  cooperation
  law
  Monetary Fund (IMF)
  peace
Japanese Peace Bell
Joint Programme on AIDS
Korean Armistice Agreement
Lake Success, NY
land mines
literacy
mediation
member state
military action
Montreal Protocol
Mozambique
Namibia
New York City
Nicaragua
nonproliferation
nuclear disarmament
Nuclear Test Ban Treaty
nuclear weapons
observer
Pakistan
peace agreement
peaceful means
peacekeeping
  mission
  operations
peacemaking
permanent member
poverty
preventive diplomacy
quality of life
quiet diplomacy
rapporteur
reconstruction
refugee

relief agency
right of asylum
Russian Federation
safety standards
San Francisco Conference (1945)
sanctions
Secretariat
secretary-general
Security Council
self-determination
self-government
settlement
smallpox
social development
Somalia
sovereign nations
sovereignty
Soviet Union
special committees
starvation
states
Suez crisis
telecommunication
trademarks
treaties
Treaty on the Non-Proliferation of Nuclear Weapons (NPT)
Treaty on the Protection of the Ozone
  Layer
tribunal
truce
trust territories
Trusteeship Council
UN
  Charter
  Development Programme
  forces
  headquarters
  Transitional Authority
United Kingdom
United States of America
Universal Declaration of Human
  Rights (1948)
war crimes
West Bank
woman's rights
Yalta Conference (1945)

ORGANIZATIONS

American Foreign Law Association (AFLA)
Americans for the Universality of UNESCO (AUU)
Association for Women in Development (AWID)
Committee of Science and Technology in Developing Countries (COSTED-IBN)
Food and Agriculture Organization (FAO)
Human Rights Watch (HRW)
International Association of Educators for World Peace (IAEWP)
International Atomic Energy Agency (IAEA)
International Civil Aviation Organization (ICAO)
International Council for Health, Physical Education, Recreation, Sport, and
    Dance (ICHPERSD)
International Court of Justice
International Fund for Agricultural Development (IFAD)
International Labor Organization (ILO)
International Maritime Organization (IMO)
International Telecommunication Union (ITU)
Panamerican/PanAfrican Association (PPA)
Students Association of UNESCO
World Intellectual Property Organization (WIPO)
UNESCO Association/U.S.A. (UA/USA)
UNESCO International Institute for Educational Planning (IIEP)
United Nations Educational, Scientific and Cultural Organization (UNESCO)
United Nations Industrial Development Organization (UNIDO)
U.S. Chamber of Shipping
Universal Postal Union (UPU)
World Association of Veterinary Laboratory Diagnosticians (WAVLD)
World Bank
World Court
World Export Processing Zones Association (WEPZA)
World Health Organization (WHO)
World Intellectual Property Organization (WIPO)
World Meteorological Organization (WMO)
World Organization for Early Childhood Education U.S. National Committee

KEY PEOPLE

Annan, Kofi
Boutros-Ghali, Boutros
Bunche, Ralph
de Cuellar, Javier Perez
Hammarskjold, Dag

Hull, Cordell
Lie, Trygve
Roosevelt, Eleanor
Thant, U
Waldheim, Kurt

WEB SITES

Coalition for a Strong United Nations
http://www.igc.apc.org/csun/
UNICEF USA
http://www.unicefusa.org/

United Nations
http://www.un.org/

United Nations Children's Fund (UNICEF)
http://www.unicef.org/

United Nations CyberSchoolBus
http://www.un.org/Pubs/CyberSchoolBus/

United Nations Educational, Scientific and Cultural Organization (UNESCO)
http://www.unesco.org/

Veterans

Keywords may be searched singly or in combination with other words using Boolean operators *and*, *or*, or *not*.

active duty
Arlington National Cemetery
armed forces
Armistice Day
auxiliary
burial benefits
Civil War
counseling
dependent survivor
disability pension
education
employment
enlisted personnel
federal aid
GI Bill of Rights
health care
home loans
homelessness
honorable discharge
hospitalization
insurance
Korean War (1950–1953)
medical treatment
memorial affairs
Memorial Day
military
    conflict

personnel
record
service
veteran
missing in action (MIA)
national cemeteries
officer
pension
Persian Gulf War
post-traumatic stress disorder
prisoner of war (POW)
rehabilitation
service
Servicemen's Readjustment Act (1944)
Spanish-American War (1898)
survivor
training allowance
unknown soldier
VA hospital
veteran's benefits
Veterans Day
veteran's education
Vietnam veterans
Vietnam War (1954–1975)
war
wartime
World War I (1914–1918)
World War II (1939–1945)

ORGANIZATIONS

American Legion
American Military Retirees Association (AMRA)
American Military Society (AMS)

American Veterans Committee
American Veterans of World War II, Korea, and Vietnam
Centennial Legion of Historic Military Commands (CLHMC)
Jewish War Veterans of the United States of America (JWV)
Midwest Committee for Military Counseling (MCMC)
Military Law Task Force (MLTF)
U.S. Veterans Bureau
Veterans Administration
Veterans of Foreign Wars of the United States

WEB SITES

Department of Veterans Affairs
http://www.va.gov/

Military Order of the Purple Heart (MOPH)
http://www.purpleheart.org/

National Cemetery System
http://www.cem.va.gov/

National Reunion Registry
http://www.militaryusa.com/reunions.html

U.S. Navy Memorial Foundation
http://www.lonesailor.org/

USS Missouri Memorial Association
http://www.ussmissouri.com/

Vietnam War (1954–1975)

Keywords may be searched singly or in combination with other words using Boolean operators *and*, *or*, or *not*.

active duty
Advance Guard Youth
Agent Orange
air cavalry
air force
airborne
AK-47
allied forces
Amerasian
amphibious landing
antipersonnel mine
armored personnel carrier
armored troop carrier (ATC)
army
Army of the Republic of Vietnam
artillery
assault
B-52
base camp
battalion
Binh Dinh Province
body bag
body count
brigade
Cambodia
Cambodian Communist Party
Can Lao
Cao Dai
casualties
cavalry
cease-fire
Central Highlands
Central Intelligence Agency (CIA)

Charlie
Chieu Hoi
civil action program
Civilian Irregular Defense Group
Cochin-China
combat assault
combat rations
commando
communist
containment policy
corps
counterinsurgency
Dac Cong
Dai Doan Ket
Dai Viet
defense
demarcation zone (DMZ)
Democratic Republic of Vietnam
deployment
Dien Bien Phu, Battle of
District Mobile Company
domino theory
elephant grass
evacuation
extraction
Field Force Vietnam
4-F
free
   -fire zone
    strike zone
    World Military Assistance Forces
freedom bird
French Indochina

friendly fire
Geneva Accords (1954)
Geneva Convention (1949)
Green Beret
ground troops
guerrilla
guerrilla warfare
Gulf of Tonkin Resolution (1964)
Hanoi
Hanoi Hilton
helicopters
Highlands
Hmong
Ho Chi Minh trail
Hoa Hao
Hoa Loa Prison
howitzer
Hue
Huey
I Corps
II Corps
III Corps
IV Corps
Imperial Citadel
in-country
Indochina
infantry
installation
intelligence
Iron Triangle
Joint Chiefs of Staff
jungle
Kampuchea
Kent State
Khe Sanh
Khmer Rouge
Khmer Serei
kill zone
killed in action (KIA)
Kit Carson scout
labor camp
landing zone (LZ)
land mine
Lao Dong
Laos
Long Binh
Long Range Reconnaissance Patrol
    (LRRP)

Luc Luong Dac Biet (LLDB)
M-16
Main Force Battalion
malaria
Marine Amphibious Force
Marine Corps
Mat Tran
mechanical ambush
Med Cap
medevac
Medical Civil Action Program
medical evacuation
Mekong Delta
military
    advisers
    Assistance Command/Vietnam
        (MACV)
    command
    draft
    intelligence
    payment currency (MPC)
    region
missing in action (MIA)
mobile advisory team (MAT)
mobile army surgical hospital (MASH)
Monday pills
Montagnard
MR IV
Mr. Charles
My Lai
Nam
napalm
National Liberation Front (NLF)
navy
negotiated peace
New Socialist Man
North Vietnamese
North Vietnamese Army (NVA)
Nung
occupation
Operation Ranch Hand
ordnance
paramilitary
paratrooper
Paris Accords
Pathet Lao
patrol
Peoples Army of Vietnam (PAVN)

People's Liberation Armed Forces
  (PLAF)
People's Revolutionary Party (PRP)
personnel
platoon
political prison
Popular Forces (PF)
post-traumatic stress disorder
prisoner of war (POW)
province
Provisional Revolutionary Government
reconnaissance by fire (RBF)
reeducation camp
regiment
Regional Forces (RF)
Republic of Vietnam
resistance
Rolling Thunder
rotation
rules of engagement
Saigon
Saigon River
sea huts
SEAL
Second Indochina War
Sereika
17th Parallel
short-timer
Snoopy mission
solacium payments
sortie
South Vietnam
South Vietnamese
Southeast Asia Treaty Organization
  (SEATO)
Special Forces
squad

Strategic Air Command
strategic hamlet program
Students for a Democratic Society
  (SDS)
surface-to-air missile (SAM)
tactical support
Tan Son Nhut
territorial forces evaluation system
  (TFES)
Tet Offensive (1968)
Thailand
Thi-Tinh River
Thua Thien Province
Tonkin Gulf
tour of duty
trauma
triage
U.S. Army Republic of Vietnam
  (USARV)
U.S. Operations Mission (USOM)
veteran's education
veterans
Viet Cong (VC)
Viet Cong Infrastructure (VCI)
Viet Minh
Vietcong
Vietnam Veterans
Vietnam Veterans Memorial
Vietnamese
  Allied Independence League
  Communist Party
  Liberation Front
  Popular Forces
Vietnamization
the Wall
WESPAC tour
white phosphorus
Yen Bai Uprising

ORGANIZATIONS

American Legion Auxiliary (ALA)
American Veterans Committee (AVC)
America's Victory Force (AVF)
Citizen Soldier (CS)
Friends of the Vietnam Veterans Memorial (FVVM)
Indochina Institute (II)
National League of Families of American Prisoners and Missing in Southeast
  Asia
Nationalist Party of Vietnam

Red Badge of Courage (RBC)
Soldiers of Freedom (SF)
USS Intrepid Association of Former Crew Members (USSIAFCM)
Veterans of the Vietnam War (VVnW)
Viet Nam Quoc Dan Dang (VNQDD)
Vietnam Combat Veterans (VCV)
Vietnam Helicopter Pilots Association (VHPA)
Vietnam Veterans Against the War (VVAW)
Vietnam Veterans Against the War Anti-Imperialist
Vietnam Veterans Institute (VVI)
Vietnam Women's Memorial Project (VWMP)

KEY PEOPLE

Cambodia
Lon Nol
Pol Pot (Saloth Sar)
Sihanouk, Norodom

United States
Abzug, Bella
Acheson, Dean
Agnew, Spiro
Baez, Joan
Ball, George
Blassie, Michael J.
Bunker, Ellsworth
Calley, William L.
Carter, James Earl, "Jimmy"
Chervony, Eddie E.
Clifford, Clark
DeBellevue, Charles B.
Dewey, A. Peter
Dulles, John Foster
Eisenhower, Dwight D.
Ellsberg, Daniel
Fonda, Jane
Ford, Gerald R.
Fulbright, William
Gritz, James, "Bo"
Haig, Alexander
Humphrey, Hubert
Johnson, Lyndon Baines
Kelley, Paul B.
Kennedy, John Fitzgerald

Kissinger, Henry Alfred
Laird, Melvin R.
Lansdale, Edward G.
Lin, Maya
Mansfield, Mike
Martin, Graham
McCain, John
McNamara, Robert S.
Nixon, Richard M.
Olds, Robin
Ritchie, Richard S.
Rostow, Walt W.
Rusk, Dean
Scruggs, Jan C.
Westmoreland, William

North Vietnam
Dong, Pham Van
Giap, Vo Nguyen
Ho Chi Minh
Le Duc Tho
Le Duan

South Vietnam
Diem, Ngo Dinh
Khanh, Nguyen
Minh, Duong Van
Nhu, Ngo Dinh
So, Huynh Phu
Thieu, Nguyen Van

Vietnam
Bao Dai, Emperor of Annam

WEB SITES

The American Experience: Vietnam
http://www.pbs.org/wgbh/pages/amex/vietnam/intro.html

The Hunt for Master Sergeant Hunt
http://www.tteam.com/hosting/HUNT/index.html

Operation Ranch Hand: Herbicides in Southeast Asia, 1961–1971
http://cpcug.org/user/billb/ranchhand/ranchhand.html

POW/MIA Homepage
http://lcweb2.loc.gov/pow/powhome.html

Sons and Daughters in Touch
http://www.sdit.org/

Vietnam Veterans Memorial Fund (VVMF)
http://www.vvmf.org/

Vietnam Veterans' War Stories
http://www.war-stories.com/WarStory.htm

World War I (1914–1918)

Keywords may be searched singly or in combination with other words using Boolean operators *and*, *or*, or *not*.

Africa
African history
air raid
air supremacy
airship
alliance
Allies
American Expeditionary Force (AEF)
antinationalism
Antwerp
Argonne Forest
armament
armistice
Asian history
assassination
Associated Powers
Austria-Hungary
autonomy
Balkan Wars (1912–1913)
Battle of
    Albert (1914)
    Amiens (1918)
    Flanders (1914)
    Gaza (1917)
    Jutland (1916)
    Passchendaele (1917)
    Tannenberg (1914)
    the Marne (1914)
    the Somme (1916)
Belgium
bombing
British Expeditionary Force (BEF)
Bulgaria

capitulation
carrier pigeons
casualty
Central Powers
colonialism
conscription
Dawes Plan
declaration of war
disarmament
Eastern Front
Europe
European history
foreign markets
foreign policy
France
front
Germany
Great
    Britain
    Powers
    War
Hapsburg
Hindenburg Line
imperialism
independent state
Industrial Revolution
invasion
Italy
Japan
Lusitania
Luxembourg
militarism
military

alliance
expansion
mobilization
Morocco
national self-determination
nationalism
naval warfare
neutrality
offensive
Ottoman empire
Pacific
Pact of London (1914)
Pan-Serbian
Panslavism
Paris Peace Conference (1919)
reparations
revolution
rivalry
Russia
Sarajevo
Schlieffen plan
self-defense
Serbia

settlement
shell shock
submarine warfare
surrender
tank
territory
Treaty of
    Brest-Litovsk (1918)
    Bucharest (1918)
    Versailles (1919)
trench warfare
Triple Alliance
Triple Entente
Turkey
United States of America
Vimy Ridge (1917)
war-guilt clause
Western Front
wireless communication
World War II (1939–1945)
Young plan
zeppelin
Zimmerman Telegram

ORGANIZATIONS

Army Records Society (ARS)
Belgian American Educational Foundation (BAEF)
Central Powers
League of Nations
League of World War I Aviation Historians
National Chapter of Canada IODE
Reparations Commission
Second Bombardment Association (SBA)
Society of Ration Token Collectors (SRTC)
Western Front Association (WFA)
World War I Aeroplanes (WWI AERO)

KEY PEOPLE

Austria
Archduke Franz Ferdinand

Canada
Bishop, William Avery

France
Clemenceau, Georges
Joffre, Joseph Jacques Césaire
Pétain, Henri Philippe

Germany

Bethman-Hollweg, Theobald von
Emperor William II (Kaiser Wilhelm)
Franz Josef (Francis Joseph I)
Kluck, Alexander von
Richthofen, Manfred von

Greece
Venizelos, Eleftherios

Great Britain
Allenby, Edmund

Asquith, Herbert Henry
Grey, Edward
Haig, Douglas
Hamilton, Ian
King George V
Lawrence, Thomas Edward (Lawrence
     of Arabia)
Lloyd-George, David

Italy
Díaz, Armando

Russia
Czar Nicholas II

Turkey
Enver Pasha

United States
House, Edward M.
Lansing, Robert
Pershing, John Joseph
Rickenbacker, Eddie
Wilson, Woodrow

WEB SITES

The Great War
http://www.infosites.net/general/the-great-war/

The Great War and the Shaping of the Twentieth Century
http://www.pbs.org/greatwar/

The Great War Society
http://www.mcs.net/~mikei/tgws/index.htm

Photos of the Great War
http://www.ukans.edu/~kansite/ww_one/photos/greatwar.htm

World War I Document Archive
http://www.lib.byu.edu/~rdh/wwi/

World War II (1939–1945)

Keywords may be searched singly or in combination with other words using Boolean operators *and*, *or*, or *not*.

African history
Afrika Korps
air raids
air war
airborne
aircraft
Allies
amphibious force
armistice
Asian history
atomic bomb
Australia
Austria-Hungary
Axis
Axis of Powers pact
battle fatigue
Battle of
   Albert
   Arras
   Aubers Ridge
   Britain (1940)
   Cambrai
   Cape Esperance
   Cape Matapan
   Coronel
   Dogger Bank
   El Alamein
   Festubert
   Flanders
   Java Sea
   Jutland
   La Bassée
   Le Cateau

Leyte Gulf
Loos
Messines
Midway (1942)
Mons
Neuve Chappelle
Sambre
St. Quentin
Sulva Bay
Tannenberg
the Argonne
the Atlantic
the Bulge (1944–1945)
the Coral Sea (1942)
the Marne
the River Ancre
the Scarpe
the Selle
the Somme
Verdun
Yser
Belgium
Bismarck
blitzkrieg
blockade
Blucher offensive
Bockscar
Bulgaria
Canada
capitulation
Casablanca Conference (1943)
China
coalition

combatants
communism
concentration camp
Covenant of the League of Nations
cryptography
cipher
Czechoslovakia
D-Day (1944)
Denmark
dictatorship
Dunkirk
Eastern Front
Eben-Emael
Egypt
English Channel
Enigma
Enola Gay
Europe
European Recovery Program
expansionism
fascism
Fascist Party
Fat Man
Finland
First Battle of Ypres
Fourteen Points
France
Free French
French Resistance
Friedensturm offensive
führer
Georgette offensive
German National Socialist (Nazi) Party
Germany
gestapo
global
Gneisenau offensive
Great Britain
Greece
Guadalcanal
Guam
Hamburg
Hiroshima
Holland
Holocaust
Hong Kong
Hungary
Indochina

industrial capacity
infantry
invasion
Iron Guard
isolationism
Italy
Iwo Jima
Japan
kamikaze
Korean War (1950–1953)
League of Nations
Lend-Lease Act (1941)
liberation
Liberation of France
Lidice, Czechoslovakia
lightning war
Little Boy
the Little Ships
long-range rocket
Low Countries
Luftwaffe
Luxembourg
Manchukuo
Manhattan Project
Marianas Turkey Shoot (1944)
Marshall Plan
Michael offensive
Midway
militaristic
military
Miracle of Dunkirk
Moscow
motorized division
Munich Agreement (1938)
Munich Pact (1938)
Nagasaki
nationalistic
Navajo code
Nazi Party
Nazi persecution
Nazis
Nazi-Soviet Pact (1939)
Netherlands
neutrality
Normandy invasion
North Africa
Norway
occupation

occupying powers
Okinawa
Operation Dynamo
Overlord
P.G. 78
Pacific Fleet
panzer division
Paris Peace Conference
Pearl Harbor, HI
Philippines
Poland
Potsdam Conference (1945)
Potsdam Declaration (1945)
prisoner of war (POW)
propaganda
Race to the Sea
racism
Red Army
reparations
Resistance
Romania
Rome-Berlin-Tokyo Axis
Rosie the Riveter
Royal Air Force (RAF)
Royal Canadian Air Force
scorched-earth policy
Second Battle of
    Amiens
    Bapaume
    Cambrai
    Le Cateau
    the Marne
    Ypres
Serbia
settlement
Siege of Leningrad
Siegfried Line

Singapore
Solomon Islands
Soviet Union
Spanish civil war (1936–1939)
Spring Offensive
SS
Stalingrad
strategic air offensive
submarine warfare
Sudetenland
Tehran Conference (1944)
Third Battle of Ypres
Third Reich
totalitarianism
Treaty of Brest-Litovsk
Treaty of Versailles (1919)
U-boat
Union of Soviet Socialist Republics
    (USSR)
United Nations Declaration
United States
V-E (Victory in Europe) Day
Versailles Treaty
Vichy France
Vietnam War (1954–1975)
Vimy Ridge
V-J (Victory in Japan) Day
War
    in the Pacific
    of attrition
    Relocation Authority
warfare
Warsaw Pact
Western Front
World War I (1914–1918)
Yalta Conference (1945)
Yugoslavia

ORGANIZATIONS

British Expeditionary Forces (BEF)
Combined Chiefs of Staff (CCS)
National Socialist German Workers' Party
North Atlantic Treaty Organization
Supreme Headquarters Allied Expeditionary Forces (SHAEF)
Tuskegee Airmen
United Nations (UN)
Women's Army Corps (WAC)

KEY PEOPLE

Finland
Mannerheim, Carl G.

France
Daladier, Edouard
de Gaulle, Charles
Pétain, Henri Philippe

Germany
Bonhoeffer, Dietrich
Hitler, Adolf
Manstein, Erich von
Mengele, Josef
Rommel, Erwin
Schindler, Oskar
Steinhilper, Ulrich

Great Britain
Chamberlain, Neville
Churchill, Winston
Cotton, Sidney
Dempsey, Miles C.
Montgomery, Bernard Law

Italy
Mussolini, Benito

Japan
Emperor Hirohito
Sugihara, Chiune
Tojo Hideki
Yamamoto Isoroku

Poland
Gnys, Wladek
Komorowski, Tadeusz

Soviet Union
Molotov, Vyacheslav Mikhailovich
Stalin, Joseph
Vasilyevsky, Aleksandr M.
Zhukov, Georgy

United States
Bradley, Omar N.
Buckner, Simon B., Jr.
Einstein, Albert
Eisenhower, Dwight D.
Hodges, Courtney H.
MacArthur, Douglas
Marshall, George Catlett
Miller, Glenn
Murphy, Audie
Nimitz, Chester William
Oppenheimer, Robert
Patton, George S.
Pyle, Ernie
Roosevelt, Franklin Delano
Sarnoff, David
Tibbets, Paul
Truman, Harry S

Yugoslavia
Tito, Josip Broz

WEB SITES

George Rarey's World War II Air Force Cartoon Journals
http://www.rarey.com/sites/rareybird/

Nagasaki Atomic Bomb Museum
http://wwwus1.nagasaki-noc.ne.jp/~nacity/na-bomb/museum/museum.html

Powers of Persuasion: Poster Art of World War II
http://www.nara.gov/exhall/powers/powers.html

Return to Midway
http://www.nationalgeographic.com/features/98/midway/

A Teacher's Guide to the Holocaust
http://fcit.coedu.usf.edu/holocaust/default.htm

U.S. Air Force Museum
http://www.wpafb.af.mil/museum/index.htm

Women Come to the Front
http://lcweb.loc.gov/exhibits/wcf/wcf0001.html

PHILOSOPHY & RELIGION

Amish

Keywords may be searched singly or in combination with other words using Boolean operators *and*, *or*, or *not*.

The Adventurer
agrarian
Anabaptist
Ausbund
Back Door Amish
Beachy Amish
believer's baptism
Church Amish
cooperative farming
dawdyhaus
Dordrecht Confession of Faith (1632)
Dutch Country
Holmes County, OH
holy experiment
House Amish

Lancaster County, PA
Mennonite
New Order Amish
Old Order Amish
Ordnung
Pennsylvania Dutch
Pennsylvania German (PG)
Plain People
shunning
Strasbourg Anabaptist conferences
Swartzentruber Amish
Swiss Brethren
Swiss Mennonites
Wisconsin v. Yoder (1972)

ORGANIZATIONS

Casselman River Amish and Mennonite Historians
Lancaster Mennonite Historical Society (LMHS)

KEY PEOPLE

Ammann, Jakob
Ammann, Uli
Herr, John
Hertzler, Jacob
Penn, William
Philips, Dirk

Simons, Menno
Smucker, Moses
Wisler, Jacob
Yoder, Kore
Zielinski, John M.

WEB SITES

The Amish and "the Plain People"
http://www.800padutch.com/amish.html

Amish Heartland
http://www.amish-heartland.com/

The Amish in Northern Indiana
http://www.goshen.edu/~lonhs/SamYoder.html

Amish Shopping Mall
http://www.amishshoppingmall.com/

Mennonite Central Committee
http://www.mcc.org/

Mennonite Information Center
http://www.800padutch.com/mennctr.html

National Committee for Amish Religious Freedom (NCARF)
http://holycrosslivonia.org/amish/

Cults

Keywords may be searched singly or in combination with other words using Boolean operators *and*, *or*, or *not*.

ancient philosophy
apocalypse
brainwashing
Branch Davidians
deprogramming
doomsday cults
Druids
Heaven's Gate
Jonestown, Guyana
Kanungu, Uganda
mind control
Movement for the Restoration of the
    Ten Commandments of God

New Age movement
occultism
parapsychology
People's Temple
religion
Satanism
sects
thought reform
totalism
vampire
voodoo
Waco, TX
witchcraft

KEY PEOPLE

Applewhite, Marshall
Jones, Jim
Kibwetere, Joseph
Koresh, David (Vernon Howell)

Mwerinde, Credonia
Nostradamus
Ryan, Leo J.
Kibwetere, Joseph

ORGANIZATIONS

American Family Foundation (AFF)
Christian Research Institute International (CRI)
Individual Freedom Federation (IFF)
Maynard Bernstein Resource Center on Cults
Personal Freedom Outreach (PFO)
Skeptics Society
Spiritual Counterfeits Project (SCP)
USCCCN National Clearinghouse on Satanic Crime in America
Vampire Research Center (VRC)
Watchman Fellowship

WEB SITES

Doomsday, Destructive Religious Cults
http://www.religioustolerance.org/destruct.htm

FACTNet International (Fight Against Coercive Tactics Network)
http://www.factnet.org/

reFOCUS: Recovering Former Cultists' Support Network
http://www.refocus.org/

Rick Ross
http://www.rickross.com/

TruthQuest Institute
http://www.truthquest.org/

Ethics

Keywords may be searched singly or in combination with other words using Boolean operators *and*, *or*, or *not*.

absolute truth
absolutism
agnosticism
altruism
animal rights
atheism
autonomy
bioethics
business ethics
categorical imperative
chance
code of conduct
code of ethics
compassion
compatibilism
confidentiality
conflict
conflict of interest
consequences
consequentialism
credibility
culture
decision making
defense
desire
determinism
dignity
divine command theory
dolor
egoism
enlightenment
entitlement
enviroethics

environmental ethics
equality
ethical
  egoism
  relativism
  theory
ethnicity
eudaemonism
eudaemonistic utilitarianism
euthanasia
evil
excellence
experience
fairness
feelings
framework
freedom
gender
group
guidelines
harm
hedon
hedonistic utilitarianism
heteronomy
honesty
honor
human
  reason
  rights
  spirit
humanitarian ethics
hypothetical imperative
ideal

impartiality
imperative
inclination
individual
inquiry
integrationist
integrity
intellectual freedom
investigation
irrational
isolationism
judgment
justice
law
maxim
medical ethics
metaethics
moral
   beliefs
   calculus
   development
   obligation
   pluralism
   rights
   standard
   system
   theory
morality
morals
narcissism
natural law
natural rights
naturalism
negative rights
nihilism
nirvana
nonconsequentialist
normative ethical relativism
obligation
order
particularity
peace
personal ethical theory
perspective
phenomenalism
philosophy
phronesis
pluralism

position
positive rights
premise
pressure
prima facie duty
principle
priority
privacy
psychologism
public policy
punishment
ramifications
rational
reason
reconciliation
relativism
religion
religious freedom
respect
reward
rights
rule
rule utilitarian
self-determination
self-interest
separatist
skepticism
spirit
subjectivism
supererogatory
systematic
teleological
theory
tolerance
tradition
transcendental
truth
unconditional
universal law
universality
universalizability
utilitarianism
value
virtue
virtue ethics
will
wisdom
work ethic

ORGANIZATIONS

American Catholic Philosophical Association (ACPA)
American Humanist Association (AHA)
American Institute of Medical Ethics
Association for Practical and Professional Ethics (APPE)
Ayn Rand Institute (ARI)
Center for Interdisciplinary Research in Bioethics (CIRB)
Center for Process Studies (CPS)
Evangelical Philosophical Society (EPS)
Foundation for Philosophy of Creativity (FPC)
Hastings Center (HC)
Institute for Philosophy and Public Policy (IPPP)
Institute for the Advancement of Philosophy for Children (IAPC)
International Association of Ethicists (IAE)
International Phenomenological Society (IPS)
Natural Law Society (NLS)
Society for Business Ethics (SBE)

KEY PEOPLE

Fourth Century B.C.
Aristotle

Eighteenth Century
Kant, Immanuel

Nineteenth Century
Marx, Karl
Nietzsche, Friedrich

Twentieth Century
Boisjoly, Roger
Crouch, Robert A.
Moore, G. E.
Ruggiero, Vincent Ryan
Russell, Bertrand
Sartre, Jean-Paul
Wolpe, Gerald

WEB SITES

American Philosophical Association
http://www.udel.edu/apa/

Guide to Philosophy on the Internet
http://www.earlham.edu/~peters/philinks.htm

Institute for Global Ethics
http://www.sourcemaine.com/ethics/

LegalEthics.com
http://www.legalethics.com/

Medical Ethics: Where Do You Draw the Line?
http://www.learner.org/exhibits/medicalethics/

Systems, Values and Organizations
http://sysval.org/

Online Ethics Center for Engineering and Science
http://onlineethics.org/

Philosophy

Keywords may be searched singly or in combination with other words using Boolean operators *and*, *or*, or *not*.

abstract
abstraction
action
actuality
ad hominem argument
adequacy
aesthetics
affirmation
agape
agnosticism
alienation
altruism
ambiguity
analysis
anarche
antithesis
aporetic method
argument from design
assent
association
atheism
autonomy
axiom
beauty
being
belief system
beliefs
blank slate
Buddhism
categorical imperative
categories
causation
certainty

chaos theory
Christianity
cogito, ergo sum
cognitive process
coherence
communicability
concept
conclusion
Confucianism
consciousness
consent
consequence
consequentialism
consistency
constructivism
contradiction
conventialism
cosmology
critical component
critical questioning
critique
data
death
debate
deconstruction
deduction
denial
deontology
determinism
dialectic
dialectical method
dialogue
dignity

dualism
duty
education
egoism
element
emotion
empiricism
Enlightenment
epistemology
eros
essence
estrangement
ethical
   intellectualism
   intuition
   naturalism
ethics
eudaemonism
euthanasia
event
evoke
examination
existence
existentialism
experience
explanation
fact
faith
fallibilism
family resemblance
fate
first philosophy
form
formalism
foundation
free will
good
hedonism
hermeneutics
hermeutics
Hinduism
historicism
holism
holistic approach
human experience
human nature
humanism
humility

idealism
identity
imagination
immaterial substance
independence
individualism
induction
inference
inquiry
institutions
interpretation
intuition
Islam
Judaism
justification
knowledge
language
law
Leibniz's law
linguistics
literature
logic
logical atomism
logical positivism
Marxism
materialism
maxim
meaning
metaphilosophy
metaphysics
metascience
method
methodology
mind
modernism
monism
moral
   action
   claims
   relativism
mysticism
natural religion
natural selection
naturalism
nature
nominalism
Occam's Razor
omnipotence

omniscience
ontology
operator
origin
paradox
perception
personal identity
perspective
phenomenology
philosophical
   anthropology
   method
   theology
philosophy of language
philosophy of man
Platonism
pluralism
polis
political philosophy
position
possible world
postmodernism
potentiality
practical wisdom
pragmatism
premise
prescription
presupposition
principle of noncontradiction
proposition
quantifier
questioning
rational inquiry
realism
reason
reasoning
regional sciences
regression
religion

rights
romanticism
rule
Russell's paradox
science
scientific method
self-direction
semantics
semiotics
sentence
set
social and political philosophy
social contract
social philosophy
Socratic method
sophist
speech act
sublime
substance
syllogism
synthetic
Taoism
theoretical wisdom
theory
theory of knowledge
thinking
thought
three-valued logic
tolerance
traditionalism
transcendentalism
truth
understanding
universals
universe
verification
Vienna Circle
virtue
Western philosophy
wisdom

ORGANIZATIONS

American Catholic Philosophical Association (ACPA)
American Philosophical Association (APA)
Association for Informal Logic and Critical Thinking (AILACT)
Association for Research and Enlightenment (ARE)
Council for Philosophical Studies (CPS)
Council for Research in Values and Philosophy (RVP)
Family of Humanists (FH)

Foundation for Philosophy of Creativity (SPC)
Institute for the Advancement of Philosophy for Children (IAPC)
Institute of Advanced Philosophic Research (IAPR)
International Association of Ethicists (IAE)
Philosophical Research Society (PRS)
Skeptics Society
Society for Natural Philosophy (SNP)
Society for the Advancement of American Philosophy (SAAP)

KEY PEOPLE

Sixth Century B.C.
Confucius
Thales

Fifth Century B.C.
Plato
Protagoras
Socrates

Fourth Century B.C.
Aristotle

Fifth Century
Augustine of Hippo

Thirteenth Century
Aquinas, Thomas

Fourteenth Century
William of Ockham

Sixteenth Century
Copernicus, Nicolaus

Seventeenth Century
Descartes, René
Galileo (Galileo Galilei)
Locke, John

Eighteenth Century
Berkeley, George
Kant, Immanuel

Newton, Isaac
Rousseau, Jean Jacques

Nineteenth Century
Comte, Auguste
Darwin, Charles Robert
Engels, Frederick
Hegel, Georg Wilelm Friedrich
James, William
Kierkegaard, Søren
Marx, Karl
Mill, John Stuart
Nietzsche, Friedrich
Peirce, Charles Sanders

Twentieth Century
Adler, Alfred
Baudrillard, Jean
Buber, Martin
Camus, Albert
Dewey, John
Durkheim, Émile
Freud, Sigmund
Heidegger, Martin
Moulton, Janice
Russell, Bertrand
Schlick, Moritz
Whitehead, Alfred North
Wittgenstein, Ludwig

WEB SITES

Greek Philosophy Archive
http://graduate.gradsch.uga.edu/archive/Greek.html

Society for Philosophical Inquiry
http://www.philosopher.org/

Stanford Encyclopedia of Philosophy
http://plato.stanford.edu/

Women in Philosophy
http://billyboy.ius.indiana.edu/WomenInPhilosophy/WomeninPhilo.html

Religion

Keywords may be searched singly or in combination with other words using Boolean operators *and*, *or*, or *not*.

affirmative action
agnostic
antidisestablishmentarianism
anti-Semitism
apocalypse
atheist
Bahá'í
beliefs
Bible
Buddhism
Buddhist
caste
Catholic
Celticism
chaplain
Christian
Christianity
church
clergy
comparative religion
Confucianism
congregation
conservative
conversion
cosmogony
creation
creationism
cryptoreligion
cult
culture
culture conflict
deity
denomination

devil
divine
doctrine
dogma
entity
eschatalogy
eschaton
ethical instruction
ethics
ethnic groups
ethnic studies
ethnicity
evil
evolution
existence
faith
freedom from religion
freedom of worship
genesis
gnosis
god
God
good
grace
hajj
Hare Krishna
healing
heathen
Heaven
Hebrew
Hell
henotheism
heresy

heretic
hermeneutics
Hindu
holy
humanist
hymns
ideology
interfaith
intermarriage
irreligion
Islam
Jews
Judaism
kabbalah
liberal
liturgy
manuscript
meaning
meditation
messiah
minister
missionary
moderate
modernism
monotheism
moral
mystic
mysticism
myth
naturalism
New Age
non-Western civilization
nonprofit organization
nun
orthodox
pagan
pantheism
parochial school
Pentecost
philosophy
polytheism
practice
prayer
priest
priestess
proselytism

Protestant
pseudoreligion
Quran
Rastafarianism
reincarnation
religious
    conflict
    differences
    discrimination
    holidays
    organizations
    studies
revelation
righteousness
ritual
sacrament
sacred
salvation
Santera
savior
school prayer
Scientology
Scripture
Second Coming
sect
secular
Sikhism
sin
skeptic
spiritual
spiritualist
state-church separation
Subud
symbolism
Taoism
teachings
theism
theology
tradition
traditionalism
Trinity
truth
values
voodoo
Wicca
yoga
Zoroastrianism

ORGANIZATIONS

Association for the Sociology of Religion (ASR)
Council of Societies for the Study of Religion (CSSR)
Global Congress of the World's Religions (GCWR)
Institute on Religion in an Age of Science (IRAS)
International Association for the History of Religions (IAHR)
National Council on Religion and Public Education (NCRPE)
New Age World Religious and Scientific Research Foundation
    (NAWRSRF)
Religious Research Association (RRA)
Religious Speech Communication Association (RSCA)
Society for the Scientific Study of Religion (SSSR)
Society of Biblical Literature (SBL)
Society of Christian Ethics (SCE)
Women's Alliance for Theology, Ethics and Ritual (WATER)
World Archaeological Society (WAS)

KEY PEOPLE

First Century
Jesus Christ

Fifth Century
Geneviève

Seventh Century
Muhammad

Fifteenth Century
Joan of Arc

Sixteenth Century
Teresa of Ávila

Seventeenth Century
Bourignon, Antoinette
Hutchinson, Anne

Nineteenth Century
Brown, Olympia
Eddy, Mary Baker
Seton, Elizabeth Ann

Wise, Isaac M.

Twentieth Century
Bhagavati, Ma Jaya Sati
Dalai Lama
Day, Dorothy
Graham, Billy
Harris, Barbara C.
Holmes, Ernest
Houteff, Victor
Kaplan, Mordecai M.
Koresh, David (Vernon Howell)
Morgan, Gertrude
Mother Teresa of Calcutta
Peale, Norman Vincent
Roberts, Oral
Robertson, Pat
Schuller, Robert H.
Tillich, Paul Johannes

WEB SITES

Americans United for Separation of Church and State
http://www.au.org/

Council on Spiritual Practices
http://www.csp.org/

Gays for God
http://www.gaysforgod.org/

Ontario Consultants on Religious Tolerance
http://www.religioustolerance.org/

Virtual Religion Index
http://religion.rutgers.edu/vri/

World Jewish Congress
http://www.wjc.org.il/

Witchcraft

Keywords may be searched singly or in combination with other words using Boolean operators *and, or,* or *not.*

afterlife
Akasha
alchemy
Alexandrian witch
altar
amulet
angel
animals
Apollonian
the Art
Art Magickal
astral plane
astral projection
astrology
athame
atheism
aura
balance
balefire
Beltane
biorhythm
birthstone
black magic
blessing
Bolline
Book of Shadows
British Traditional Wicca
Burning Times
calendar
candle
Candlemas
cardinal signs
cauldron

Celtic
chakra
chalice
channeling
chaos
charge
Charge of the Goddess
charging
charm
Christianity
cingulum
circle casting
clairvoyance
color
cone of power
conjure
consecration
Correspondences
cosmic
Court of Oyer and Terminer
coven
covendom
covenstead
craft
crypt
crystal
crystal ball
cult
curse
daemon
daughter-coven
death
deity

demon
Devil
divination
dowsing
drawing down the moon
dream
Earth
eclectic witch
elder
elements
enchantment
energy
energy ball
equinox
evil
evocation
exorcism
faeries
familiar
festival
fire
fortune-telling
four elements
fragrance
Gardnerian witch
gemstone
god
goddesses
Great Rite
Greater Sabbats
Grimoire
Halloween
Hallows
Hallows Eve
handfasting
harmony
healing
hedgewitch
Hephaestic Transference
herb
herbalism
hereditary witch
hex
hexagram
high priest
high priestess
human aura
humility

incantation
initiation
karma
Lammas
Law of Threefold Return
left-hand path
Lesser Sabbats
lore
lower astral
lucid dreaming
lucky charm
magician
magick
Magickal Arts
meditation
Middle Ages
mirror
moon phases
mother-coven
mystic
neo-pagan
November Eve
numerology
occult
ogham stick
out-of-body experience (OOBE)
pagan
pentagram
phenomenon
planet
postulant
powders of inheritance
poytheism
practice
protection
psychic
punishment
rebirth
ritual
rune
Sabbat
sabbath
Salem
Salem Witch Trials (1692)
Satanism
scrying
scrying mirror
seeker

seven chakras
shadow world
Shamanism
sleep
solstice
sorcerer
sorcery
spell
spirit
spiritual
star sign
stone
superstition
symbols
talisman
tarot
temple
therapy
third degree

tolerance
torture
totem
tradition
traditional witch
transmutation
transportation
trust
upper astral
wand
water
Western
Wheel of the Year
white witchcraft
Wicca
wiccan
witch-hunt
witches
wizard
Yule

ORGANIZATIONS

Church and School of Wicca
Congregationalist Witchcraft Association (CWA)
Ordo Sinistri Vivendi
Pagan/Occult/Witchcraft Special Interest Group (POWSIG)
Spiritual Counterfeits Project (SCP)

KEY PEOPLE

Twelfth Century
Artephius

Thirteenth Century
Arnold of Villanova
Bacon, Roger
Peter of Abano
Scot, Michael

Fourteenth Century
Kyteler, Alice

Fifteenth Century
Bolingbroke, Roger
Cobham, Eleanor
Sabellicus, Georgius

Sixteenth Century
Agrippa von Nettesheim, Henry
    Cornelius
Cardan, Jerome
Earl of Bothwell
Faustus, Johannes

Fian, John
Nostradamus (Michel de Notre-Dame)
Sampson, Agnes
Wierus, John

Seventeenth Century
Bavan, Madeleine
Beuther, David
Gaufridi, Louis
Gowdie, Isobel
Smith, Isobel
Style, Elizabeth
Tuchet, Eleanor

Eighteenth Century
Cagliostro, Alessandro
Dashwood, Francis
Schröpfer, Johann Georg
Weishaupt, Adam

Twentieth Century
Frost, Gavin

Frost, Yvonne

Gardner, Gerald
Sanders, Alex

WEB SITES

Ashlynn's Grove: A Pagan Information Resource
http://paganism.com/ag/index2.html

Salem, Massachusetts, Witch Trials
http://www.salemweb.com/witches.htm

The Witches' League for Public Awareness
http://www.celticcrow.com/

The Witches' Web
http://www.witchesweb.com/

The Witching Hours
http://www.goth.net/~shanmonster/witch/

SCIENCE & TECHNOLOGY

Agriculture

Keywords may be searched singly or in combination with other words using Boolean operators *and*, *or*, or *not*.

abnormal farm
absentee owner
adult farm education
agribusiness
AGRICOLA
agricultural
   chemistry
   colleges
   engineering
   supply
   trends
Agricultural Act (1956)
agriculture products
agrochemical
agronomy
animal
   caretakers
   husbandry
   science
aquaculture
bee-keeping
biotechnology
breeding
cash grains
cooperative farm
cover crop
crop-processing occupations
cropland
dairy farm
dairy farmers
experiment station
experimental farm
extension agent

farm
   labor
   management
   occupations
   operator
farmers
Federal Agricultural Improvement
     and Reform Act (1996)
Federal Commodity Acreage Program
feed
   industry
   science
   store
fertilizers
field crops
fish farm
fishery
floriculture
Food, Agriculture, Conservation, and
     Trade Act (1990)
food demand
Food Security Act (1985)
food supply
forage crops
forestry
fruit and nut crops
grains
grazing
grove
harvest
harvest season
harvesting
herbicides

horticulture
hydrology
hydroponics
insecticides
institutional farm
irrigation
land-grant university
land use
livestock
migrant workers
mill
nursery plants
nursery stock
off-farm agricultural occupation
orchard
organic farming
part-time farmers
pasture
pest management
pesticides
pests
plant
  disease
  genetics
  growth

pathology
sciences
pollination
poultry
precision farming
ranch
reforestation
research farm
rotation
seasonal employment
seasonal laborers
sharecropper
silo
soil
  building
  conservation
  science
sustainable agriculture
tenant farmers
timber tract
tractors
thresher
veterinary medicine
vineyard
world food supply
zoology

ORGANIZATIONS

Agricultural and Industrial Manufacturers Representatives Association (AIMRA)
American Crop Protection Association (ACPA)
American Feed Industry Association (AFIA)
Commodity Credit Corporation (CCC)
Crop Insurance Research Bureau (CIRB)
Future Farmers of America (FFA)
International Association of Fairs and Expositions (IAFE)
National Agri-Marketing Association (NAMA)
National Association of Farm Broadcasters (NAFB)
National BioEnergy Industrial Association (NBIA)
National Grain and Feed Association (NGFA)
Southern Cotton Association (SCA)
Western Fairs Association (WFA)

KEY PEOPLE

Eighteenth Century
Pinckney, Eliza Lucas
Tull, Jethro

Nineteenth Century
McCormick, Cyrus

Twentieth Century
Aboagye, Gertrude S.
Borlaug, Norman E.
Carver, George Washington
Chase, Mary Agnes Meara

Evans, Alice Catherine
Grandin, Temple
Hind, E. Cora
Kindinger, Paul
King, Louisa
Overman, Amegda J.

Patch, Edith Marion
Rodale, J.I.
Shiva, Vanadana
Tamang, Saraswati
Thoft, Bob
White, Elizabeth Coleman

WEB SITES

Agriculture Network Information Center (AgNIC)
http://www.agnic.nal.usda.gov/

American Crop Protection Association (ACPA)
http://www.acpa.org/

American Farm Bureau
http://www.fb.com/

National Farmers Union
http://www.nfu.org/

Council for Agricultural Science and Technology (CAST)
http://www.cast-science.org/

Food and Agriculture Organization of the United Nations
http://www.fao.org/

Organic Farming Research Foundation
http://www.ofrf.org

U.S. Department of Agriculture
http://www.usda.gov/

West Virginia University Fruit Web
http://www.caf.wvu.edu/kearneysville/wvufarm1.html

Anthropology

Keywords may be searched singly or in combination with other words using Boolean operators *and*, *or*, or *not*.

acculturation
anthropocentricity
anthropoid
anthropological linguistics
anthropometry
antiquity
archaeology
biblical archaeology
biological anthropology
Bronze Age
chronometric dating
civilization
communal cult
creation science
cross-cultural studies
cultural
   anthropology
   context
   determinism
   pluralism
diachronic linguistics
dig
domestication
Egyptology
enculturation
ethnicity
ethnocentrism
ethnography
ethnohistory
ethnology
eugenics
evolution
evolutionary ecology

excavation
extinction
Gloger's rule
habitat
Human Relations Area Files (HRAF)
Iron Age
lineage
linguistic theory
linguistics
marine archaeology
material culture
methodological individualism
microrace
natural selection
osteology
paleoanthropology
paleontology
parallelism
phylogeny
phylum
physical anthropology
population
prehistory
primatology
remains
Sapir-Whorf hypothesis
semantics
seriation
social
   anthropology
   class
   science research
   scientist

standing
studies
socialization
socioculture

sociolinguistics
Stone Age
synthetic theory of evolution
taxonomy
theism

ORGANIZATIONS

American Academy of Forensic Sciences (AAFS)
American Anthropological Association
American Association of Physical Anthropologists (AAPA)
American Ethnological Society (AES)
Association of Black Anthropologists (ABA)
Central States Anthropological Society (CSAS)
Institute for the Study of Man (ISM)
National Association for the Practice of Anthropology (NAPA)
New England Antiquities Research Association (NEARA)
Society for Cultural Anthropology (SCA)
South American Explorers Club (SAEC)

KEY PEOPLE

Eighteenth Century
Winckelmann, Johann Joachim

Nineteenth Century
Darwin, Charles Robert
Evans, Arthur John
Petrie, William Matthew Flinders
Schliemann, Heinrich

Twentieth Century
Bates, Daisy Mae
Bell, Gertrude Margaret Lowthian
Boas, Franz
Breuil, Henri Edouard Prosper
Caton-Thompson, Gertrude
Childe, Vere Gordon
Deloria, Ella Cara
Fletcher, Alice Cunningham
Freyre, Gilberto
Galdikas, Birute
Gardner, Ann
Garrod, Dorothy Annie Elizabeth
Gimbutas, Marija

Goldman, Hetty
Goodall, Jane
Hawes, Harriet Boyd
Heyerdahl, Thor
Howells, William White
Hurston, Zora Neale
Kidder, Alfred Vincent
Kroeber, Alfred Louis
Leakey, Louis Seymour Bazett
Leakey, Mary Douglas
Leakey, Richard Erskine Frere
Lewis, Oscar
Lowie, Robert Harry
Mead, Margaret
Murray, Margaret Alice
Perry, William J.
Radcliffe-Brown, A. R.
Redfield, Robert
Smith, Grafton Elliot
Sudarkasa, Niara
Weidenreich, Franz

WEB SITES

American Anthropological Association
http://www.ameranthassn.org/

Archaeological Institute of America (AIA)
http://www.archaeological.org/

ArchNet
http://archnet.uconn.edu/

Department of Anthropology, National Museum of Natural History, Smithsonian Institution
http://nmnhwww.si.edu/departments/anthro.html

Society for Applied Anthropology (SFAA)
http://www.sfaa.net/

Astronomy

Keywords may be searched singly or in combination with other words using Boolean operators *and*, *or*, or *not*.

Alpha Centauri
Andromeda Galaxy
apogee
archaeoastronomy
asteroid
asteroid belt
astrolab
astrology
astrometry
astronomical
   constants
   unit (AU)
astrophysics
atmosphere
aurora
  australis
  borealis
big bang theory
black hole
blue moon
bow shock
Bruce Medal
celestial mechanics
centrifugal force
comet
constellation
Copernican theory
corona
cosmic year
cosmology
cosmos
crater
dark matter

doppler effect
double star
Earth
eclipse
Encke's comet
Gaia hypothesis
galaxy
gamma ray
geosphere
geosynchronous orbit
gravitation
gravitational pull
gravity
Great Red Spot
greenhouse effect
Hale-Bopp comet
Halley's comet
Hubble space telescope
inflationary theory
interplanetary magnetic field (IMF)
ionosphere
Jovian planet
Jupiter
kelvin (K)
Lagrangian point
light year
lunar eclipse
Magellan
magnetic field
magnetosphere
magnetotail
magnitude
Mars

Mercury
mesosphere
meteor
meteor shower
meteorite
meteoroid
Milky Way galaxy
moon
Mount Palomar, CA
nebula
nebulae
Neptune
neutron star
new moon
Newton
north celestial pole
northern lights
nova
nuclear fusion
observatory
perihelion
photosphere
planetariums
planetary motion
planetoid
planets
plasma
plasma wave
Pluto
pulsar
quasar
radiation
radiation belts
radio stars
radio telescope
radiometry
red giant
red shift
regolith
Roche limit
satellite
Saturn
Shoemaker-Levy 9
shooting star
solar
    cycle

eclipse
flare
nebula
system
wind
solar-terrestrial environment
space
    exploration
    sciences
    weather
spectroscope
spectroscopy
spectrum analysis
star
    chart
    system
stishovite
stratosphere
sun
sunspot
sunspot cycle
supergiant
superior planets
supernova
synodic month
tectonics
tektite
telemetry
telescope
theory of relativity
thermosphere
tholus
tidal force
topography
trajectory
trojans
troposphere
ultraviolet
Uranus
Van Allen belts
velocity
Venus
wavelength
white dwarf
X-ray
zodiac
zodical light

ORGANIZATIONS

Amateur Astronomers Association (AAA)
American Institute of Physics (AIP)
American Museum of Natural History (AMNH)
International Astronomical Union (IAU)
International Union of Radio Science (IURS)
Mauna Kea Observatory, HI
Origin Science Association (OSA)
Palomar Observatory, CA
Radio Science (USNC-URSI)
Society for Popular Astronomy (SPA)
Stonehenge Study Group (SSG)

KEY PEOPLE

Sixth Century B.C.
Pythagoras

Fourth Century B.C.
Eudoxus of Cnidus

Third Century B.C.
Aristarchus of Sámos
Eratosthenes of Cyrene

Second Century
Ptolemy (Claudius Ptolemaeus)

Fifth Century
Hypatia of Alexandria

Thirteenth Century
Bacon, Roger

Fifteenth Century
Leonardo da Vinci

Sixteenth Century
Brahe, Tycho (Tyge Ottesen)
Copernicus, Nicolaus

Seventeenth Century
Galileo (Galileo Galilei)
Harriot, Thomas
Huygens, Christiaan
Kepler, Johannes
Marius, Simon
Wren, Christopher

Eighteenth Century
Halley, Edmund
Herschel, William
Lagrange, Joseph Louis
Newton, Isaac

Nineteenth Century
Adams, John Couch
d'Arrest, Heinrich Louis
Bond, William Cranch
Galle, Johann Gottfried
Le Verrier, Urbain Jean Joseph
Mitchell, Maria
Schiaparelli, Giovanni Virginio
von Fraunhofer, Joseph

Twentieth Century
Barnard, Edward Emerson
Bell-Burnell, Susan Jocelyn
Burbidge, Eleanor Margaret
Cannon, Annie Jump
Einstein, Albert
Hale, George Ellery
Hawking, Stephen William
Helin, Eleanor Francis
Hogg, Helen Sawyer
Hubble, Edwin Powell
Jansky, Karl Guthe
Jernigan, Tamara E.
Leavitt, Henrietta Swan
Lowell, Percival
Newcomb, Simon
Oort, Jan Hendrik
Payne-Gaposchkin, Cecelia
Penzias, Arno
Pickering, William Henry
Sagan, Carl
Tombaugh, Clyde
Van Allen, James A.
Whiting, Sarah Frances

WEB SITES

Astronomy Picture of the Day
http://antwrp.gsfc.nasa.gov/apod/

Hubble Space Telescope Public Pictures
http://oposite.stsci.edu/pubinfo/pictures.html

NASA Observatorium
http://observe.ivv.nasa.gov/

The Nine Planets
http://seds.lpl.arizona.edu/nineplanets/nineplanets/

Skyview: The Internet's Virtual Telescope
http://skyview.gsfc.nasa.gov/skyview.html

Aviation & Aeronautics

Keywords may be searched singly or in combination with other words using Boolean operators *and*, *or*, or *not*.

A-10 Thunderbolt II (Warthog)
aerial surveillance
aerodynamics
aerofoil
aeronautics
aerospace
   industry
   science
   technology
aileron
airbus
aircraft
   carrier
   design
   mechanics
   pilot
airline
airline transport pilot
airship
air show
airspace
airspeed
air traffic control
automatic speech recognition (ASR)
automation systems
autopilot
aviation
   mechanics
   psychology
   technology
aviator
aviatrix
azimuth

B-2 stealth bomber
B-52 Stratofortress
Bell X-1
Bendix Trophy Race
biplane
biennial flight review
bluecoat
camber
canard
certificated flight instructor
climatology
cockpit
cockpit data recorder
controlled airspace
controlled flight
controller
Curtiss JN-4
dirigible
Distinguished Flying Cross
Federal Aviation Regulations
flight
   data recorder
   deck
   instrumentation
   number
   plan
   school
   simulator
   technology
   training
flying club
Fokker D.VII
free flight

fuselage
Glamorous Glennis
glider
global positioning system (GPS)
gyroplane
hangar
helicopter
high-speed roll-coupling
instrument flight rules (IFR)
jet airliner
jet engine
MiG
Moller Skycar
navigation
navigator
NEXRAD (next Generation radar)
oceanic control
passenger transport
pilot
private pilot
privatization
runway

single-engine plane
Sopwith Camel
space
   exploration
   sciences
   systems
   travel
spacecraft design
The Spirit of St. Louis
Spruce Goose
Strategic Air Command
supersonic
Tactical Air Command
tail number
tailhook
tailwing
terminal radar approach control
   (TRACON)
thermodynamics
uncontrolled airspace
velocity
visual flight rules (VFR)
zeppelin

ORGANIZATIONS

Academy of Model Aeronautics (AMA)
Aerospace Industries Association of America (AIA)
Aircraft Mechanics Fraternal Association
Allied Pilots Association
American Helicopter Society (AHS)
American Institute of Aeronautics and Astronautics (AIAA)
Association of Naval Aviation (ANA)
Aviation Research Laboratory
Center for Advanced Aviation System Development (CAASD)
Civil Air Patrol (CAP)
Council of Defense and Space Industry Associations (CODSIA)
Interior & Arctic Alaska Aeronautical Foundation (IAAAF)
National Aeronautic Association of the U.S.A. (NAA)
National Aeronautics and Space Administration (NASA)
National Association of State Aviation Officials (NASAO)
National Transportation Safety Board
Royal Aeronautical Society (RAeS)
U.S. Department of Transportation

KEY PEOPLE

Flight Pioneers
Arnold, Henry H., "Hap"
Brown, Willa
Coleman, Bessie

Corrigan, Douglas, "Wrongway"
Crossfield, Scott
Doolittle, Jimmy
Earhart, Amelia

Gipson, Annette
Hughes, Howard
Lindbergh, Charles
Post, Wiley
Quimby, Harriet

Scott, Blanche
Turner, Roscoe
Wright, Orville
Wright, Wilbur
Yeager, Chuck

WEB SITES

Air Line Pilots Association, International
http://www.alpa.org/

Aircraft Owners and Pilots Association (AOPA)
http://www.aopa.org/

Experimental Aircraft Association (EAA)
http://www.eaa.org/

Federal Aviation Administration (FAA)
http://www.faa.gov/

NASA Dryden Flight Research Center Aircraft Gallery
http://www.dfrc.nasa.gov/gallery/index.html

National Air and Space Museum, Smithsonian Institution
http://www.nasm.si.edu/

National Air Traffic Controllers Association (NATCA)
http://home.natca.org/natca/

The Ninety-Nines: International Organization of Women Pilots
http://ninety-nines.org/

San Diego Aerospace Museum
http://www.AerospaceMuseum.org/

Sun 'n Fun EAA Fly-In
http://www.sun-n-fun.com/

U.S. Air Force Museum
http://www.wpafb.af.mil/museum/index.htm

Biological Sciences

Keywords may be searched singly or in combination with other words using Boolean operators *and, or,* or *not.*

agriculture
agronomy
anatomy
animal
anthropology
biochemistry
biodiversity
bioengineering
biofeedback
biological safety
biology
biomathematics
biome
biomechanics
biomedical engineering
biomedical ethics
biomedicine
bionics
biophysics
biospeleology
biotechnology
cardiovascular system
botany
cell biology
chromotography
circadian rhythms
cytology
deductive reasoning
developmental biology
digestive system
earth science
ecology
ecosystem

embryology
entomology
environmental science
epidemiology
ethology
evolution
exercise physiology
exobiology
food technology
genetic engineering
genetics
geochemistry
geophysics
heredity
ichthyology
immunology
integrative physiology
invertebrate
kinetics
kingdom
life science
marine biology
mathematical biology
mathematics
medicine
microbiology
molecular biology
mycology
nervous system
natural selection
neuroscience
ornithology
paleontology

parasitology
pharmacology
phenology
physiology
plant
primatology
psychobiology
psychophysiology
radiation biology
radiobiology

respiratory system
robotics
skeletal system
social biology
sociobiology
structural biology
systematics
taxonomy
vertebrate
veterinary medicine
zoology

ORGANIZATIONS

American Academy of Arts and Sciences
American Association for the Advancement of Science (AAAS)
American Institute of Biological Sciences (AIBS)
American Society of Naturalists (ASN)
American Society of Plant Taxonomists (ASPT)
Animal Behavior Society (ABS)
Association for Science, Technology and Innovation (ASTI)
Association for Tropical Biology (ATB)
Botanical Society of America (BSA)
Coalition for Education in the Life Sciences (CELS)
Ecological Society of America (ESA)
Electrophoresis Society
Human Biology Association (HBA)
International Association for Ecology
International Biometric Society (IBS)
International Committee on Microbial Biology (ICOME)
International Council of Research
National Science Foundation (NSF)
Organization of Biological Field Stations (OBFS)
Phycological Society of America (PSA)
Royal Society of London
Scientists and Engineers for Secure Energy (SE2)
Society for Industrial Microbiology (SIM)

KEY PEOPLE

Nineteenth Century
Anning, Mary
Darwin, Charles Robert
Mendel, Gregor
Pasteur, Louis

Twentieth Century
Britton, Elizabeth Knight
Carson, Rachel Louise
Carver, George Washington
Chase, Mary Agnes Meara
Clapp, Cornelia M.

Cobb, Jewel Plummer
Eigenmann, Rosa Smith
Fossey, Dian
Friend, Charlotte
Goodall, Jane
Harvey, Ethel Browne
Hogue, Mary Jane
Hyde, Ida H.
Lancefield, Rebecca Craighill
Lorenz, Konrad
McClintock, Barbara

Platt, Julia Barlow   Wong-Staal, Flossie
Stevens, Nettie Maria   Young, Roger Arliner

WEB SITES

BIOSCI
http://www.bio.net/

Life Sciences Data Archive (LSDA)
http://lsda.jsc.nasa.gov/

National Institute for Biological Standards and Control (NIBSC)
http://www.nibsc.ac.uk/

Pasteur Institute
http://web.pasteur.fr/welcome-uk.html

Philosophy of Biology
http://mind.phil.vt.edu/biology/

Salk Institute for Biological Studies
http://www.salk.edu/

World Species List
http://www.envirolink.org/species/

Biotechnology

Keywords may be searched singly or in combination with other words using Boolean operators *and, or,* or *not.*

aging
agricultural products
alteration
animal food
animals
anthroposophy
bacteria
biocatalysis
biochemical engineering
biochemistry
biodegradable
bioinformatics
biological sciences
biology
biomedicine
bioremediation
bovine growth hormone (BGH)
breeding
breeds
Bt corn
cancer
cells
chemical analysis
chemical engineering
chemistry
chromosomes
cloning
combinatorial chemistry
corn
crops
cross-breeding
cultivation
cytology

decomposition
desirable characteristics
disease
DNA (deoxyribonucleic acid)
DNA sequencing
donor
double helix
drug therapy
drugs
economics
embryology
energy
enzymes
eugenics
experimentation
fermentation
food
    additives
    production
    science
forensic DNA testing
Frankenfoods
Frostban
fuels
gene splicing
gene therapy
genetic
    engineering
    manipulation
    material
genetics
genomics
green revolution

growth
herbicides
heredity
hormones
Human Genome Project
human protein
hybridization
hybrids
individualism
industrial waste disposal
insects
interbreeding
knockout mice
medicine
metabolism
microbial ecology
microbiology
microenvironment
molecular biology
monoclonal antibodies (MAb)
morality
moratorium
mutation
nucleic acids
nutrition

patents
pesticides
pharmacology
plant cells
plant pests
plants
pollutants
power technology
production
proteins
radiation biology
radiology
recombinant DNA
reproduction
research and development
selective breeding
single-cell proteins (SCP)
species
sterility
terminator seeds or crops
vaccine
vaccinia
vector
viruses
world food supply
xenotransplantation

ORGANIZATIONS

Agricultural Research Institute (ARI)
American Association of Pharmaceutical Scientists (AAPS)
American Chemical Society (ACS)
American Society for Microbiology (ASM)
Beef Improvement Federation (BIF)
Biotechnology and Biological Sciences Research Council
Biotechnology Industry Organization (BIO)
CAB International (CABI)
Council for Responsible Genetics (CRG)
Institute for Laboratory Animal Research (ILAR)
Institute for Theological Encounter with Science and Technology (ITEST)
Institute of Food Technologists (IFT)
International Centre for Genetic Engineering and Biotechnology
International Plant Biotech Network (IPBNet)
International Society for Horticultural Science (ISHS)
International Union of Biochemistry and Molecular Biology (IUBMB)
Monsanto Corporation
National Institutes of Health (NIH)
Public Voice for Food and Health Policy (PVFHP)
U.S. Coalition for Life (USCL)
U.S. Food and Drug Administration (FDA)

World Medical Association (WMA)

KEY PEOPLE

Canada
Armstrong, John

France
Ballivet, Christine

Germany
Schleyer, Manfred
Simon, Meinhard

Holland
van Bueren, Edith Lammerts
Verhoog, Henk

Switzerland
Arber, Werner

Wirz, Johannes

United Kingdom
Crick, Francis
Heaf, David

United States
Bloch, Konrad
Borlaug, Norman Ernest
Boyer, Herbert
Cohen, Stanley
Levi-Montalcini, Rita
Seed, Richard
Singer, Maxine
Watson, James

WEB SITES

Animal and Plant Health Inspection Service, Plant Protection and Quarantine
http://www.aphis.usda.gov/ppq/

Biotechnology and Scientific Services, U.S. Department of Agriculture
http://www.aphis.usda.gov/bbep/bp/

Biotechnology Information Resource
http://www.nal.usda.gov/bic/

Council for Responsible Genetics (CRG)
http://www.gene-watch.org/

Genetic Engineering News
http://www.genengnews.com/

Got Bgh?
http://www.graficamm.com/~ari/bgh.html

International Forum for Genetic Engineering (Ifgene)
http://www.anth.org/ifgene/

Mothers for Natural Law
http://www.safe-food.org/

National Biotechnology Information Facility
http://www.nbif.org/

SciWeb: The Life Science Home Page
http://sciweb.com/index.html

Students for Alternatives to Genetic Engineering (SAGE)
http://www.sage-intl.org/

Cloning

Keywords may be searched singly or in combination with other words using Boolean operators *and*, *or*, or *not*.

adult somatic cell cloning
asexual replication
assisted reproductive technology
biotechnology
celebrity cloning
child replacement
clones
commercial applications
DNA (deoxyribonucleic acid)
Dolly
genetic engineering
genetic selection
human cloning
legislation
medical applications

moral consequences
Multiplicity (1996)
nuclear transfer
public policy
public reaction
regulation
replication
reproductive medicine
Sleeper (1973)
somatic cell nuclear transfer
somatic mutations
stem cells
third-party clone source
totipotent cells

ORGANIZATIONS

American Cryonics Society (ACS)
National Bioethics Advisory Commission (NBAC)

KEY PEOPLE

Researchers
Bishop, Michael
Briggs, Robert
Foote, Robert H.
Kato, Yoko
King, Thomas
Perry, Tony
Prather, Randall S.

Renard, Jean-Paul
Seed, Richard
Seidel, George
Tsunoda, Yukio
Wakayama, Teruhiko
Wicker, Randolfe H.
Willadsen, Steen
Wilmut, Ian

WEB SITES

Cloning: A Special Report
http://www.nsplus.com/nsplus/insight/clone/clone.html

Cloning Ethics
http://members.tripod.com/~cloning/

The Cloning of a Sheep Called Dolly
http://biowin.kribb.re.kr/topic/ethics/cloning/cloning004.htm

Human Cloning Foundation
http://www.humancloning.org/

Missyplicity Project
http://www.missyplicity.com/

Roslin Institute
http://www.ri.bbsrc.ac.uk/

Computer Science

Keywords may be searched singly or in combination with other words using Boolean operators *and, or,* or *not.*

animation
Apple
   Computer
   Macintosh
   QuickTime
applications
artificial intelligence (AI)
artificial languages
ASCII
asynchronous learning network (ALN)
automation
CD-Rewritable (CD-RW)
CD-ROM (compact disc read-only
   memory)
CMI
compact disc (CD)
computer
   -assisted design (CAD)
   -assisted instruction (CAI)
   -based training (CBT)
   graphics
   literacy
   -managed instruction (CMI)
   programs
   virus
CPU (central processing unit)
cybernetics
data processing
database management systems
desktop computers
desktop publishing
distance education
DOS (disc operating system)

DVD (digital versatile disc)
electronic
   bulletin boards
   commerce
   gaming
   mail (e-mail)
   publishing
Electronic Numerical Integrator and
     Computer (ENIAC)
encryption
graphic user interface (GUI)
hypertext
IBM PC
imaging technology
information
   networks
   science
   systems
   technology
The Internet
intranet
local area network (LAN)
management information systems
   (MIS)
microcomputers
microprocessors
modems
Moore's Law
MS-DOS
object linking and embedding (OLE)
operating system (OS)
personal computer (PC)
programming languages

RAM (random access memory)
ROM (read-only memory)
selective dissemination of information
    (SDI)
telecommunication
telecommuting
telephone communications systems

UNIVAC
Unix
very-large scale integration (VLSI)
wide area network (WAN)
word processing
World Wide Web
Y2K crisis (year 2000 crisis)

ORGANIZATIONS

American Society for Cybernetics (ASC)
Association for Information Systems (AIS)
Association of Information Technology Professionals
British Interactive Multimedia Association
Computer Professionals for Social Responsibility (CPSR)
Computing Research Association (CRA)
International Society for Technology in Education (ISTE)
International Society of Applied Intelligence (ISAI)
Society for Industrial and Applied Mathematics (SIAM)

KEY PEOPLE

**Computer Scientists &
Mathematicians**
Allen, Fran
Borg, Anita
Clarke, Edith
Easley, Annie
Glasgow, Janice
Hopper, Grace Murray
Hudlicka, Eva
Kolodner, Janet
Lanier, Jaron
Leibniz, Gottfried Wilhelm von
Lovelace, Ada Byron
Napier, John
Pratt, Lori
Sanford, Linda
Shannon, Claude Elwood

Inventors, Hardware
Babbage, Charles
Bush, Vannevar

Cray, Seymour R.
Eckert, J. Presper
Gelernter, David
Hoover, Erna Schneider
Jobs, Steven
Mauchly, John
Moore, Gordon
Noyce, Robert
Packard, David
Turing, Alan Mathison
Von Neumann, John
Wang, An
Wosniak, Steve

Inventors, Software
Allen, Paul
Ballmer, Steve
Gates, Bill
Norton, Peter
Ritchie, Dennis
Wirth, Nicholas

WEB SITES

Apple Computer
http://www.apple.com/

Association for Women in Computing (AWC)
http://www.awc-hq.org/

Association of Online Professionals
http://www.aop.org/

Computer Law Association (CLA)
http://cla.org/

IEEE Communications Society
http://www.comsoc.org/

Microsoft Corporation
http://www.microsoft.com

Dinosaurs

Keywords may be searched singly or in combination with other words using Boolean operators *and, or,* or *not.*

aetosaur
allosaurus
Alvarez impact theory
ammonite
archosaur
Archosauria
aves
biostratigraphic correlation
bipeds
brontosaurus
carnivores
Carnosauria
Cleveland-Lloyd deposit
Cretaceous Period
Cretaceous-Tertiary (K-T)
Crocodylia
Dinosauria
directional selection
disruptive selection
eggs
Ejecta Layer
Eocene
evolution
exaptation
extinction
giganotosaurus
Gondwana
Hennigian systematics
herbivores
ichthyosaur
Jurassic Period
K-selection
K-T meteorite impact

labyrinthodont
Lagerstatte deposit
Late Cretaceous Period
Late Triassic Period
Laurasia
Lepidosauria
Linnaean hierarchy
Maastrichtian
Magic Layer
Mesozoic Era
meteorites
mosasaur
natural selection
nonavian dinosaurs
Ornithischia
paleontology
Panthalassa
parallelism
parsimony
Phanerozoic Eon
phylogenetic
phytoplankton
phytosaurs
plesiomorphic
plesiosaur
preadaptation
predator-prey ratio
Predentata
primitive mesotarsal (PM) ankle
pterosaur
Pterosauria
quadruped
r-selection

rudistid
Saurischia
shocked quartz
Siderophile element
stishovite
stratigraphy

taphonomy
tektites
Tethys Sea
Theropoda
Triassic Period
Triceratops
tyrannosaurus rex

ORGANIZATIONS

American Museum of Natural History (AMNH)
Dinosaur Society (DS)
International Organization of Paleobotany (IOP)
International Society of Cryptozoology (ISC)
National Speleological Society (NSS)
Palaeontographical Society
Palaeontological Association
Paleontological Research Institution (PRI)
Paleontological Society (PS)
Paleopathology Association (PPA)
Society for Sedimentary Geology (SEPM)
Society for the Study of Evolution (SSE)
Society of Vertebrate Paleontology (SVP)

KEY PEOPLE

**Paleontologists, Discoverers, &
Explorers**
Alvarez, Luis
Alvarez, Walter
Andrews, Roy Chapman
Brett-Surman, Michael K.
Carpenter, Kenneth
Cope, Edward Drinker
Currie, Phillip J.
Davidson, Jane
Farlow, James O.

Hageman, Steven J.
Harwood, David M.
Holtz, Thomas R., Jr.
Horner, John R.
Johnson, Claudia C.
Marsh, Othniel Charles
Meyer, David L.
Milner-Halls, Kelly
Olshevsky, George
Sereno, Paul

WEB SITES

Dinosaur Eggs
http://www.nationalgeographic.com/features/96/dinoeggs/

The Dinosauria
http://www.ucmp.berkeley.edu/diapsids/dinosaur.html

Dinosaurs at the Smithsonian
http://photo2.si.edu/dino/dino.html

Giganotosaurus: T. rex Meets His Match
http://www.acnatsci.org/gigapage/

Hadrosaurus foulkii
http://www.levins.com/dinosaur.html

Royal Tyrrell Museum
http://www.tyrrellmuseum.com/

DNA Testing

Keywords may be searched singly or in combination with other words using Boolean operators *and*, *or*, or *not*.

AFLP
amino acids
behavioral genetics
biological warfare
biomedical technology
biotechnology
blood sample
blood testing
complementary DNA (cDNA)
confidentiality
crime laboratory
disease prevention
DNA (deoxyribonucleic acid)
    chain
    databank
    fingerprinting
    profiling
    segment
    typing

employment
ethics
forensic medicine
forensic science
gene therapy
genetic disorders
genetic engineering
genetics
genome mapping
homology
human gene therapy
Human Genome Project
Jones v. Murray (1992)
messenger RNA (mRNA)
polymerase chain reaction (PCR)
recombinant DNA
restriction fragment length polymor-
    phism (RFLP)
ribonucleic acid (RNA)
transfer RNA (tRNA)

ORGANIZATIONS

American Prosecutors Research Institute (APRI)
National Association of Criminal Defense Lawyers (NACDL)

KEY PEOPLE

Criminal Defendants
Andrews, Tommy Lee
Mengele, Joseph
Pitchfork, Colin
Simpson, Orenthal James (O. J.)

Law Enforcement
Jeffreys, Alec J.

Scheck, Barry

Researchers
Baltimore, David
Berg, Paul
Chargaff, Erwin
Crick, Francis Harry Crompton
Franklin, Rosalind Elsie

Hershey, Alfred Day
Khorana, Har Gobind
Kornberg, Arthur
Nirenberg, Marshall Warren

Northrop, John Howard
Singer, Maxine
Todd, Alexander
Watson, James Dewey

WEB SITES

Centre for DNA Fingerprinting and Diagnostics (CDFD)
http://salarjung.embnet.org.in/

DNA Diagnostics Center
http://www.dnacenter.com/

Human Genome Project
http://www.ornl.gov/hgmis/home.html

Micro Diagnostics
http://www.microdx.com/

Northern Bioidentification Service
http://www.mts.net/~northern/

Progeny
http://www.progeny2000.com/

Earthquakes

Keywords may be searched singly or in combination with other words using Boolean operators *and*, *or*, or *not*.

accelerometer
active fault
aftershocks
animal behavior
bedrock
Benioff zone
brittle-ductile boundary
building codes
building construction
continental plates
detection
earthquake-resistant design
elastic dislocation theory
epicenter
fault
    bend
    creep
forecast
foreshocks
Fourier amplitude spectrum
frequency
geology
geomorphology
geophysics
Green's function
landslides
lithosphere
Love wave
magnitude
magnitude scale
microearthquake
Modified Mercalli Intensity scale
Mohorovičic discontinuity

natural disasters
New Madrid earthquakes (1811–1812)
Newmark analysis
Newport-Inglewood fault
plate tectonics
pore pressure
prediction
P-wave (primary)
radioactive carbon (14C)
Rayleigh wave
Richter scale
Ring of Fire
Rossi-Forel scale
San Andreas fault
San Jacinto fault
seismology
seismometer
seismometry
Sierra Madre fault
Southern California Seismographic
       Network
tectonic plates
tremor
tsunami
tsunami magnitude (Mt)
Turkish earthquakes (1999)
upper mantle
velocity
volcanic arc
volcano
Wadati-Benioff zone
wavelength
weakness

wedge   zone

ORGANIZATIONS

American Institute of Inspectors
California Earthquake Society
California Engineering Foundation (CEF)
Earthquake Engineering Research Institute (EERI)
European Seismological Commission (ESC)
International Association of Seismology and Physics of the Earth's Interior
International Seismological Centre (ISC)
National Association of Catastrophe Adjusters (NACA)
National Earthquake Information Center
National Information Service for Earthquake Engineering (NISEE)
Seismological Society of America (SSA)
Society for Earthquake and Civil Engineering Dynamics

KEY PEOPLE

Researchers   Lehmann, Inge
Benioff, Hugo   Love, A.E.H.
Ewing, William Maurice   Mohoroviçic, Andrija
Gutenberg, Beno   Richter, Charles F.
Heng, Zhang   Wadati, Kiyoo
Jeffreys, Harold   Winthrop, John

WEB SITES

1906 San Francisco Earthquake
http://quake.wr.usgs.gov/more/1906/

Make Your Own Seismogram! Berkeley Digital Seismic Network
http://quake.geo.berkeley.edu/bdsn/make_seismogram.html

Mid-America Earthquake Center
http://mae.ce.uiuc.edu/

St. Louis University Earthquake Center
http://www.eas.slu.edu/Earthquake_Center/quakemaps.html

U.S. Geological Survey Current Seismicity
http://quake.wr.usgs.gov/QUAKES/CURRENT/

Endangered Species

Keywords may be searched singly or in combination with other words using Boolean operators *and, or,* or *not.*

acid rain
adaptation
African black rhinoceros
air pollution
animal species
assessment
auk
background rate of extinction
balance
bald eagle
biodiversity
biology
breeding
California condor
captive breeding
capture
climate
conservation
conservation biology
critical habitat
cryptozoology
defense
deforestation
ecosystem
Endangered Species Act (1973)
evolution
exploitation
export
extermination
extinction
fauna
food chain
food web

forest
genetic diversity
habitat
   destruction
   fragmentation
   restoration
hunting
import
intervention
invertebrate
ivory
loss
management
Marine Mammal Protection Act (1972)
medicines
Migratory Bird Conservation Act (1929)
natural resources
natural selection
neglect
non-native
passenger pigeon
pesticides
petitions
plant species
poachers
pollution
population
predators
preservation
products
propagation
protected habitat

protection
rain forest
rare species
recovery
reintroduction
release
relocation
reproduction
reserve
restoration
self-sustenance
survival

sustainablity
threatened species
trade
trap
turtles
water pollution
web of life
wetlands
whales
whooping cranes
zoology
zoos

ORGANIZATIONS

Habitat Conservation Plan (HCP)
Natural Resources Defense Council
World Conservation Union (IUCN)
World Wildlife Fund

KEY PEOPLE

Authors & Scientists
Carson, Rachel
Evans, Brock
Featherstone, Roger
Finney, Kevin
George, Andrew

Metcalfe, Melissa
Meyers, Norman
Miller, George
Minette, Mary
Vincent, Brian
Weiner, Heather

WEB SITES

Asian Conservation Awareness Progamme (ACAP)
http://www.jackiewild.com/

Endangered Species Coalition
http://www.stopextinction.org/

Luna: The Stanford Giant
http://www.lunatree.org

National Wildlife Federation: Endangered Habitats
http://www.nwf.org/nwf/endangered/

The Raptor Center
http://www.raptor.cvm.umn.edu/

Threatened Animals of the World
http://www.wcmc.org.uk/data/database/rl_anml_combo.html

U.S. Fish and Wildlife Service
http://www.fws.gov/

The Wild Ones
http://www.thewildones.org/

Energy

Keywords may be searched singly or in combination with other words using Boolean operators *and*, *or*, or *not*.

advanced power systems
alternative energy source
atomic energy
building operation
by-product
chemical energy
climate control
coal
conservation
   of energy
   of matter
   technology
consumer
customer utilization
depletion
diffusion
direct energy conversion
ecology
electrical energy
electricity
emission
energy audit
energy policy
environmental
   assessment
   impact
   standards
fossil fuels
fuel consumption
fuels
gas
geosciences
geothermal energy

hazardous waste management
heat
heat recovery
hydroelectric power
hydroelectricity
joules
kinetic energy
lasers
life cycle costing
materials handling
matter
mechanical energy
mechanics
mining
motor vehicles
natural gas
natural resources
nuclear energy
nuclear power
nuclear power plant
oil
optics
petroleum industry
physics
pollution
potential energy
power plant
power technology
quantum mechanics
radiant energy
radiation
relativity
renewable energy sources

solar energy
strategic petroleum reserve
substation
synthetic fuels
thermal
thermal energy
thermodynamics

thermonuclear power
tidal energy
transmission
underground
utilities
water resources
wind energy

ORGANIZATIONS

Association for Commuter Transportation (ACT)
Bio-Electro-Magnetics Institute (BEMI)
Congressional Coal Group (CCG)
Consumer Energy Council of America Research Foundation (CECA/RF)
Energy Frontiers International
Environmental Action Foundation (EAF)
Environmental and Energy Study Conference (EESC)
Friends of the Earth (FOE)
International Rivers Network (IRN)
Interstate Oil and Gas Compact Commission (IOGCC)
National Energy Resources Organization (NERO)
National Recycling Coalition (NRC)
Nuclear Free America (NFA)
Organization of Petroleum Exporting Countries (OPEC)
U.S. Association for Energy Economics (USAEE)

WEB SITES

Earthship Internet Community
http://www.earthship.org/

Hoover Dam
http://www.hooverdam.com/

Maine Solar House
http://www.solarhouse.com

Nuclear Energy Institute
http://www.nei.org/

U.S. Department of Energy
http://www.energy.gov/

Veggie Van
http://www.veggievan.org/

Engineering

Keywords may be searched singly or in combination with other words using Boolean operators *and, or,* or *not.*

accident prevention
acoustics
aerodynamics
aeronautics
aerospace engineering
agricultural engineering
agriculture
application
applied mathematics
aqueduct
architectural drafting
architecture
automatic control
automation
automotive engineering
biomedical engineering
blueprints
chemical engineering
circuit
civil engineering
coastal engineering
communication systems
computer
   -assisted design (CAD)
   engineering
   graphics
   science
computerization
conservation
construction
crystallization
dams
design

dissolution
distillation
dock
efficiency
electric power
electrical engineering
electromechanics
electronics
engineering
   drawing
   ethics
   software
   technology
engineers
environment
environmental engineering
equilibrium
ergonomics
extraction
feedback
fiber optics
filtration
fluid mechanics
force
geodetic engineering
geology
geophysics
hazards
highway engineering
human factors engineering
hydraulic engineering
hydraulics
industrial engineering

industrial safety
irrigation
machinery
manufacturing
marine engineering
material science
mathematics
mechanical
   design
   drawing
   engineering
mechanics
metallurgy
microelectronics
microminiaturization
military engineering
mineralogy
mining
natural science
naval architecture
naval engineering
nuclear engineering
nuclear technology
oceanography
optical engineering
orthographic projection
petroleum engineering

power technology
production
productivity
quality management
reclamation
reliability engineering
safety
sanitation
scientific method
semiconductor
sequence
site development
software engineering
structural engineering
structures
surveying
systems engineering
technical illustration
technology
telecommunications
thermodynamics
time study
very large-scale integration (VLSI)
water treatment
water-supply system
welding engineering

ORGANIZATIONS

American Association for the Advancement of Science (AAAS)
American Cartographic Association (ACA)
American Railway Bridge and Building Association (ARBBA)
Commission on Professionals in Science and Technology (CPST)
IEEE Professional Communication Society (PCS)
International Engineering Consortium (IEC)
National Academy of Engineering
National Association of County Engineers (NACE)
U.S. Army Corps of Engineers

KEY PEOPLE

Croatia
Tesla, Nikola

France
Diesel, Rudolf
Eiffel, Gustave
Peregrinus, Petrus

Italy
Leonardo da Vinci

United Kingdom
Brunel, Isambard Kingdom
Smeaton, John

United States
Armstrong, Edwin Howard
Baum, Eleanor
Bechtel, Stephen Davison
Bell, Alexander Graham

Bragg, Elizabeth
Bramley, Jenny Rosenthal
Burr, Theodore
Bush, Vannevar
Carrier, Wills
Chawla, Kalpana
Clarke, Edith
Dolby, Ray
Edison, Thomas Alva
Flugge-Lotz, Irmgard

Gleason, Kate
Holly, Krisztina
Iacocca, Lee
Kavandi, Janet Lynn
Mahowald, Misha
McCoy, Elijah
Roebling, Emily Warren
Roebling, John A.
Shavers, Cheryl
Shirley, Donna
Thayer, Sylvanus

WEB SITES

Engineering Ethics
http://lowery.tamu.edu/ethics/

The Jason Project
http://www.jasonproject.org/

Multidisciplinary Center for Earthquake Engineering Research (MCEER)
http://mceer.buffalo.edu/

Society of Women Engineers (SWE)
http://www.swe.org/

United Engineering Foundation
http://www.uefoundation.org/

Food

Keywords may be searched singly or in combination with other words using Boolean operators *and*, *or*, or *not*.

additives
agricultural revolution
agriculture
alcoholic beverages
analysis
baby food
bacteria
baked goods
beverage industry
biochemistry
biotechnology
cafeteria
calories
canning
carbohydrates
catering
chemistry
condiments
consumer
   product
   research
   science
cookery
cooking
cropland
dairy industry
dehydration
developed countries
developing countries
diet
dietetic foods
dietitians
distribution

distributor
drying
economics
enzymes
essential nutrients
famine
farming
fast food
fats
ferment
fermented foods
flavor
food
   commodities
   demand
   handling
   market
   poisoning
   processing
   pyramid
   safety
   science
   service
   supply
   technology
   web
freeze-drying
freezing
fresh foods
frozen foods
fruits
functional foods
future consumption

game
genetically modified foods or crops
grains
grocery stores
harvest
hospitality industry
hunger
hygiene
Industrial Revolution
ingredients
inspection
irradiation
labels
legislation
malnutrition
marine products
marketing
meatpacking
merchandising
microbiology
minerals
nutrients
nutrition
nutritional quality
nutritional value
organic
packaging
patents
pesticides
pet food
pre-packaged
preservation

processing
produce
producers
proteins
public health
quality control
recommended daily allowance (RDA)
refrigeration
regulation
retailing
rickets
salmonella
salting
scientific revolution
scurvy
seafood
seasoning
smoking
soy
spices
spoilage
standards
starvation
storage
supermarkets
toxicology
transport
vegetarian
vending machines
vitamins
wine and spirits
world food supply

ORGANIZATIONS

American Frozen Food Institute (AFFI)
American Institute of Food Distribution
Center for Science in the Public Interest (CSPI)
Food Distributors International
Food Processors Institute (FPI)
Foodbanking, Inc. (FI)
International Association of Food Industry Suppliers
National Food Processors Association (NFPA)
National Frozen Food Association (NFFA)
National Grocers Association (NGA)

KEY PEOPLE

Activists, Lawmakers, &
Restaurateurs
Forster, E. M.

Goldsmith, James Michael
Grierson, Bill
Hatch, William Henry

Kessler, David A.
Kroc, Roy
McGovern, George Stanley

Orr, John Boyd
Sinclair, Upton Beale, Jr.
Wiley, Harvey Washington
Zink, Donald

WEB SITES

FoodNet
http://foodnet.fic.ca/

U.S. Food and Drug Administration (FDA)
http://www.fda.gov/

Geography

Keywords may be searched singly or in combination with other words using Boolean operators *and, or,* or *not.*

area study
atlas
cartography
climate
climatology
county
cultural isolation
demography
developed nations
developing nations
dialects
distribution
ecology
economic geography
economic geology
environment
ethnic distribution
feminist geography
foreign countries
geomorphology
geophysics
historical geography
human geography
hydrology
map skills
maps
metropolitan
mineralogy

natural resources
oceanography
paleontology
physical divisions
physical geography
political divisions
population distribution
poverty
racial distribution
region
regional characteristics
regional studies
relocation
remote sensing
rural
   environment
   geography
   population
sedimentology
site analysis
social geography
social science
stratigraphy
tectonics
topography
transportation
urban
urban geography
world geography

ORGANIZATIONS

American Association for the Advancement of Science (AAAS)
American Congress on Surveying and Mapping (ACSM)

American Friends of the Hakluyt Society
American Geographical Society (AGS)
Association for Geographic Information (AGI)
Association of American Geographers (AAG)
Association of Social and Behavioral Scientists (ASBS)
Canadian Association of Geographers (CAG)
Geographical Association (GA)
International Political Science Association (IPSA)
National Council for the Social Studies (NCSS)
Royal Geographical Society (RGS)
Society for the History of Discoveries (SHD)
Western Association of Map Libraries (WAML)

KEY PEOPLE

Second Century
Ptolemy, Claudius

Sixteenth Century
Mercator, Gerhardus
Ortelius, Abraham
Waldseemüller, Martin

Nineteenth Century
Humboldt, Alexander von

Morse, Jedidiah
Ritter, Karl
Vidal de la Blache, Paul

Twentieth Century
Bowman, Isaiah
Davis, William Morris
Gaile, Gary
Willmott, Cort

WEB SITES

Geo-Globe
http://library.advanced.org/10157/

GeoWeb Interactive
http://www.ggrweb.com/

Heritage Antique Maps
http://www.HeritageAntiqueMaps.com/

U.S. Department of State's Geographic Learning Site (GLS)
http://geography.state.gov/index.html

U.S. Geological Survey
http://www.usgs.gov/

Global Warming

Keywords may be searched singly or in combination with other words
using Boolean operators *and, or,* or *not.*

acid rain
aerosol propellants
air
anthropogenic
atmosphere
biosphere
bromine
carbon dioxide (CO_2)
carbon tetrachloride
CFC (chlorofluorocarbon)
chlorine
climate
climatic change
coal
combustion
controlled substances
decomposition
deforestation
Earth Summit (1992)
ecosystem
electromagnetic radiation
electromagnetic spectrum
emissions
enhanced greenhouse effect
equilibrium temperature
exhaust
fluorine
fossil fuel
fully halogenated CFCs
gamma rays
glaciers
global climate change (GCC)
greenhouse effect

greenhouse gases
halocarbons
halon
hydrochlorofluorocarbons
Industrial Revolution
infrared
infrared band
infrared radiation
mesosphere
methane (CH_4)
methyl bromide
methyl chloroform
microwaves
Montreal Protocol (1987)
natural gas
nitrogen
nitrous oxide (N_2O)
oil
organic material
oxygen
ozone
    hole
    layer
photosphere
photosynthesis
pollutants
pollution
propellants
radio waves
renewable energy
respiration
smog
solar power

solar radiation
solvents
stratosphere
thermal equilibrium
thermosphere
trace gases
troposphere

ultraviolet light
ultraviolet to visible
visible light
water vapor
wavelength
wind energy
X-rays

ORGANIZATIONS

American Association for Fuel Cells
American Hydrogen Association (AHA)
Center for Environmental Information (CEI)
Citizens Alliance Saving the Atmosphere and the Earth (CASA)
Climate Network Europe
Environmental and Contamination Research Center
Global Warming International Center (GWIC)
Greenhouse Crisis Foundation (GCF)
Intergovernmental Panel on Climate Change
Society for Environmental Truth (SET)

WEB SITES

Montreal Protocol on Substances that Deplete the Ozone Layer
http://www.tufts.edu/departments/fletcher/multi/texts/BH906.txt

Policy.com Issue of the Week: Global Warming
http://www.policy.com/issuewk/97/1006/

Sierra Club Global Warming Campaign
http://www.toowarm.org/home.html

Union of Concerned Scientists (UCS)
http://www.ucsusa.org/

U.S. Environmental Protection Agency Global Warming Site
http://www.epa.gov/globalwarming/

Hazardous Substances

Keywords may be searched singly or in combination with other words using Boolean operators *and*, *or*, or *not*.

absorption
acute health effects
adverse effect
aerosol
agriculture
asbestos
asphixiants
birth defects
by-products
carcinogens
chemical
   hygiene plan
   reaction
   substance
chronic health effects
Clean Air Act
combustion
corrosive
decontamination
deposits
detection
dichlorodiphenyltrichloroethane (DDT)
disposal
disposal facility
dumping
emergency preparedness
emissions
endangered species
environment
environmental impact
environmental influences
explosion
exposure

flammability
fumes
garbage
gases
generator
groundwater
hazardous materials
hazardous waste
health hazard
identification
imminent hazard
industrial waste
industrialization
infection
ingestion
inhalation
laboratory safety
landfill
lead
leak
liability
mercury
mortality
negligence
neurotoxin
neutralization
occupational exposure
occupational safety and health
ozone
paint
pesticide
physical health
pollutant

pollution
pollution prevention
production
public health
radiation
reaction
recovery
refuse
regulation
removal
Resource Conservation and Recovery
   Act (RCRA, 1976)
respirator
respiratory toxic agent
safety
sanitation

sludge
soils
solid waste
Solid Waste Disposal Act (1965)
spill
storage
toxic waste
toxicity
toxins
transportation
uncombined radical
vapors
ventilation
wastes
water

ORGANIZATIONS

Air and Waste Management Association (A&WMA)
Association of Container Reconditioners
Association of Metropolitan Sewerage Agencies (AMSA)
Board of Certified Hazard Control Management (BCHCM)
Center for Chemical Process Safety (CCPS)
Center for Hazardous Materials Research (CHMR)
Conference on Safe Transportation of Hazardous Articles (COSTHA)
Environmental Action Foundation (EAF)
Ground Water Protection Council (GWPC)
Hazardous Materials Control Resources Institute (HMCRI)
Hazardous Waste Management Association
Hazardous Waste Treatment Council (HWTC)
Household Hazardous Waste Project (HHWP)
Legal Environmental Assistance Foundation (LEAF)
Manufacturers Alliance for Productivity and Innovation (MAPI)
Spill Control Association of America (SCAA)

WEB SITES

Asbestos Removal Contractors Association (ARCA)
http://www.arca.org.uk/

Environmental Network
http://www.environmentalnetwork.com/

Hazardous Materials Advisory Council (HMAC)
http://www.hmac.org/

Hazardous Substance Research Centers (HSRC)
http://www.hsrc.org/hsrc/html/index.html

Solid and Hazardous Substances
http://water.usgs.gov/public/eap/env_guide/solid_haz.html

Insects

Keywords may be searched singly or in combination with other words using Boolean operators *and*, *or*, or *not*.

adaptation
agriculture
animal host
ants
antennae
Apterygota
arthropod phylum
bees
beetle
Blattaria
bugs
caterpillars
cerci
cicadas
cocoon
Coleoptera
Collembola
colony
decomposition
Dermaptera
Dictyoptera
Diplura
Diptera
ecdysis
eggs
Embioptera
entomology
Ephemeroptera
exoskeleton
flight
foregut
growth
Grylloblattodea

Hemiptera
Heteroptera
hindgut
Homoptera
horticulture
housefly
Hymenoptera
hypermetamorphosis
hyperparasitism
imago
insect society
Insecta
insecticides
invertebrate
Isoptera
jaws
labia
larvae
Lepidoptera
life cycle
Mallophaga
Malpighian tubules
Mantodea
maturity
Mecoptera
Megaloptera
mesothorax
metamorphosis
metathorax
midgut
molting
moths
Neuroptera

nymph
ocelli
Odonata
ommatidia
Orthoptera
ovipositor
paedogenesis
palp
parasites
pests
Phasmida
pheromones
Phthiraptera
Plecoptera
pollination
predators
prolegs
prothorax
Protura
Psocoptera
Pterygota
pupa

Raphidiodea
reproduction
scavengers
sclerotization
Siphonaptera
Siphonculata
social insects
spiracles
stages
stick insect
Strepsiptera
struts
symbiotic
thorax
Thysanoptera
Thysanura
tracheae
Trichoptera
veins
wings
wingspread
Zoraptera

ORGANIZATIONS

Academy of Natural Sciences (ANS)
American Entomological Society (AES)
American Museum of Natural History (AMNH)
Association of Applied Biologists (AAB)
CAB International (CABI)
Entomological Society of Canada (ESC)
National Pest Control Association (NPCA)
Young Entomologists' Society (YES)

KEY PEOPLE

Researchers
Bates, Henry Walter
Bilsing, Sherman Weaver
Frazier, James L.
Knipling, Edward Fred
Koehler, Carlton S.
Mally, Fred W.

Malpighi, Marcello
McPherson, J. E.
Quisenberry, Sharron
Ries, Donald T.
Swammerdam, Jan
Tauber, Catherine A.
Weismann, August

WEB SITES

Class: Insecta
http://www.insecta.com/

Entomological Society of America (ESA)
http://www.entsoc.org/

Insect Chat, Iowa State University
http://cgi.ent.iastate.edu/chat/

Insects on the Web
http://bugbios.com/

Iowa State University Entomology Image Gallery
http://www.ent.iastate.edu/imagegallery/

The Philadelphia Insectarium
http://www.insectarium.com/

Internet

Keywords may be searched singly or in combination with other words using Boolean operators *and*, *or*, or *not*.

acceptable use policy (AUP)
ActiveX
address
AltaVista
anonymous FTP
Apple Quicktime VR
applet
Archie
archive
ARPA Internet
ARPAnet (Advanced Research Projects
    Agency Network)
ASCII (American Standard Code for
    Information Interchange)
asynchronous transfer mode (ATM)
baud rate
Bitnet
bits per second (bps)
Boolean operation
broadband
browser
BrowserWatch
bulletin board system (BBS)
byte
cable modem
cache
chat room
Communications Decency Amendment
    (CDA)
CU-SeeMe
CyberPatrol
CyberSitter
cyberspace

cyberwarfare
database
dedicated line
denial of service attack
desktop videoconferencing
dial-in connection
digital divide
domain name
electronic mail (e-mail)
emoticon
encryption
ethernet
Eudora
Federal Communications Commission
    (FCC)
fiber optics
file
file transfer protocol (FTP)
filter
firewall
frame
freenet
freeware
frequently asked questions (FAQ)
graphical user interface (GUI)
handheld
hardware
home page
host
hypertext
HyperText Markup Language
    (HTML)
icon

integrated services digital network (ISDN)
Internet-based training (IBT)
Internet relay chat (IRC)
Internet service provider (ISP)
intranet
Java
keypals
link
listserv
local area network (LAN)
Lynx
mail bombing
mailbox
megabyte (MB)
metadata
Microsoft Internet Explorer
Microsoft Windows
mirror site
modem
MOO (MUD object-oriented system)
MUD (multi-user dimension)
National Public Telecomputing Network (NPTN)
NCSA Mosaic
Net Computer (NC)
Net Nanny
netiquette
Netscape Navigator
network interface card (NIC)
newbie
newsgroups
online service provider

plug-in
point-to-point protocol (PPP)
protocol
public reflector
serial line interface protocol (SLIP)
server
shareware
Shockwave
simple mail transfer protocol (SMTP)
software
Standard Generalized Markup Language (SGML)
Surf Watch
T1 network connection
T3 network connection
Telecommunications Act of 1996
telnet
terminal emulation
transmission control protocol/Internet protocol (TCP/IP)
uniform resource locator (URL)
UNIX
urban legends
USENET
Virtual Reality Modeling Language (VRML)
virus
Web site
Web-based training (WBT)
Webmaster
wide area information servers (WAIS)
wide area network (WAN)
World Wide Web (WWW)

ORGANIZATIONS

America Online
Apple Computer
CERN (European Laboratory for Particle Physics)
CompuServe
Digital Equipment Corporation
Educational Resources Information Center (ERIC)
Electronic Frontier Foundation (EFF)
International Business Machines (IBM)
Internet Telephony Consortium
InterNIC
Merit Network Information Center
Microsoft Corporation
National Center for Supercomputing Applications (NCSA)
National Science Foundation Network (NSFNET)

New York State Education and Research Network (NYSERNet)
Prodigy
Recreational Software Advisory Council (RSAC)
SafeSurf
Silicon Graphics
Sun Microsystems
Voice on the Net Coalition
WebCrawler
World Wide Web Consortium (W3C)
Yahoo!

KEY PEOPLE

Andreeson, Marc
Ballmer, Steve
Berners-Lee, Tim
Case, Steve
Cerf, Vinton
Crispen, Patrick
Gates, Bill
Gilster, Paul

Grobe, Michael
Kahn, Robert
Mitnick, Kevin
Montulli, Lou
Morris, Robert
Postel, Jon
Rezac, Charles
Stoll, Clifford

WEB SITES

Deja.com
http://www.deja.com/

Hobbes' Internet Timeline v5.0
http://info.isoc.org/guest/zakon/Internet/History/HIT.html

International Forum on the White Paper (IFWP)
http://www.ifwp.org/

Internet2 Project
http://www.internet2.edu/

Liszt: The Mailing List Directory
http://www.liszt.com/

W3C: World Wide Web Consortium
http://www.w3.org/

Webgrrls International
http://www.webgrrls.com/

Web Police
http://www.web-police.org/

Mathematics

Keywords may be searched singly or in combination with other words using Boolean operators *and, or,* or *not.*

absolute
absolute value
achievement
acute angle
addition
algebra
algorithm
angle
application
applied mathematics
aptitude
arc
Archimedes' constant
arithmetic
average
axiom
axis
binomial
calculation
calculator
calculus
causal models
chance
chaos theory
chi square
circle
computation
computer literacy
conic
constant
cosine
counting
cryptography

data
decimal
denominator
diagram
diameter
difference
digit
discrete mathematics
discriminant analysis
division
effect size
ellipse
entropy
equation
estimate
estimation
exponent
expression
extrapolation
extreme
factor
Fermat's last theorem
finite
formula
fractal
fraction
frequency
function
game theory
general mathematics
generalizability
geometric concepts
geometry

golden mean
graph
heuristics
hypotenuse
hypothesis
hypothesis testing
inequality
infinite
information theory
integer
interpolate
intersection
intuition
Isosceles triangle
item response theory
Kepler's equation
line
linear programming
linguistics
logarithm
logic
Ludolphine number
Markov processes
mathematical
  concepts
  models
  modes
mathematicians
mathematics anxiety
matrix
mean
measurement
median
metric
mode
model
modern mathematics
monomial
Monte Carlo method
multiple
multiplication
multivariate analysis
negative
nonparametric statistics
norm
notation
number
  concepts

system
  theory
numbers
numeracy
numerator
numeric
obtuse angle
operations
operations research
order
parallel
percentage
perfect number
permutation
pi
place
plane
plot
point
polygon
polynomial
positive
power
practical mathematics
prime
probability
problem
problem sets
problem solving
product
proof
properties
Pythagorean theorem
quadratic
quantitative
quantity
quantum mechanics
quartic
quartile
quotas
radius
range
ratio
rational number
real number
reciprocal
rectangle
remedial mathematics

right angle
robustness
root
scale
scaling
scatter plot
science process skills
scientific notation
secant
sentences
sequence
set
set theory
sign
significant digit
sine
solution
space
square
square root
standard deviation
statistics
structural equation models
subtraction
sum
symbolic logic

symbols
symmetry
systems analysis
table
tangent
technical mathematics
term
test theory
theorem
theta
topology
transformations
triangle
trigonometry
unit
value
variable
vector
Venn diagram
vertex
vocabulary
volume
whole number
word frequency
word problems
zero

ORGANIZATIONS

American Association for the Advancement of Science (AAAS)
Association for Physical and Systems Mathematics (APSM)
Association for Symbolic Logic (ASL)
Association for Women in Mathematics (AWM)
Conference Board of the Mathematical Sciences (CBMS)
Econometric Society (ES)
Fibonacci Association (FA)
Industrial Mathematics Society (IMS)
International Centre for Pure and Applied Mathematics (ICPAM)
Mathematical Association
Mathematical Association of America (MAA)
School Science and Mathematics Association (SSMA)
Society for Natural Philosophy (SNP)
Society for the Advancement of Economic Theory (SAET)
Special Interest Group on Numerical Mathematics (SIGNUM)
Women and Mathematics Education (WME)

KEY PEOPLE

Sixth Century B.C.
Pythagoras
Fourth Century B.C.

Euclid

Third Century B.C.
Archimedes

Second Century
Ptolemy (Claudius Ptolemaeus)

Fourth Century
Hypatia

Sixteenth Century
Van Ceulen, Ludolph

Seventeenth Century
Bernoulli, Jakob
Descartes, René
Fermat, Pierre de
Huygens, Christiaan
Kepler, Johannes
Pascal, Blaise
Piscopia, Elena Lucrezia Cornaro
Wallis, John
Wren, Christopher

Eighteenth Century
Agnesi, Maria Gaetana
Bernoulli, Daniel
Bernoulli, Johann
Newton, Isaac

Nineteenth Century
Fourier, Jean Baptiste
Gauss, Carl Friedrich
Germain, Sophie
Herschel, Caroline
Herschel, John Frederick William

Lovelace, Ada Byron
Poisson, Siméon Denis
Somerville, Mary Fairfax

Twentieth Century
Browne, Marjorie Lee
David, Florence Nightingale
Erdös, Paul
Ladd-Franklin, Christine
Granville, Evelyn Boyd
Hawking, Stephen William
Hazlett, Olive Clio
Hennel, Cora Barbara
Hilbert, David
Mandelbrot, Benoit
Merrill, Winifred Edgerton
Neumann, Hanna
Newson, Mary Frances Winston
Péter, Rózsa
Polubarinova-Kochina, Pelageya
       Yakovlevna
Rees, Mina
Scott, Charlotte Angas
Sinclair, Mary Emily
Taussky-Todd, Olga
Turing, Alan
Wheeler, Anna Pell
Wiles, Andrew
Young, Grace Chisholm

WEB SITES

American Mathematical Society (AMS)
http://www.ams.org/

American Statistical Association
http://www.amstat.org/

MacTutor History of Mathematics Archive
http://www-groups.dcs.st-and.ac.uk/~history/

Mathmania
http://www.theory.csc.uvic.ca/~mmania/

Math Archive
http://bsuvc.bsu.edu/~d004ucslabs/

Professor Stephen Hawking
http://www.damtp.cam.ac.uk/user/hawking/

Society for Industrial and Applied Mathematics (SIAM)
http://www.siam.org/

National Parks & Preserves

Keywords may be searched singly or in combination with other words using Boolean operators *and*, *or*, or *not*.

animals
archaeological site
biodiversity
biology
conservation
culture
development
ecosystem
environment
excavation
fire prevention
forestry
funding
geology
historic preservation
historic towns
historical
   event
   site
landscapes
maintenance
management
Mission 66
national
   battlefield
   military park
   monument
   park
   parks movement

Park Service Organic Act (1916)
preserves
river
seashore
trails system
trust
natural habitat
natural resources
nature reserve
plant life
prehistory
preservation
protection
public lands
ranger
recreation
research
restoration
scenery
scenic trail
Serengeti National Park
tours
visitors
wilderness
wildlife
wildlife reserve
Yellowstone Act (1872)
Yellowstone National Park
Yosemite National Park

ORGANIZATIONS

Abundant Wildlife Society of North America (AWS)
Adirondack Council (TAC)

Big Thicket Conservation Association (BTCA)
Civilian Conservation Corps
Council for the Preservation of Rural England
Ford's Theatre Society (FTS)
Foundation of National Parks and Environmental Action
Greater Yellowstone Coalition (GYC)
Heritage Trails Fund (HTF)
Mount Rushmore National Memorial Society (MR)
National Conference of State Historic Preservation Officers (NCSHPO)
National Council on Public History (NCPH)
National Park Hospitality Association (NPHA)
Organization of American Historians (OAH)
Save the Redwoods League (SRL)
Southwest Parks and Monuments Association (SPMA)
Student Conservation Association (SCA)
Theodore Roosevelt Association (TRA)
U.S. Department of the Interior
Wolf Trap Foundation for the Performing Arts (WTFPA)
World Wildlife Fund (WWF)

KEY PEOPLE

Albright, Horace M.
Cammerer, Arno B.
Catlin, George
Dickenson, Russell E.
Drury, Newton B.
Golden, Steve
Hartzog, George B., Jr.
Kennedy, Roger G.
Mather, Stephen T.

Mott, William Penn, Jr.
Muir, John
Ridenour, James M.
Rockefeller, John D., Jr.
Roosevelt, Franklin Delano
Roosevelt, Theodore
Stanton, Robert
Wilson, Woodrow
Wirth, Conrad L.

WEB SITES

National Park Foundation (NPF)
http://www.nationalparks.org/

National Park Trust (NPT)
http://www.parktrust.org/

National Parks and Conservation Association (NPCA)
http://www.npca.org/home/npca/

ParkNet: The National Park Service Place on the Web
http://www.nps.gov/

Parks and History Association
http://www.parksandhistory.org/

Oceanography

Keywords may be searched singly or in combination with other words using Boolean operators *and, or,* or *not.*

absorption
abyssal plain
advection fog
Aguaje
albacore
algae
Ama
amoeba
ampullae of Lorenzini
anadromous
Antarctic Circle
aphotic zone
aquaculture
archipelagic plain
Arctic Circle
Aristotle's lantern
Atlantis
atoll
autotroph
Azores-Bermuda high
barnacles
barrier beach
barrier reef
basin
bathythermograph
bay
beach
Beaufort wind scale
benthos
berm
Bermuda triangle
biological noise
biological oceanography

bioluminescence
black smokers
bony fish
brachiopods
breakwater
Callao painter
Calypso
cathodic protection
cephalopod
cetaceans
chemical oceanography
chemosynthesis
chlorinity
chlorophyll
coelacanth
coelenterates
commercial ocean fishing
continental
    drift
    rise
    shelf
    slope
Copenhagen water
copepod
coral reef
Coriolis effect
crustacean
currents
deep scattering layer (DSL)
deep-sea channel
deep-sea hydrothermal vents
deepwater wave
denitrification

density current
desalination
detritus
diapir
discontinuity layer
Discovery I
diurnal tide
diving
downwelling
eau de mer normal
echo sounder
echolocation
ecology
ecosystem
eelgrass
El Niño
epifauna
equatorial countercurrent
estuary
euphausiids
euphotic zone
evolution
fan valley
Fata Morgana
fathometer
fishery
fishing industry
fjord
floor
food chain
food web
fringing reef
fulmar
fungus
Galathea
gastropods
gastrozooids
geochemistry
geography
geological oceanography
geophysics
global warming
gravity wave
greenlings
gulf
guyot
gymbretoxin
habitable zones

hadal
hexactinellida
high seas
hurricane
hydrogen sulfide
hydrography
hydrologic cycle
hydrology
hydrostatic pressure
iceberg
ichthyology
infragravity wave
inland sea
International Decade of Ocean Explo-
        ration (IDOE)
iron-manganese nodules
isopods
Jason Jr.
jetty
kelp
king wave
krill
lateral line
latitude
law of the sea
limpet
littoral zones
longitude
long-period wave
longshore current
manganese nodules
Mariana Trench
mariculture
marine
    air
    biology
    biotechnology
    bird
    mammal
    medicine
    optics
    pollution
    sediments
maritime
mata-malu
medusae
meiobenthos
mermaid's purses

meroplankton
meteorology
microplankton
Mid-Ocean Ridge
MODE (Mid-Ocean Dynamics Experi-
    ment)
Mohr titration
monoculture
nannoplankton
nautical chart
nautilus
neritic zone
neutron activation analysis (NAA)
nitrogen cycle
noise
normal water
ocean
    circulation
    currents
    engineering
    gases
    geothermal deposits
    pollution
    water
oceanic birds
oceanic zone
oceanography
offshore oil well
oil spill
osmosis
oxygen cycle
parts per million (PPM)
parts per thousand (PPT)
pharmaceuticals
pharma-sea
phosphorus cycle
photic zone
photophore
photosynthesis
phototaxis
physical oceanography
phytoplankton
pinniped
plaice
planetary carbon cycle
plankton
plant life
plate tectonics

pogy
pollution
polychaetes
polyculture
polymetalic sulfides
polyp
pompano
pressure
protozoa
pteropod ooze
quad
quadrature
quahaug
radiation fog
radiolarian ooze
red clay
red tide
redox potential
remora
ridge
rip current
robotic submarine
Romanche Gap
rust
salinity
salinity-temperature-depth recorder
salt
    cycle
    dome
    gland
sapropel
sea
    anemone
    -birds
    farming
    Grant Program
    grass
    ice
    level
    lilies
    noise
    state
seafloor spreading
seafoam
Seasat-A
seashells
seashore paspalum
seawall

seawater
seaweeds
seiche
seismic sea-wave warning system
        (SSWWS)
semidiurnal tide
seven seas
shadow zone
shallow-water wave
shelf channel
shoal
shoreline
Sibbald's Rorqual
silicon dioxide
silt grass
Snell's law
sonar
sonobuoy
sound
sounding
spacecraft oceanography
sponges
spring tide
squaloid
storm surge
strait
submarine canyon
substrate
sulfur cycle
suspension current
swell

symbiosis
syzygy
teleosts
teredo
thermocline
tidal bore
tide
tornado
toxicant
transducer
transoceanic
trans-tidal waves
trench
trough
tsunami
turbot
turtle grass
typhoon
U.S. Fishery Conservation Zone
upslope fog
upwelling
venomous marine life
water
    cycle
    exchange
    -spout
    tagging
wave period
wavelength
Winkler titration
World Ocean Circulation Experiment
        (WOCE)

ORGANIZATIONS

British Marine Life Study Society
Center for Oceans Law and Policy (COLP)
Coastal Engineering Research Council (CERC)
The Coastal Society (TCS)
Coastal States Organization (CSO)
Cousteau Society
Fleet Numerical Meteorology & Oceanography Center (FNMOC)
IEEE Oceanic Engineering Society (OES)
Institute for Exploration
Interamerican Tropical Tuna Commission
International Association for the Physical Sciences of the Ocean (IAPSO)
International Council for the Exploration of the Sea (ICES)
International Oceanographic Foundation (IOF)
International Tsunami Information Center (ITIC)
Marine Technology Society (MTS)

National Geographic Society (NGS)
National Ocean Industries Association (NOIA)
North American Society for Oceanic History (NASOH)
Ocean Society
Oceanic Society (OS)
Oceanography Society (TOS)
Pacific Ocean Research Foundation (PORF)
Sea Education Association (SEA)
Sea Fisheries Research Institute (SFRI)
University Corporation for Atmospheric Research (UCAR)
U.S. National Committee for the Scientific Committee on Oceanic Research (USNCSCOR)

KEY PEOPLE

Belgium
Piccard, Auguste

Finland
Palmen, Erik Herbert

France
Cousteau, Jacques Yves

Germany
Humboldt, Alexander von

Holland
Vening Meinesz, Felix Andries

Norway
Nansen, Fridtjof
Sverdrup, Harald Ulrik

Switzerland
Linnaeus, Carolus

United Kingdom
Bullard, Edward Crisp

Cook, James
Darwin, Charles Robert

United States
Ballard, Robert
Bowditch, Nathaniel
Ewing, William Maurice
Goldberg, Edward D.
Guyot, Arnold Henry
Heezen, Bruce Charles
Iselin, Columbus O'Donnell
Johnson, Martin Wiggo
Maury, Matthew Fontaine
Redfield, Alfred Clarence
Sears, Mary
Shepard, Francis Parker
Spiess, Fred Noel
Spilhaus, Athelstan Frederick
Stommel, Henry Melson
Tharp, Marie

WEB SITES

American Society of Limnology and Oceanography (ASLO)
http://www.aslo.org/

Greenpeace International
http://www.greenpeace.org/index.shtml

The JASON Project
http://www.jasonproject.org/

SeaWiFS Project
http://seawifs.gsfc.nasa.gov/SEAWIFS.html

Scripps Institution of Oceanography (SIO)
http://sio.ucsd.edu/

Woods Hole Oceanographic Institution (WHOI)
http://www.whoi.edu/home/

Physical Sciences

Keywords may be searched singly or in combination with other words using Boolean operators *and*, *or*, or *not*.

accelerator
aeronautics
alchemy
alloy
alpha ray
antielectron
applied sciences
astronomy
astrophysics
atmosphere
atom
atomic
   theory
   weight
Avogadro's law
big bang theory
biochemistry
bioengineering
biomathematics
biomechanics
biomedicine
bionics
biophysics
Boyle's law
cartography
cell
charge
chemical reaction
chemical thermodynamics
chemicals
chemistry
cloud chamber
composition

compound
conservation
   of energy
   of mass
continental drift
cosmic radiation
cosmic ray
cosmology
cryogenics
crystallography
Curie temperature
diffusion
earth science
earthquake
Edison effect
electric circuit
electrical
electricity
electrochemistry
electromagnetic radiation
electron
electronics
element
elementary particles
elements
emission
energy
engineering
erosion
evolution
experimentation
fault
fission

fluid mechanics
forces
fusion
gas
gauge theory
geochemistry
geochronology
geodetics
geodynamics
geography
geologic time
geology
geomorphology
geoscience
gravity
heat
historical geology
hydrology
iatrochemistry
iatrophysics
inductive reasoning
inorganic chemistry
instrumentation
interaction
ion
ionization
irradiation
isotope
kinetic theory of gases
kinetics
landform
laser (light amplification by stimulated
    emission of radiation)
laws of thermodynamics
light
liquid
macroscopic
magnetic
magnetism
mass
material
materials science
mathematics
matter
measurement
mechanics
metallurgy
metals

meteorology
micropaleontology
microscope
mineral
mineralogy
modern science
molecule
momentum
neutral
neutron
Newtonian mechanics
nominalism
nuclear
    physics
    reaction
    reactor
    science
nucleus
observation
oceanography
optical telescope
optics
organic chemistry
origin
paleobotany
paleontology
paleozoology
parity
particle accelerator
particle physics
particles
periodic table
petrology
pharmacology
phlogiston
photoelectricity
photon
physical
    chemistry
    geology
    property
physicochemical
physics
pi-meson
Planck's constant
planetary science
plasma
plasma physics

plate tectonics
polarization
positron
postulate
proof
properties
proton
quantum mechanics
quantum theory
quark
radio astronomy
radioactivity
reagent
realism
relativity
Renaissance
resistance
robotics
rock
scholasticism
scientific
    instrument
    method
    revolution
    theory
sedimentary geology
sedimentation
seismology
signal transduction
soil science
solid
solid state physics
space
spark chamber

spectroscopy
statistical mechanics
stereochemistry
stratigraphy
structuralism
structure
subatomic
subparticle
substance
superconductivity
symmetry
technology
telescope
temperature
theoretical calculation
theories
theory of relativity
thermal
thermodynamics
thermonuclear
time
topography
transmutation
uncertainty principle
unified field theory
universal law of gravitation
universe
Van de Graaff generator
volcano
volume
water
wave mechanics
wave motion
world
X-rays

ORGANIZATIONS

American Academy of Arts and Sciences
American Association for the Advancement of Science
American Association of Petroleum Geologists
American Geological Institute
American Geophysical Union
American Petroleum Institute
British Association for the Advancement of Science
European Laboratory for Particle Physics (CERN)
Geological Society of America
International Bureau of Weights and Measures

KEY PEOPLE

Fourth Century B.C.
Aristotle
Euclid
Theophrastus

Third Century B.C.
Eratosthenes

Sixteenth Century
Agricola, Georgius
Brahe, Tycho
Copernicus, Nicholas
Leonardo da Vinci

Seventeenth Century
Boyle, Robert
Huygens, Christiaan
Kepler, Johannes
Steno, Nicolaus
Torricelli, Evangelista
van Helmont, Jan Baptista

Eighteenth Century
Cavendish, Henry
Franklin, Benjamin
Newton, Isaac

Nineteenth Century
Avogadro, Amedeo
Becquerel, Antoine Henri
Berzelius, Jöns Jakob
Buckland, William
Curie, Pierre
Dalton, John
Faraday, Michael
Fresnel, Augustin Jean
Gauss, Karl Friedrich
Gibbs, Willard
Halley, Edmund
Herschel, John Frederick William
Hertz, Heinrich Rudolf
Ohm, Georg Simon
Richards, Ellen Henrietta Swallow
Volta, Alessandro

Twentieth Century
Bardeen, John
Blodgett, Katherine
Brattain, Walter Houser
Carr, Emma Perry
Cooper, Leon N.

Cori, Gerty
Curie, Maria Sklodowska
de Broglie, Louis
Dirac, Paul Adrien Maurice
Dresselhaus, Mildred Spiewak
Einstein, Albert
Elion, Gertrude Belle
Fermi, Enrico
Feynman, Richard Phillips
Flanigen, Edith M.
Franck, James
Gabor, Dennis
Glaser, Donald Arthur
Glashow, Sheldon Lee
Goeppert-Mayer, Maria
Gould, Gordon
Hahn, Otto
Hawking, Stephen William
Heisenberg, Werner
Hess, Victor Franz
Hodgkin, Dorothy Crowfoot
Jackson, Shirley Ann
Joliot-Curie, Frédéric
Joliot-Curie, Irène
Joule, James Prescott
Kamerlingh Onnes, Heike
Landau, Lev Davidovich
Lee, Tsung-Dao
Lucid, Shannon W.
Marconi, Guglielmo
McClintock, Barbara
Meitner, Lise
Michelson, Albert Abraham
Millikan, Robert Andrews
Mössbauer, Rudolf
Onnes, Heike Kamerlingh
Oppenheimer, J. Robert
Pauli, Wolfgang Ernst
Perrin, Jean Baptiste
Planck, Max
Powell, Cecil Frank
Richter, Burton
Ride, Sally K.
Röntgen, Wilhelm Conrad
Ruska, Ernst August Friedrich
Schrödinger, Erwin
Shockley, William Bradford

Teller, Edward
Thomson, George Paget
Thomson, Joseph John
Thornton, Kathryn C.
Tomonaga, Shin'ichiro
Townes, Charles H.
Urey, Harold Clayton
Van de Graaff, Robert J.
van der Waals, Johannes Diderik

von Laue, Max
Walton, Ernest
Weber, Mary Ellen
Wegener, Alfred
Weinberg, Steven
Wigner, Eugene Paul
Wilson, Charles Thomson Rees
Yang, Chen Ning
Yukawa, Hideki

WEB SITES

American Chemical Society
http://www.acs.org/

American Physical Society
http://www.aps.org/

Biophysical Society
http://www.biophysics.org/biophys/society/biohome.htm

Chemical Heritage Foundation
http://www.chemheritage.org/

Physical Science Laboratory (PSL), New Mexico State University
http://www.psl.nmsu.edu/

UIC Thermodynamics Research Laboratory
http://www.uic.edu/~mansoori/TRL_html

Plate Tectonics

Keywords may be searched singly or in combination with other words using Boolean operators *and*, *or*, or *not*.

African plate
aftershock
Antarctic/Indian plate
anticline
arc
aseismic
asthenosphere
Australian plate
basalt
basin
Benioff zone
breccia
collision
compression
configuration
continent
continental
   crust
   drift
   margin
   plate
convection
convergence
convergent plate movements
cooling
core
crest
crust
crustal material
damage
deep-focus
deformation
density

dip
dip-slip
displacement
divergence
divergent plate movements
dome
drift
ductile
dynamics
earth
earth science
earthquake
element
energy
epicenter
European plate
fault
felsic
focus
fold
fossil
fracture
fracture zones
friction
geologic time
geology
geophysics
geosyncline
global tectonics
Gorda plate
heat
heat flow
hydrothermal vent

igneous
intraplate
junction
land
lateral movement
lateral plate movements
lava
liquid
lithosphere
mafic
magma
magnetic field
magnometer
mantle
mantle convection
margin
Mercalli intensity scale
mesosphere
metamorphic
metamorphosis
microplate
midocean ridge
midplate
migration
mineral
motion
mountain belt
movement
Nazca plate
North American plate
ocean basin
ocean floor
oceanic crust
oceans
ophiolites
Pacific plate
paleobiogeography
paleomagnetic
paleontology
Pangea
peridotite
pillow
plane
plate subduction
plates
plume
rate of movement
recurrence

recycling
release
Richter scale
ridge
rift
Ring of Fire
rock
rock formation
rupture
San Andreas fault
seafloor spreading
sediment
seismic
   event
   wave
seismograph
seismology
shallow-focus
shear
sial
sima
slab
slide
smokers
South American plate
spreading centers
Strickler's Second Law of GeoFantasy
strike
strike-slip
structure
subduction
subduction zone
submarine
supercontinent
surface
suture
syncline
tension
thermal convection
thrust
topography
transform fault
trench
tube worms
ultramafic
upper mantle
velocity
volcanic chain

volcanic islands
volcanism
volcano

water
zone
zones of convergence
zones of divergence

ORGANIZATIONS

Commission for the Geological Map of the World (CGMW)
European Geophysical Society (EGS)
Geological Society of America (GSA)
International Association on the Genesis of Ore Deposits (IAGOD)
Subcommission for Tectonic Maps of the Commission for the Geological Map of
the World (STMCGMW)

KEY PEOPLE

Researchers
Barazangi, Muawia
Benioff, Hugo
Bullard, Edward Crisp
Dietz, Robert Sinclair
Dorman, James

Hall, James
Hess, Harry
LePichon, Xavier
Ophiolite, Josephine
Wegener, Alfred
Wilson, J. Tuzo

WEB SITES

Active Tectonics
http://www.muohio.edu/tectonics/ActiveTectonics.html

GPS Time Series
http://sideshow.jpl.nasa.gov/mbh/series.html

Tectonic Plate Motion
http://cddisa.gsfc.nasa.gov/926/slrtecto.html

This Dynamic Earth: The Story of Plate Tectonics
http://pubs.usgs.gov/publications/text/dynamic.html

Pollution

Keywords may be searched singly or in combination with other words using Boolean operators *and*, *or*, or *not*.

absorption
acid
   deposition
   precipitation
   rain
   soot
acidity
acute health effect
aerosol
afterburner
air
   pollution
   quality
   quality planning
airborne
aldehyde
alternative fuel
ambient air quality
antinoise
aquatic pollution
aquatic toxicology
aromatic
asbestos
asthma
atmosphere
average rate of emission
bacteria
best available control technology
      (BACT)
British thermal unit (BTU)
burn day
cancer
capture efficiency

carbon
   dioxide (CO_2)
   monoxide (CO)
carcinogen
catalytic converter
chemical
chemical reaction
chlorine
chlorofluorocarbon (CFC)
chronic health effect
Clean Air Act (1970)
Clean Water Act (1977)
cleanup
climate
coefficient of haze (COH)
colorless
combustion
commons
compound
congestion
conservation
construction
contaminants
contamination
control
copper
death
demographics
density
deposits
deterioration
diet
disease

disease control
dispersal
disposal
dump
dust
earplugs
earth
ecological factor
ecology
ecosystem
effluent
electric motor
emission offset
emissions
enforcement
environmental
   action
   impact
   influence
   standard
epidemiology
ethanol
exhaust
exposure
exposure level
extinction
extraction
Exxon Valdez
Federal Clean Air Act (1970)
federal regulations
fluorine
food chain
fossil fuel
freshwater pollution
fuel
fugitive emission
global
   climate change (GCC)
   temperature
   warming
greenhouse effect
greenwashing
ground pollution
groundwater
growth management
hazard
hazardous
   air pollutant (HAP)

   materials
   waste
haze
health
health risk
hearing
hearing loss
heat
heavy metals
herbicides
hydrocarbon
illness
immune system
incineration
indoor air pollution
industrial
   discharge
   waste
industry
land pollution
land use
landfill
lead
lead poisoning
legal limits
life cycle
liquid
   membrane system
   propane
Love Canal, NY
low-emission vehicle (LEV)
manufacturing
marine pollution
mass transit
maximum level
methanol
mining
mitigation
mobile source
monitor
motor
   oil
   vehicle
   vehicle inspection
National Ambient Air Quality Standards (NAAQS)
National Emission Standards for Hazardous Air Pollutants (NESHAP)

natural gas
nitrogen oxides (NOx)
noise
noise pollution
nonindustrial
nonmethane organic compounds
nonvehicular
oil
oil spill
olefin
organic compound
oxides of nitrogen
ozone layer
particles
particulate matter
pesticide
petroleum
photochemical reaction
photochemical smog
physical environment
physical health
poisons
pollutant
pollutant standards index (PSI)
population
power plants
prevention
primary pollutant
public health
public welfare
quality of life
radiant
radiation
radiation effects
radioactive waste
radon
reactive organic gases (ROG)
reasonably available control technology (RACT)
recycling
reduction
refuse
regulation
release
Ringelmann chart
risks
runoff
secondhand noise

seepage
septic
sewage
sewage treatment
skimmer
smog
smoke
smokestack
soil
solid waste
solvent
sound
source
spill
standards
storage tank
stratosphere
stress
substance
sulfur dioxide (SO_2)
survival
tanker
testing
thermal
tinnitus
total suspended particulates (TSP)
toxic
    air
    air contaminant (TAC)
    best available control technology (TBACT)
    emission
toxicity
toxicology
transit
transportation
transportation control measure (TCM)
trash
troposphere
ultraviolet radiation
urban environment
vegetation
virus
volatile organic compound (VOC)
warming
waste
    disposal
    management

wastewater
wastewater treatment

water pollution
water supply
wildlife

ORGANIZATIONS

Air and Waste Management Association (A&WMA)
American Association for Aerosol Research (AAAR)
Association of Local Air Pollution Control Officials (ALAPCO)
Association of State and Interstate Water Pollution Control Administrators (ASIWPCA)
Association of State and Territorial Solid Waste Management Officials (ASTSWMO)
Center for Clean Air Policy (CCAP)
Center for Hazardous Materials Research (CHMR)
Center for Waste Reduction Technologies (CWRT)
Citizens for a Better Environment (CBE)
Citizens for Alternatives to Chemical Contamination (CACC)
Clean Water Action (CWA)
Consumer Energy Council of America Research Foundation (CECA/RF)
Earth Ecology Foundation (EEF)
Earth Regeneration Society (ERS)
Environmental Law Institute (ELI)
Greenhouse Crisis Foundation (GCF)
Group Against Smokers' Pollution (GASP)
Institute of Clean Air Companies (ICAC)
International Bicycle Fund (IBF)
National Conference of Local Environmental Health Administrators (NCLEHA)
National Oil Recyclers Association (NORA)
National Pollution Prevention Roundtable (NPPR)
Natural Areas Association (NAA)
Natural Resources Defense Council (NRDC)
Rodale Institute (RI)
Seacoast Anti-Pollution League (SAPL)
Spill Control Association of America (SCAA)
Water Environment Federation (WEF)

WEB SITES

COPA (Coalition Opposed to PCB Ash in Monroe County, Indiana)
http://copa.org/

The Greens/Green Party USA
http://www.greenparty.org/

Keep America Beautiful
http://www.kab.org/

Noise Pollution Clearinghouse
http://www.nonoise.org/

Pollution Online
http://www.pollutiononline.com/

Pollution Probe
http://www.pollutionprobe.org/

U.S. Environmental Protection Agency (EPA)
http://www.epa.gov/

Rain Forests

Keywords may be searched singly or in combination with other words using Boolean operators *and*, *or*, or *not*.

agriculture
alternative fibers
Amazon jungle
atmosphere
ayahuasca
biodiversity
biosphere
canopy
carbon dioxide
clear-cut
climate
conservation
consumption
crops
culture
deforest
deforestation
destruction
developing nation
development
diversity
ecology
ecosystem
endangered
environment
equator
extinction
extraction
farm
fertile
food
food supply
forest

forest product
global warming
greenhouse effect
habitat
hydrologic cycle
indigenous
industrialization
industry
inhabitant
jungle
land
life
logging
meat industry
medicine
mining
native
nature
nutrient
old growth
oxygen
pharmaceutical
planet
plant
pollution
primary forest
production
protection
rain
recycling
secondary forest
soils
species

survival
sustainability
sustainable
system
temperature
timber
tree

tropical
tropical climates
understory
vegetation
vines
water
wildlife
wood fiber

ORGANIZATIONS

Bank Information Center (BIC)
Big Island Rainforest Action Group (BIRAG)
Conservation Foundation
Conservation International (CI)
Dian Fossey Gorilla Fund International
Earthstewards Network
Friends of the Earth—Brazil (FOEB)
Global Response
International Rivers Network (IRN)
Rainforest Information Centre (RIC)
South and Meso-American Indian Rights Center (SAIIC)
Tropical Forest Foundation (TFF)
Xerces Society (XS)

WEB SITES

Amazon Interactive
http://www.eduweb.com/amazon.html

Rainforest Action Network (RAN)
http://www.ran.org/

Rainforest Alliance
http://www.rainforest-alliance.org/

Tongass Clearinghouse
http://www.tongass.com/

Tropical Rainforest Coalition
http://www.rainforest.org/

Space Exploration

Keywords may be searched singly or in combination with other words using Boolean operators *and*, *or*, or *not*.

aerospace technology
Apollo-Soyuz Project
asteroid belt
astronomical unit (AU)
astronomy
astrophysics
Atlas missile
atmosphere
atomic structure
atomic theory
aurora
Baikonur Cosmodrome
Cape Canaveral
capsule
centrifugal force
Challenger disaster
Columbia space shuttle
comet
cosmic year
Earth
earth science
Explorer
Friendship 7
Gaia hypothesis
galaxy
geology
geospace
geosphere
geosynchronous orbit
gravitational pull
gravity
Halley's comet
Hubble space telescope

International Space Station
interplanetary
interplanetary magnetic field (IMF)
Johnson Space Center
Jupiter
Laika
light years
lunar
    landing
    research
    rover
Magellan
magnetic field
magnetosphere
magnetotail
manned spaced flight
Mariner
Mars lander
Mars Pathfinder
mathematics
Mercury Seven
Milky Way galaxy
Mir space station
moon
National Aeronautics and Space Administration (NASA)
navigation
Neptune
orbit
photosphere
physics
Pioneer missions
planet

planetarium
Pluto
Project Apollo
Project Gemini
Project Mercury
propulsion
quantum mechanics
Redstone Arsenal
Salyut I
Saturn
Skylab
solar system
solar-terrestrial environment
Soviet Union space program
Soyuz
space
   exploration
   race
   shuttle
   station

spacecraft
speed of light
Sputnik
star
stratosphere
sun
surface
time
trajectory
troposphere
universe
Uranus
vacuum
velocity
Venera
Venus
Viking Project
Vostok
Voyager

ORGANIZATIONS

American Astronautical Society (AAS)
American Institute of Aeronautics and Astronautics (AIAA)
Association of Space Explorers—U.S.A. (ASE-USA)
British Interplanetary Society (BIS)
Institute for Theological Encounter with Science and Technology (ITEST)
International Academy of Astronautics (IAA)
International Astronomical Union (IAU)
International Space Exploration and Colonization Company (ISECCo)
United Nations Committee on the Peaceful Uses of Outer Space (COPUOS)
U.S. Space Education Association (USSEA)
World Space Foundation

KEY PEOPLE

Challenger Mission
Jarvis, Gregory B.
McAuliffe, S. Christa
McNair, Ronald E.
Onizuka, Ellison S.
Resnik, Judith A.
Scobee, Francis, "Dick"
Smith, Michael J.

Mercury Seven
Carpenter, M. Scott
Cooper, Leroy Gordon, Jr.
Glenn, John H., Jr.
Grissom, Virgil I., "Gus"

Schirra, Walter M., Jr.
Shepard, Alan B., Jr.
Slayton, Donald K., "Deke"

Soviet Union
Gagarin, Yuri
Tereshkova, Valentina V.
Titov, Gherman

Other Figures
Aldrin, Edwin, "Buzz"
Armstrong, Neil
Chaffee, Roger B.
Einstein, Albert
Eisenhower, Dwight D.

Goddard, Robert

Hire, Kathryn P., "Kay"

Kennedy, John Fitzgerald

Killian, James R., Jr.

Lovelock, James

Lucid, Shannon W.

Ride, Sally K.

von Braun, Wernher

Webb, James E.

White, Edward H.

WEB SITES

NASA Astronaut Biographies
http://www.jsc.nasa.gov/Bios/

NASA: National Aeronautics and Space Administration
http://www.nasa.gov/

National Space Society (NSS)
http://www.nss.org/

Orbital Space Settlements
http://science.nas.nasa.gov/Services/Education/SpaceSettlement/

PlanetScapes
http://planetscapes.com/

U.S. Space Camp
http://www.spacecamp.com/

Women of NASA
http://quest.arc.nasa.gov/women/intro.html

Technology & Invention

Keywords may be searched singly or in combination with other words using Boolean operators *and*, *or*, or *not*.

accounting
aerospace technology
agriculture
applied sciences
appropriate technology
auto mechanics
automation
biotechnology
computer
   -assisted design (CAD)
   -assisted instruction (CAI)
   -assisted manufacturing
   literacy
   -oriented programs
computers
construction
consumer science
cosmetology
cultural literacy
culture lag
cybernetics
design requirement
developed nations
developing nations
dislocated workers
drafting
economic progress
education-work relationship
educational technology
electromechanical technology
electronics
emerging occupations
energy education

engineering
engineering technology
etiology
forestry
genetic engineering
graphic arts
horology
hydraulics
industrial arts
industrialization
information
   literacy
   technology
   transfer
inventions
journalism
laboratory technology
manufacturing
marketing
masonry
material culture
mechanics
medicine
metallurgy
metalworking
mining
navigation
obsolescence
optometry
patents
plumbing
power technology
quality of life

radiology
reprography
research
   and development
   and development centers
   utilization
robotics
scientific and technical information
scientific literacy
skilled occupations
systems development

technical assistance
technological literacy
technology transfer
trades
transportation
use studies
water treatment
welding
wildlife management
woodworking
work environment

ORGANIZATIONS

Affiliated Inventors Foundation (AIF)
Association for the Promotion and Advancement of Science Education (APASE)
International Tesla Society (ITS)
Monmouth Antiquarian Society (MAS)
Netherlands Design Institute
Newcomen Society of the United States (NSUS)
Ryan Foundation International (RYFO)
Women Inventors Project
World Intellectual Property Organization (WIPO)

KEY PEOPLE

Eighteenth Century
Arkwright, Richard
Newcomen, Thomas
Watt, James

Nineteenth Century
Babbage, Charles
Bell, Alexander Graham
Bessemer, Henry
Burbank, Luther
Davy, Humphry
Deere, John
Edison, Thomas Alva
Maxim, Hiram Stevens

Mushet, Robert Forester
Woods, Granville T.

Twentieth Century
Carver, George Washington
Drew, Charles
Hounsfield, Godfrey
Morgan, Garrett A.
Mullis, Kary
Sikorsky, Igor I.
Whittle, Frank
Wright, Orville
Wright, Wilbur
Zworykin, Vladimir Kosma

WEB SITES

African American Invention Express
http://www.invention-express.com/

Alliance for Public Technology (APT)
http://www.apt.org/

Georgia Tech School of History, Technology, and Society
http://www.hts.gatech.edu/

Women in Technology International (WITI)
http://www.witi.com/

Scientists for Global Responsibility
http://www.sgr.org.uk/

Transportation

Keywords may be searched singly or in combination with other words using Boolean operators *and, or,* or *not.*

access
aerospace
air
   freight
   passenger
   pollution
   transportation
aircraft
airport
airport terminal
alternative fuels
alternative transportation modes
Americans with Disabilities Act (ADA, 1990)
articulated coach
Automatic Vehicle Control Systems (AVCS)
average daily traffic (ADT)
aviation
bikeway
bituminous surface treatment (BST)
bridge
busway
cargo
carpool
carpool lane
Clean Air Act Amendments of 1990
clean-fuel vehicle (CFV)
common carrier
commuter
   air service
   rail service
compressed natural gas (CNG)

congestion
congestion management system (CMS)
construction
county road
demographics
diesel fuel
driving
efficiency
electric vehicle
emission standards
environmental impact
expressway
feeder service
fixed rail
fixed-route transit
fixed-schedule transit
freeway
fuel oil
funding
gas tax
gasoline
global positioning satellite navigation
grade crossing
grade separation
grid
ground transportation
hauling
hazardous materials
heavy rail
high-occupancy vehicle (HOV)
high-speed rail
highway
hydrogen

industrial park
infrastructure
inspection
Intelligent Transportation System (ITS)
Intelligent Vehicle Highway Systems
    (IVHS)
Interstate Highway System
light rail
liquefied natural gas (LNG)
low-emission vehicle (LEV)
maglev
marine terminal
mass transit
median
monorail
motor
    carrier
    fuel
    vehicle
    vehicle fleet
National Ambient Air Quality Stan-
    dards (NAAQS)
National Highway System (NHS)
network
odometer tax
off-road vehicle
paratransit
park-and-ride
parking
people-mover
Pershing Map
point-to-point
pollutant
privatization
public
    facility
    transit

transportation
railroad yard
rapid transit
regional transit
reversible lane
road construction
rush hour
safety
seaway
seismic retrofit
shuttles
single-occupancy vehicle (SOV)
smart highway
speed trap
subway
superhighway
terminal
through traffic
toll road
tolls
tourism
traffic
    control
    flow
    signal
    taming
transit agency
transit authority
transitway
transportation control
transportation demand management
    (TDM)
transportation planning
vanpool
vehicle miles traveled (VMT)
vehicular traffic
voucher

ORGANIZATIONS

American Association of Port Authorities (AAPA)
American Association of State Highway & Transportation Officials (AASHTO)
American Public Transit Association (APTA)
American Railway Development Association (ARDA)
Association for Commuter Transportation (ACT)
Association for Transportation Law, Logistics, and Policy
Federal Aviation Administration (FAA)
Federal Highway Administration (FHWA)
Federal Transit Administration (FTA)
Intergovernmental Organisation for International Carriage by Rail (OTIF)

International Federation of Air Line Pilots Associations (IFALPA)
International Municipal Signal Association (IMSA)
National Association of Governors' Highway Safety Representatives (NAGHSR)
National Bus Traffic Association (NBTA)
National Safety Council (NSC)
Transportation Alternatives (TA)
U.S. Department of Transportation (DOT)
Women's Transportation Seminar (WTS)

KEY PEOPLE

Business Leaders
Armour, Philip Danforth
Butterfield, John
Collins, Edward Knight
Durant, Thomas Clark
Fargo, William George
Grace, William Russell
Harriman, Edward Henry
Judah, Theodore Dehone
McKay, Donald
Vanderbilt, Cornelius

Inventors & Engineers
Ford, Henry

Fulton, Robert
Olds, Ransom Eli
Selden, George B.
Shreve, Henry Miller
Sprague, Frank Julian
Stevens, John

Political Leaders
Calhoun, John Caldwell
Eisenhower, Dwight D.
Fish, Hamilton
Hoover, Herbert Clark

WEB SITES

American Society of Highway Engineers
http://www.highwayengineers.org/

Metropolitan Transportation Authority, NY
http://www.mta.nyc.ny.us/index.html

National Transportation Safety Board (NTSB)
http://www.ntsb.gov/

Transport Web
http://www.transportweb.com/

Vercomnet
http://www.vercomnet.com/

Volcanoes

Keywords may be searched singly or in combination with other words using Boolean operators *and*, *or*, or *not*.

active volcano
andesite
ash
ashfall
asthenosphere
ava fountain
basalt
bomb
caldera
cap
central vent
cinder
cinder cone
clastic
cloud
collapse
column
composite volcano
compound volcano
conduit
cone
core
crater
crust
curtain of fire
dacite
debris avalanche
debris flow
delta
depression
dolomite
dome
dormant volcano

dust
ejecta
energy
episode
eruption
eruption cloud
evacuation
explosion
expulsion
fallout
fault
fissure
flank eruption
flow
fracture
fragment
fumarole
gas
geothermal
glass
Hawaii
heat
hot spot
hyaloclastite
hydrothermal
inactive volcano
intrusion
lahar
lapilli
lava
    bomb
    flow
    lake

shield
  tube
liquid
liquid rock
lithosphere
magma
magma chamber
mantle
midocean ridge
Mont Pelee
Mount St. Helen's
mountain
mudflow
nuee ardente
obsidian
overflow
Pacific Rim
pahoehoe
Pele's hair
Pele's tears
phreatic eruption
phreatomagmatic
pillow lava
plastic
plate tectonics
plinian eruption
plug
plug dome
plutonic
power
pumice

pyroclastic
repose
rhyolite
rift zone
rock
scoria
seismic
shield
shield volcano
slope
solid
steam
stratosphere
stratovolcano
stream
Stromboli
summit
summit eruption
surface
tephra
tremor
tube
tuff
vent
vesicle
Vesuvius
volcanic
  activity
  arc
  neck
  rock
volcanology

ORGANIZATIONS

American Geophysical Union (AGU)
European Volcanological Association (SVE)
French Amateur Federation of Mineralogy and Paleontology (FAFMP)
International Association of Volcanology and Chemistry of the Earth's Interior
  (IAVCEI)
International Tsunami Information Center (ITIC)
International Union of Geodesy and Geophysics (IUGG)
Surtsey Research Society (SRS)

KEY PEOPLE

Researchers
Barberi, Franco
Calvari, Sonia
Cashman, Kathy
Heliker, Christina

Kauahikaua, Jim
Monticelli, Teodoro
Neal, Tina
Thordarson, Thor
Westgate, John

Wright, Thomas L.

WEB SITES

Krakatau Volcanic Island
http://www.irfamedia.com/lampung/krakatau.htm

Lava Beds National Monument, CA
http://www.nps.gov/labe/

Michigan Technological University Volcanoes Page
http://www.geo.mtu.edu/volcanoes/index.html

Volcano Watch
http://hvo.wr.usgs.gov/volcanowatch/

Volcano World
http://volcano.und.nodak.edu/

Water

Keywords may be searched singly or in combination with other words using Boolean operators *and, or,* or *not.*

acid rain
acids
aeration
analysis
aquarium
aquatic sport
atmosphere
augmentation
boil
bound water
canal
catalyst
chemical analysis
chemical engineering
chemistry
chlorination
chlorine
civil engineering
climate
cloud
condensation
conservation
conservation of natural resources
dam
demineralization
depleted resources
desalination
dew
dike
disease control
distillation
distribution systems
drainage

drinking
drinking water
drought
ecology
electrodialysis
elements
energy conservation
engineering works
environmental standards
erosion
estuary
evaporation
filtration
flash evaporation
flood
flood control
fluoridation
fluorides
fog
free water
freeze
freshwater
gas
geothermal energy
groundwater
H_2O
hard water
health
heavy water
humidity
hydrates
hydraulics
hydrogen-oxygen compound

hydrological cycle
hydrology
hydrolysis
ice
impurity
ionization
irrigation
lakes
liquid state
marine life
maritime education
meteorology
moisture
natural drinking water
ocean engineering
oceanography
pollution
potable
precipitation
protoplasm
public health
pure water
purification
quality
rain
recycling
reservoir
river oceans
river pollution
sanitation
saturation
seawater
sedimentation
sleet
sludge
snow
soft water
soil conservation
solid

solid waste
solvent
spring
steam
storage
stream
stream pollution
substance
supply
temperature
thermal environment
treatment
tritium oxide
urban environment
use
utilities
waste disposal
wastewater
  reuse
  treatment
water
  cycle
  law
  -power
  purification
  quality
  quality management
  resources
  softening
  supply
  table
  treatment
  utility management
  vapor
  -works
watershed
waterway
weather
well
wetlands

ORGANIZATIONS

American Association of Port Authorities (AAPA)
Association of Metropolitan Sewerage Agencies (AMSA)
Bureau of Reclamation
Inter-American Center for the Integral Development of Water and Land Re-
    sources
International Water Resources Association (IWRA)
National Environmental Health Association (NEHA)

National Institutes for Water Resources (NIWR)
Paper Industry Management Association (PIMA)
World Association of Soil and Water Conservation (WASWC)

KEY PEOPLE

Researchers
Cavendish, Henry
Fahrenheit, Gabriel Daniel
Gay-Lussac, Joseph Louis

Grosse, Aristid
Humboldt, Alexander von
Lavoisier, Antoine Laurent

WEB SITES

Cambridge Water Department, MA
http://www.ci.cambridge.ma.us/~Water/

The Potomac Conservancy
http://www.potomac.org/

Rouge River National Wet Weather Demonstration Project
http://www.waynecounty.com/rougeriver/

Soil and Water Conservation Society
http://www.swcs.org/

U.S. Environmental Protection Agency Office of Wetlands, Oceans, and Watersheds
http://www.epa.gov/OWOW/

WaterWiser: The Water Efficiency Clearinghouse
http://www.waterwiser.org/

Weather & Climate

Keywords may be searched singly or in combination with other words using Boolean operators *and*, *or*, or *not*.

acid rain
Advanced Weather Information Processing System (AWIPS)
advection
advisory
air
   mass
   pollution
   pressure
altocumulus
altostratus
anemometer
anticyclone
astrophysics
atmosphere
atmospheric phenomena
atmospheric pressure
autumn
barometer
barometric pressure
blizzards
ceiling
chinook wind
circulation
cirriform
cirrocumulus
cirrostratus
cirrus
climate
   change
   control
cloud
cold front

computer models
condensation
conditions
convergence zone
coriolis force
cumulonimbus
cumulus
cyclone
depression
dew point
Doppler radar
downburst
downdraft
drizzle
drought
dust devil
earthquake
ecology
El Niño
El Niño-Southern Oscillation
equator
evacuation
evacuation order
evaporation
fall
flash flood
flooding
fog
forecast
front
Fujita Scale
geoastrophysics
glaciology

GOES-8 (Geostationary Operational
    Environmental Satellite)
groundwater
hail
heat
heat index
high
high pressure
humidity
hurricane
hydrology
hydrosphere
ice
ice crystals
Indian summer
insulation
isobar
jet stream
knot
La Niña
land breeze
landslide
lightning
low pressure
map
meteorology
microburst
millibar
modeling
monsoon
mudslide
natural disaster
NEXRAD (next generation radar)
NOAA Weather Radio (NWR)
numerical model
occluded fronts
offshore
ozone
path
pattern
physical geography
physical oceanography
physics
pollutants
pollution
precipitation
prediction
probability

radar
rain
rain droplet
relative humidity
ridge
runoff
Saffir-Simpson Scale
sea breeze
sea surface temperature (SST)
season
seismic
shower
sky
sleet
small craft advisory
smog
snow
soil conservation
solar energy
Southern Oscillation
spring
storm
storm surge
stratus
sun
sunlight
survival kit
sustained winds
temperature
thermal
thermal environment
thunder
thunderstorm
tide
tornado
trade winds
tropical
    air mass
    depression
    storm
trough
tsunami
turbulence
typhoon
virga
visibility
volcano
warm front

warning
watch
water
water vapor
waterspout
wave
Weather Service Forecast Office
    (WSFO)

Weather Service Office (WSO)
whirlwind
wind
  -chill factor
  energy
  shear
  speed
winter
winter storm

ORGANIZATIONS

American Institute of Biomedical Climatology (AIBC)
American Meteorological Society (AMS)
American Weather Observers Supplemental Observation Network (AWOSON)
Canadian Meteorological and Oceanographic Society (CMOS)
Caribbean Meteorological Institute (CMI)
Commercial Weather Services Association (CWSA)
Earth Ecology Foundation (EEF)
International Association of Severe Weather Specialists
International Center for the Solution of Environmental Problems (ICSEP)
International Society of Biometeorology (ISB)
National Climatic Data Center (NCDC)
National Hurricane Center (NHC)
National Meteorological Center (NMC)
National Severe Storms Forecast Center (NSSFC)
National Weather Association (NWA)
Royal Meteorological Society (RMS)
Scientific Committee on Oceanic Research (SCOR)
Weather Modification Association (WMA)

KEY PEOPLE

Researchers
Aristotle
Bacon-Bercey, June
Dalton, John
Franklin, Benjamin

Fujita, Theodore
Galton, Francis
Humboldt, Alexander von
Lamarck, Chevalier de
Langmuir, Irving

WEB SITES

Center for the Study of Carbon Dioxide and Global Change
http://www.co2science.org/

Interactive Marine Observations
http://www.nws.fsu.edu/buoy/

National Weather Service
http://www.nws.noaa.gov/

Tropical Storms, Worldwide
http://www.solar.ifa.hawaii.edu/Tropical/tropical.html

UM Weather
http://cirrus.sprl.umich.edu/wxnet/

The Weather Channel
http://www.weather.com/

Wildlife

Keywords may be searched singly or in combination with other words using Boolean operators *and*, *or*, or *not*.

amphibians
animal
   behavior
   caretakers
   facilities
aquarium
biomes
birds
botany
brood cover
brush control
camouflage
canopy
carnivores
carrion
cold-blooded
communication
community
concealment
coniferous forest
conservation
controlled burning
cool forest
cool grassland
cover
daylighting
deciduous forest
den tree
desert
diurnal
diversity
dominance
ecology

ecosystem
ecotone
endangered species
escape cover
extinction
food
food supply
forage
forb
forest
forestry
game management
gamekeeping
grassland
habitat
herbivore
hibernation
home range
hunting
invertebrates
mammals
management
migration
natural resources
neotropical migrants
nesting cover
nocturnal
nondomesticated animal
offspring
omnivore
pests
plant growth
plants

pollinator
predator
preservation
prey
protozoa
reproduction
reptiles
resource management
roosting cover
scrubland
shelter
species
stewardship management
streamside management zone (SMZ)
succession
survival
temperate forest
thicket
threatened species

transition zone
tree line
trees
tropical grassland
tropical rain forest
tundra
understory
vegetation
vertebrate
veterinary medicine
warm-blooded
water resources
weeds
wetlands
wilderness
wildlife conservation
wildlife management
zoology
zoos

ORGANIZATIONS

Albert Schweitzer Council on Animals and the Environment
Committee to Abolish Sport Hunting (CASH)
Deer Unlimited of America (DUA)
Fauna & Flora International (FFI)
National Animal Damage Control Association (NADCA)
National Audubon Society
National Trappers Association (NTA)
National Wildlife Federation
Nature Protection League
People Animals Nature
Primarily Primates, Inc. (PPI)
Safari Club International (SCI)
Society for Environmental Truth (SET)
United Animal Nations (UAN)
U.S. Fish and Wildlife Service
Wildlife Conservation Fund of America (WCFA)
Wildlife Disease Association (WDA)
Wildlife Habitat Council (WHC)
Wildlife Legislative Fund of America (WLFA)
Wildlife Management Institute (WMI)
The Wildlife Society (TWS)
Young Naturalists Center

KEY PEOPLE

Researchers & Proponents
Adamson, George
Adamson, Joy
Dollinger, Bill

Fox, Camilla
Fritchman, Lynn
Grinnell, George Bird
Kushlan, James A.

Leakey, Richard Erskine Frere
Markarian, Michael
Pittman, Key

Robertson, Willis
Roosevelt, Theodore
Shoemaker, Carl

WEB SITES

Canadian Wildlife Service
http://www.cws-scf.ec.gc.ca/

Really Wild Animals
http://www.nationalgeographic.com/features/97/rwa/

U.S. Fish and Wildlife Service: Branch of Habitat Assessment
http://www.nwi.fws.gov/bha/

Watchable Wildlife
http://www.watchablewildlife.org/

Wildlife Conservation Society: Zoos and Aquarium
http://www.wcs.org/zoos/

SOCIAL ISSUES &
SOCIOLOGY

Affirmative Action

Keywords may be searched singly or in combination with other words using Boolean operators *and*, *or*, or *not*.

ability
admissions
adverse impact
affected class
African American
Age Discrimination in Employment
    Action (1967)
Alaskan Native
American Indian
bona fide occupational qualification
    (BFOQ)
California Civil Rights Initiative (CCRI)
civil rights
Civil Rights Act of 1964
college desegregation
color-blind society
cultural identification
desegregation methods
desegregation plans
disabled individual
disabled veterans
disadvantaged
discrimination
    disability
    educational
    racial
    religious
    reverse
    sex
    systematic
diversity
equal
    access

education
employment
opportunity
opportunity employer
pay
protection
Equal Employment Opportunity
    (EEO)
Equal Employment Opportunity
    Commission (EEOC)
Equal Employment Opportunity Co-
    ordinating Council (EEOCC)
equality
ethnic distribution
exclusion
fair employment
Fair Labor Standards Act (Wages and
    Hours Act, 1938)
Griggs v. Duke Power Co. (1971)
hiring guidelines
Hopwood v. Texas (1996)
marginalization
Native American
nondiscrimination
Pacific Islander
parental leave policy
protected class
quota
racial
    balance
    bias
    composition
    integration

preferences
quotas
racism
Regents of the University of California v.
    Bakke (1978)
reverse discrimination
selective admission
sex bias
sex fairness
sexism
sexual harassment
termination
Title VII of the Civil Rights Act of 1964
tokenism
underrepresentation
Uniform Guidelines on Employee Se-
    lection Procedures
women
workforce analysis

ORGANIZATIONS

American Association for Affirmative Action (AAAA)
Center for Human Services (CHS)
Employment Policy Foundation (EPF)
Equal Employment Advisory Council (EEAC)
Equal Rights Advocates (ERA)
U.S Commission on Civil Rights
U.S. Department of Labor

KEY PEOPLE

Bakke, Allan Paul
Connerly, Ward
Der, Henry
Hopwood, Cheryl
Jaye, David
Johnson, Lyndon Baines
Kennedy, John Fitzgerald
Leonard, Walter
O'Connor, Sandra Day

WEB SITES

Americans Against Discrimination and Preferences (AADAP)
http://www.aadap.org/

Americans United for Affirmative Action
http://www.auaa.org/

Campaign for a Color-Blind America
http://www.equalrights.com/

Chinese for Affirmative Action (CAA)
http://www.caasf.org/

National Association for the Advancement of Colored People (NAACP)
http://www.naacp.org/

NOW Issue Report: Affirmative Action
http://www.now.org/issues/affirm/affirmre.html

Animal Rights

Keywords may be searched singly or in combination with other words
using Boolean operators *and*, *or*, or *not*.

Ahimsa
animal
  abuse
  caretakers
  experimentation
  exploitation
  husbandry
  interests
  liberation movement
  product
  rights movement
  sacrifice
  suffering
  testing
  welfare
  Welfare Act
  welfare movement
bullfighting
circus
cloning
cruelty-free
dissection
downers
endangered species

factory farming
fashion
fishing
food chain
free range
fur farms
habitats
Humane Slaughter Act (1960)
hunting
laboratory animals
leghold traps
lower animals
meat industry
natural selection
Premarin
product testing
rodeo
slaughterhouse
speciesism
vegan
vegetarian
veterinary medicine
vivisection
zoo

ORGANIZATIONS

Alliance for Animals
Americans for Medical Progress
Animal Industry Foundation (AIF)
Animal Liberation Front
Animal Rights Coalition (ARC)
Animal Rights Network (ARN)
Citizens to End Animal Suffering and Exploitation (CEASE)

Coalition for Non-Violent Food (CONF)
Earth Liberation Front
Farm Animal Reform Movement (FARM)
Farm Sanctuary
Vegetarian Resource Group (VRG)

KEY PEOPLE

Activists

Buston, Gene
Buston, Lorri
Daley, Tim
De Rose, Chris
Fox, Michael W.
Katz, Elliot
McCartney, Linda

Neal, Barnard
Newkirk, Ingrid
Pacheco, Alex
Regan, Tom
Salt, Henry
Singer, Peter
Vlasak, Jerry

WEB SITES

American Anti-Vivisection Society (AAVS)
http://www.aavs.org/

Animal Legal Defense Fund
http://www.aldf.org/

Animal Protection Institute
http://www.api4animals.org/

Animal Rights Resource Site
http://www.animalconcerns.org/

Ark Online
http://www.arkonline.com/

Farm Sanctuary
http://www.farmsanctuary.com/

People for the Ethical Treatment of Animals (PETA)
http://www.peta.com/

Vegan Action
http://www.vegan.org/

Capital Punishment

Keywords may be searched singly or in combination with other words using Boolean operators *and*, *or*, or *not*.

abolition
capital crime
capital prosecution
China
civil liberty
clemency
comparative law
constitutional law
constitutional rights
Convention for the Protection of Human Rights of the Council of Europe (1950)
Cuba
death
   chamber
   penalty
   row
   sentence
drug kingpin death penalty
due process
electrocution
execution
extradition

federal death penalty
firing squad
Furman v. Georgia (1972)
gas chamber
Gregg v. Georgia (1976)
hanging
international law
Iran
lethal gas
lethal injection
life imprisonment
McCleskey v. Kemp (1987)
murder
natural law
Nigeria
Pakistan
postexecution syndrome
Protocol to the American Convention on Human Rights (1990)
racial bias
Saudi Arabia
Universal Declaration of Human Rights (1948)
war crimes

ORGANIZATIONS

American Civil Liberties Union—Capital Punishment Project
American Civil Liberties Union Foundation (ACLUF)
Canadians for Responsible Government (CFRG)
Capital Punishment Project (CPP)
Coalition to Abolish the Death Penalty
Committee on Justice and the Constitution (COJAC)
Feminists for Life of America (FFL)

Friends for Life (FFL)
Justice Now (JN)
Lamp of Hope Project (LHP)
National Association for the Advancement of Colored People Legal Defense and Educational Fund
Penny Resistance (PR)

KEY PEOPLE

Executed Persons
Chessman, Caryl
Gilmore, Gary
Hauptmann, Bruno Richard
Rosenberg, Ethel
Rosenberg, Julius
Sacco, Nicola
Tucker, Karla Faye

Vanzetti, Bartolomeo

Law Enforcement & Political Leaders
Becarria, Marchese di
Darrow, Clarence Seward
Livingston, Edward
Peel, Robert
Reed, Thomas Brackett
Shabaka

WEB SITES

Amnesty International and the Death Penalty
http://www.amnesty.org/ailib/intcam/dp/index.html

Court TV Legal Documents: The Death Penalty
http://www.courttv.com/map/library/capital/

Death Penalty Information Center (DPIC)
http://www.essential.org/dpic/

Death Penalty Links
http://www.clarkprosecutor.org/html/links/dplinks.htm

National Coalition to Abolish the Death Penalty (NCADP)
http://www.ncadp.org/

Prison Issues Desk: Death Penalty
http://www.prisonactivist.org/death-penalty/

Censorship

Keywords may be searched singly or in combination with other words using Boolean operators *and*, *or*, or *not*.

banned books
Bethel School District v. Fraser (1986)
Board of Education v. Pico (1982)
bookstores
civil liberties
classroom
colleges and universities
constitutional law
creation science law
elementary schools
First Amendment, Constitution of the
    United States
freedom
   of information
   of speech
   to read
Hazelwood School District v. Kuhlmeier
    (1988)

high schools
Huckleberry Finn
intellectual freedom
libraries
library materials
materials selection policies
moral rights
obscenity
pornography
pressure groups
racism
public schools
school
   censorship
   law
   library censorship
secular humanism
sex

ORGANIZATIONS

Academy of Family Films and Family Television (AFFFT)
American Booksellers Association (ABA)
American Library Association, Office of Intellectual Freedom (OIF)
Anti-Censorship and Deception Union
Civil Censorship Study Group (CCSG)
Committee on International Freedom to Publish (CIFP)
DC Feminists Against Pornography (DCFAP)
First Amendment Consumer and Trade Society (FACTS)
Foundation to Improve Television (FIT)
Free Expression Project
Free Press Association (FPA)
Freedom to Read Foundation (FTRF)
Media Coalition/Americans for Constitutional Freedom (MC/ACF)

National Campaign for Freedom of Expression (NCFE)
National Coalition Against Censorship (NCAC)
National Council of Teachers of English
Parents' Alliance to Protect Our Children (PAPOC)
People for the American Way
U.S. Supreme Court

KEY PEOPLE

Authors & Activists
Bradford, William
Comstock, Anthony
Creel, George
Dostoyevsky, Fyodor
Dreiser, Herman Theodore
Filmer, Robert
Frankfurter, Felix
Fraser, Matthew

Godwin, Mary Jo
Lawrence, David Herbert
Manley, Will
Milton, John
Pico, Steven
Solzhenitsyn, Alexander Isayevich
Twain, Mark
Weins, Leo

WEB SITES

ACLU Freedom Network: Cyber-Liberties
http://www.aclu.org/issues/cyber/hmcl.html

American Library Association Banned Books Week
http://www.ala.org/bbooks/

A Brief History of Banned Music in United States
http://www.ericnuzum.com/banned/index.html

The Censorship Files
http://www.clairescorner.com/censorship/default.htm

Electronic Frontier Foundation (EFF)
http://www.eff.org/

Families Against Internet Censorship (FAIC)
http://shell.rmi.net/~fagin/faic/

Child Abuse

Keywords may be searched singly or in combination with other words using Boolean operators *and*, *or*, or *not*.

abused children
assault and battery
battered children
battered women
Child Abuse Potential (CAP) Inventory
child
   molestation
   protection
   welfare
domestic violence
emotional abuse

family violence
Megan's law
missing children
neglect
pedophilia
prevention
psychological abuse
sexual abuse
sexual exploitation
United States v. Maxwell (1996)
verbal abuse

ORGANIZATIONS

American Professional Society on the Abuse of Children (APSAC)
Believe the Children (BTC)
Child Abuse Institute of Research (CAIR)
Child Abuse Listening and Mediation (CALM)
Child Welfare Institute (CWI)
Childhelp U.S.A.
Children's Rights of America (CRA)
Children's Watch International
End Violence Against the Next Generation (EVAN-G)
National Center for Prosecution of Child Abuse (NCPCA)
National Coalition to Abolish Corporal Punishment in Schools (NCACPS)
National Committee to Prevent Child Abuse
National Council on Child Abuse and Family Violence (NCCAFV)
Parents and Teachers Against Violence in Education (PTAVE)
Parents Anonymous (PA)

WEB SITES

Canadian Society for the Investigation of Child Abuse (CSICA)
http://www.csica.zener.com/

Child Abuse Prevention Month
http://familysource.org/abusemonth.html

Child Abuse Prevention Network
http://child.cornell.edu/

Child Welfare Research Institute
http://www.childwelfare.com/

A Citizen's Guide to Megan's Law
http://www.state.nj.us/lps/megan.htm

National Clearinghouse on Child Abuse and Neglect Information
http://www.calib.com/nccanch/

Civil Rights

Keywords may be searched singly or in combination with other words using Boolean operators *and*, *or*, or *not*.

activists
antidiscrimination legislation
apartheid
Big Six Leaders
Black Power
Bloody Sunday
Brown v. Board of Education of Topeka (1954)
busing
children's rights
civil
    disobedience
    law
    liberties
    Rights Act (1866)
    Rights Act (1875)
    Rights Act (1957)
    Rights Act (1964)
    Rights Commission
    rights legislation
    rights movement
demonstrations
Edmund Pettis Bridge, Selma, AL
Fourteenth Amendment
freedom march
freedom of speech
freedom rides
Freedom Summer
Freedom's Journal
Harper's Ferry
Liberator
Little Rock, AR
lynchings
March on Washington
Montgomery, AL
Montgomery bus boycott
nonviolent civil disobedience
Plessy v. Ferguson
protest movements
race riots
racial integration
racial segregation
reverse discrimination
school desegregation
segregation
separate but equal
sex discrimination
sit-in
Sixteenth Street Baptist Church, Birmingham, AL
slavery
tort reform
Tuskegee Institute
underground railroad
Voter Education Project
Voting Rights Act (1965)
white supremacy

ORGANIZATIONS

American–Arab Anti-Discrimination Committee (ADC)
American Civil Liberties Union (ACLU)

Black Panther Party
Center for Constitutional Rights (CCR)
Citizens' Commission on Civil Rights (CCCR)
Citizens for a Better America (CBA)
Clearinghouse on Women's Issues (CWI)
COINTELPRO
Community Service Organization (CSO)
Congress of Racial Equality (CORE)
Gay and Lesbian Advocates and Defenders (GLAD)
International League for Human Rights (ILHR)
National Antislavery Society
National Association for the Advancement of Colored People (NAACP)
National Farm Workers Association
People for the American Way (PFAW)
Southern Christian Leadership Conference (SCLC)
Student Nonviolent Coordinating Committee (SNCC)
United Farm Workers of America, AFL-CIO

KEY PEOPLE

Nineteenth Century, United States
Brown, John
Cornish, Samuel
Douglass, Frederick
Garrison, William Lloyd
Mott, Lucretia Coffin
Stevens, Thaddeus
Stowe, Harriet Beecher
Truth, Sojourner (Isabella van Wagener)
Tubman, Harriet

Twentieth Century, United States
Abernathy, Ralph
Bond, Julian
Carmichael, Stokely (Kwame Toure)
Chávez, César
Collins, Addie Mae
Du Bois, W.E.B. (William Edward Burghardt)
Evers, Medgar
Farmer, James
Hoover, J. Edgar
Jackson, Jesse
Johnson, Lyndon Baines
Kennedy, John Fitzgerald
Kennedy, Robert F.
King, Coretta Scott

King, Martin Luther, Jr.
Lee, Bill Lann
Lewis, John
Malcolm X
Marshall, Thurgood
McKissick, Floyd B.
McNair, Denise
Meredith, James
Muste, Abraham Johannes
Newton, Huey
Parks, Rosa Louise
Randolph, A. Phillip
Robertson, Carol
Robinson, Jackie
Rustin, Bayard
Shriver, Sargent
Wallace, George
Washington, Booker T.
Wells, Ida B.
Wesley, Cynthia
Wilkins, Roy
Williams, Hosea
Young, Andrew
Young, Whitney

Non-U.S. Figures
Gandhi, Mahatma
Mandela, Nelson
Tutu, Desmond

WEB SITES

The Carter Center
http://www.cartercenter.org/

Civil Rights Timeline
http://www.seattletimes.com/mlk/movement/Seatimeline.html

Leadership Conference on Civil Rights
http://www.civilrights.org/

NAACP (National Association for the Advancement of Colored People)
http://www.naacp.org/

National Civil Rights Museum
http://www.midsouth.rr.com/civilrights/

The National Urban League
http://www.nul.org/

National Voting Rights Museum and Institute
http://www.voterights.org/

Southern Poverty Law Center
http://splcenter.org/

U.S. Commission on Civil Rights
http://www.usccr.gov/

U.S. Department of Education Office for Civil Rights (OCR)
http://www.ed.gov/offices/OCR/

U.S. Department of Justice, Civil Rights Division
http://www.usdoj.gov/crt/

Community Service & Volunteerism

Keywords may be searched singly or in combination with other words using Boolean operators *and*, *or*, or *not*.

community
   center
   organizations
   resources
outreach programs
public service
service clubs

social agencies
social services
student volunteers
volunteer agencies
volunteers
youth agencies

ORGANIZATIONS

Call for Action (CFA)
Center for Community Action of B'Nai B'rith International
General Federation of Women's Clubs (GFWC)
Joint Action in Community Service (JACS)
National Service League
Points of Light Foundation
Prison Fellowship Ministries (PFM)
Project Volunteer (PV)
Volunteers of America
Women in Community Service (WICS)

KEY PEOPLE

Carter, James Earl, "Jimmy"
Carter, Rosalynn Smith

Chávez, César
Powell, Colin

WEB SITES

@grass-roots.org
http://www.grass-roots.org/

AmeriCorps
http://www.cns.gov/americorps/index.html

Habitat for Humanity International
http://www.habitat.org/

The Helping Place
http://www.helpingplace.org/

Idealist
http://www.idealist.org/

The League of Women Voters
http://www.lwv.org/

Volunteer for Our Children
http://www.child.net/volunteer.htm

Volunteer Web
http://www.epicbc.com/volunteer/

Crime

Keywords may be searched singly or in combination with other words using Boolean operators *and, or,* or *not.*

assault and battery
attorney general
ballistics
bounty hunter
bribery
burglary
Chicago Crime Commission
civil law
civil liberty
computer crimes
crime prevention
criminal history
criminal law
criminology
death penalty
domestic violence
embezzlement
family violence
felony
forensic science
forgery

fraud
homicide
incest
juvenile crime
larceny
law enforcement
Lindbergh law
loss prevention
manslaughter
Miranda rights
misdemeanor
murder
organized crime
police
prisons
prostitution
RICO Act
sexual assault
tax evasion
vandalism
violent crime
white-collar crime

ORGANIZATIONS

Canadian Criminal Justice Association (CCJA)
Center for Victims of Violent Crime (CVVC)
International Community Corrections Association (ICCA)
International Prisoners Aid Association (IPAA)
National Crime Information Center
Victims of Crime and Leniency (VOCAL)

KEY PEOPLE

Law Enforcement & Reformers
Allen, Florence Ellinwood
Bailey, F. Lee
Darrow, Clarence Seward
Dugdale, Richard Louis
Field, David Dudley
Hoover, J. Edgar
Klaas, Marc
Lindsey, Benjamin Barr
Murphy, Frank
Ness, Eliot
Pinkerton, Allan
Shang Yang
Thorndike, Edward Lee
Warren, Earl

Criminals & Criminal Defendants
Barrow, Clyde
Berkowitz, David
Boesky, Ivan
Bonney, William, "Billy the Kid"
Borden, Lizzie
Colley, William
Capone, Al
DeSalvo, Albert
Dillinger, John
Einhorn, Colin
Ferguson, Colin
Fromme, Lynette, "Squeaky"
Gacey, John Wayne
Goetz, Bernard
Gotti, John
Hauptmann, Bruno Richard
Hinckley, John W., Jr.
Hiss, Alger
Jack the Ripper
James, Jesse Woodson
Kaczynski, Theodore
Manson, Charles
McVeigh, Timothy
Menendez, Erik
Menendez, Lyle
Milken, Michael
Nichols, Terry
Parker, Bonnie
Resendez, Angel Maturino
Rolling, Danny
Sheppard, Sam
Siegel, Benjamin, "Bugsy"
Simpson, O. J.
Smith, Susan
Tadic, Dusko
Von Bulow, Claus
Williams, Wayne
Wuornos, Aileen

WEB SITES

The Crime Library
http://www.crimelibrary.com/

Federal Bureau of Investigation
http://www.fbi.gov/

Gang Land
http://www.ganglandnews.com/

National Crime Prevention Council On-Line Resource Center
http://www.ncpc.org/

National Criminal Justice Reference Service (NCJRS)
http://www.ncjrs.org/ncjhome.htm

Organized Crime: A Crime Statistics Site
http://www.crime.org/

Domestic Violence

Keywords may be searched singly or in combination with other words using Boolean operators *and, or,* or *not.*

abuse
battered women
Brady Bill (1993)
child abuse
elder abuse
family violence
firearm violence
gun control
gun regulation
homicide

intimate-partner violence
National Victimization Survey
partner abuse
post-traumatic stress syndrome
prevention
psychological abuse
sexual assault
spousal assault
stalking
Violence Against Women Act (1994)

ORGANIZATIONS

AMEND
Batterers Anonymous (BA)
Cyprus Association for the Prevention and Handling of Violence in the Family
Emerge: Counseling and Education to Stop Male Violence
Family Violence Prevention Fund (FVPF)
Injury Prevention Network
National Center for Assault Prevention
National Clearinghouse on Marital and Date Rape (NCMDR)
National Coalition Against Domestic Violence (NCADV)
National Council on Child Abuse and Family Violence (NCCAFV)
National Gay and Lesbian Domestic Violence Victims' Network
National Organization for Victim Assistance (NOVA)
National Organization of Black Law Enforcement Executives (NOBLE)
Physicians for a Violence-Free Society
Women Against Gun Violence
Women's Aid Organization (WAO)

KEY PEOPLE

Activists
Chavez, Vivian
Giggans, Patricia Occhiuzzo

Lane, Ann Reiss
Lee, Debbie
Levy, Barrie

Lytle, Alice A.
Steele, Maggie Escobedo

Criminals & Criminal Defendants
Carruth, Rae

Phillips, Lawrence
Simpson, Orenthal James (O. J.)

Victims
Adams, Cherica
Brown-Simpson, Nicole

WEB SITES

Domestic Violence Shelter Tour
http://www.dvsheltertour.org/

Family Violence Awareness Page
http://www.famvi.com/

Los Angeles Commission on Assaults Against Women (LACAAW)
http://www.lacaaw.org/home.html

National Network to End Domestic Violence
http://www.nnedv.org/

Nicole Brown Charitable Foundation
http://www.nbcf.org/

No Safe Place
http://www.pbs.org/kued/nosafeplace/

Pavnet Online: Partnerships Against Violence Network
http://www.pavnet.org/

SafetyNet Domestic Violence Resources
http://home.cybergrrl.com/dv/

Education

Keywords may be searched singly or in combination with other words using Boolean operators *and, or,* or *not.*

ACT assessment
ability grouping
academic
   adviser
   freedom
   probation
   program
   progress
   year
academy
access
accountability
accreditation
administrator
admissions
adult education
adult literacy
advanced placement
affirmative action
after school education
agricultural education
alternative assessment
alternative schools
alumni
assessment
assignment
assistantship
athletics
at-risk students
attention deficit disorder (ADD)
bachelor's degree
basal reader
benchmark

bilingual education
block schedule
board of regents
board of trustees
Brown v. Board of Education of Topeka
   (1954)
business-education partnerships
busing
campus
candidate
career
career planning
Carnegie Unit
certificate
certification
chancellor
Chapter I
charter schools
class rank
classroom
clustering
coeducation
cognition
cognitive science
collaboration
college
college school cooperation
community college
community involvement
commuters
competency-based education
compulsory education
computer-assisted instruction (CAI)

computer centers
conflict resolution
consortia
continuing education
contract
cooperative learning
core curriculum
corporal punishment
correspondence course
counseling
counselor
course load
course work
credits
critical thinking
cultural diversity
cultural literacy
curriculum
dean
dean's list
decentralization
degree
department of education
desegregation
diploma
discrimination
dissertation
distance education
distance learning
diversity
doctorate
dormitory
driver education
dropouts
dropout prevention
dyslexia
early childhood
educational
   background
   malpractice
   psychology
   reform
   tests and measurements
   trends
educationally disadvantaged
edutainment
elective courses
elementary

education
   school
emergent literacy
emotional and behavioral disorder
   (EBD)
employment
employment potential
English as a second language
enrollment
environment
equal education
equality of educational opportunity
evaluation
examination
excellence in education
exceptional children
experiential education
extracurricular
facilities
faculty
fees
fellowship
financial aid
formative evaluation
fraternity
funding
gender bias
gifted education
gifted students
Goals 2000
grade level
grade point average (GPA)
graduate
graduate school
grammar school
graphophonics
guidance
gun-free zones
Head Start
high school
higher education
home schooling
homework
honor roll
honor society
honors program
housing
humanism

ID (identification card)
illiteracy
incomplete
independent schools
independent study
individualized education plan (IEP)
Individuals with Disabilities Education
    Act (1975)
industrial arts
innovation
inservice training
instructional objective
instructional technology
integrated learning
I.Q. (intelligence quotient)
intercollegiate
Internet
internship
intramural athletics
Iowa Test of Basic Skills
job training
junior college
junior high school
juniors
language arts
latchkey children
learning disabilities
legislation
lesson plans
liberal arts
lifelong learning
literacy
magnet school
mainstreaming
master teachers
master's degree
mental age (MA)
mentoring
merit pay
middle school
migrant
migrant education
model
motivation
multicultural education
multiple intelligences
needs assessment
nondiscrimination

nontraditional
objectives
official transcript
open education
oral examination
parent-teacher cooperation
parental involvement
parochial school
partnerships
pedagogy
performance-based assessment
philosophy
phonics
physical education
placement test
policy
portfolio assessment
postbaccalaureate
postgraduate
post-secondary education
preprofessional
preschool
preservice
principal
private school
privatization
probation
professional school
professor
progressive
PTO (parent-teacher organization)
public
    education
    policy
    school
pupil
quality assessment
quarter
reading
record
referral
reform
registrar
registration
rehabilitation
religious
remedial education
remediation

report card

required courses

research

residence hall

resource allocation

retraining

retrenchment

room and board

rote memorization

sabbatical

SAT (Scholastic Aptitude Test)

SCANS Report

scholarships

school

   choice

   district

   library media center

   reform

   violence

school-based management

school choice

school-to-work transition

secondary education

semester

seminar

sexual harassment

skills

social promotion

sorority

special education

standards

student

   identification number

   teachers

   union

study abroad

study hall

summative evaluation

supplementary

support staff

teacher

certification

education

evaluation

licensing

training schools

teacher-student ratio

teaching

teaching models

team teaching

technology

telecourses

tenure

terminal degree

tests and measurements

textbook

theories of learning

thesis

Title I (Elementary and Secondary Education Act)

Title IX (Education Amendments, 1972)

Title VII (Elementary and Secondary Education Act, 1984)

transcript

transfer

transient

trimester

trustees

tuition

undergraduate

university

urban education

validation

vocational

vocational education

voucher

warehousing

Web-based instruction (WBI)

whole language

work-study

World Wide Web

year-round school calendar

ORGANIZATIONS

American Federation of Teachers

Association for Supervision and Curriculum Development (ASCD)

The College Board (TCB)

Council on International Educational Exchange (CIEE)

International Reading Association (IRA)

National Association for Bilingual Education (NABE)
National Association of Early Childhood Teacher Educators (NAECTE)
National Association of Secondary School Principals (NASSP)
National Board for Professional Teaching Standards (NBPTS)
National Coalition for Women and Girls in Education (NCWGE)
National Coalition of Title I/Chapter 1 Parents (NCTIC1P)
National Society for Experiential Education (NSEE)
U.S. Department of Education

KEY PEOPLE

Seventeenth Century
Comenius, John Amos

Nineteenth Century
Barnard, Frederick Augustus Porter
Barnard, Henry
Beecher, Catharine Esther
Bradley, Lydia Moss
Cary, Mary Shadd
Corson, Juliet
Crandall, Prudence
Froebel, Friedrich
Gallaudet, Thomas Hopkins
Granson, Milla
Greene, John Morton
Herbart, Johann Friedrich
James, William
Lyon, Mary
Mann, Horace
Smith, Sophia
Wundt, Wilhelm

Twentieth Century
Beard, Charles Austin
Bethune, Mary McCloud
Binet, Alfred
Brown, Charlotte Hawkins
Cixous, Hélène

Collins, Marva N.
Conant, James Bryant
Cooney, Joan Ganz
Crane, Julia Etta
Dewey, John
Du Bois, W.E.B. (William Edward Burghardt)
Eliot, Charles William
Escalante, Jaime
Fromm, Hanna
Haley, Margaret
Hall, G. Stanley
Hosmer, Helen M.
Judd, Charles H.
Koch, Sarah Raymond
Macy, Anne Sullivan
McDonald, Marianne
Mitchell, Grace
Montessori, Maria
Moody, Susan I.
Rice, Joseph Mayer
Scobee, June
Shalala, Donna
Sizemore, Barbara
Smith, Sally L.
Thorndike, Edward Lee (E. L.)
Washington, Booker T.

WEB SITES

21st Century Trust
http://www.21stCenturyTrust.org/

EdWeb: Exploring Technology and School Reform
http://edweb.gsn.org/

National Education Association (NEA)
http://www.nea.org/

National Institute for Literacy
http://novel.nifl.gov/

Resouces for Online Learning
http:/www.tahoeacademy.com/resources.html

Society for International Sister Schools
http://www.siss.org/

Euthanasia

Keywords may be searched singly or in combination with other words using Boolean operators *and, or,* or *not.*

active euthanasia
advance directive
AIDS (acquired immunodeficiency
    syndrome)
alert card
assisted suicide
auto-deliverance
auto-euthanasia
autonomy
bioethics
brain death
carbon monoxide
case history
case law
choice in dying
civil liberty
coma
constitutional right
constitutionality
court ruling
Cruzan v. Director, Missouri Department
    of Health (1989)
death
death with dignity
drugs
durable power of attorney
dying
end-of-life care
ethics
health care provider
health care proxy
hospice
informed consent

intervention
involuntary active euthanasia
Krischer v. McIver (1997)
law
legal authority
legal reform
legality
legalization
legislation
lethal drugs
lethal injection
life-sustaining treatment
life-threatening illness
litigation
living death
living will
medical
    battery
    futility
    history
    power of attorney
Medicare
medicide
Mercitron
mercy killing
moral issues
multiple sclerosis
murder
natural death
Hippocratic Oath
palliative care
passive euthanasia
patient autonomy

Patient Self-Determination Act
patient's rights
persistent vegetative state (PVS)
physician-assisted suicide
power of attorney
President's Commission for the Study
       of Ethical Problems in Medicine
       and Biomedical and Behavioral
       Research (1983)
pro-choice
Project on Death in America
pro-life
proxy
proxy directive
public policy

quality of life
rational suicide
right to refuse treatment
right-to-die
suicide
   clause
   machine
terminal care
terminal illness
termination of life
Vacco v. Quill (1997)
viatical settlement
voluntary
voluntary active euthanasia
Washington v. Glucksberg (1997)

ORGANIZATIONS

American Life League (ALL)
Americans for Death with Dignity (ADD)
Americans United for Life (AUL)
Center for the Rights of the Terminally Ill (CRTI)
Citizens United Resisting Euthanasia (CURE)
Compassion in Dying Federation (CID)
Human Life Foundation (HLF)
International Anti-Euthanasia Task Force (IAETF)
National Right to Life Committee (NRLC)
Protect Life in All Nations (PLAN)
U.S. Supreme Court
University Faculty for Life (UFL)
Value of Life Committee (VOLCOM)
Women Exploited by Abortion (WEBA)
World Federation of Right to Die Societies

KEY PEOPLE

Proponents
Bastable, Austin
Humphry, Derek
Kevorkian, Jack
Little, Sheila
Seguin, Marilynne
Other Figures
Bland, Anthony

Bouvia, Elizabeth
Cruzan, Nancy
Kluge, Eike-Henner
Kuhse, Helga
McLean, Sheila
Quill, Timothy
Quinlan, Karen Ann
Rodriguez, Sue

WEB SITES

Center to Improve Care of the Dying
http://www.gwu.edu/~cicd/

Choice in Dying
http://www.choices.org/

DeathNET
http://www.rights.org/deathnet/

ERGO!: Euthanasia Research and Guidance Organization
http://www.rights.org/~deathnet/ergo.html

FindLaw: Internet Legal Resources
http://www.findlaw.com/

Hemlock Society USA
http://www.hemlock.org/

Not Dead Yet!
http://acils.com/NotDeadYet/

Gambling

Keywords may be searched singly or in combination with other words using Boolean operators *and*, *or*, or *not*.

addiction
asset forfeiture
Atlantic City, NJ
baccarat
bankroll
betting
betting establishment
blackjack
bookie
cards
casino
casino advantage
chalk
chips
coins
commercial gambler
corruption
crime
debt
drugs
electronic device
financial advantage
front money
gambling
   device
   establishment
   house
   investigation
   place
game of chance
greyhound races
hole card
horses

illegal gambling
income
investigation
Las Vegas, NV
legalized gambling
loan shark
loss
lottery
mechanical device
money
money laundering
money line
narcotics
Native Americans
odds
off-the-board
one-armed bandit
organized crimes influence
pari-mutuel
parlay
parlor
poker
progressive slots
promoter
racing
racketeering
raids
regulation
roulette
roulette wheel
season
slot machine
sports

sports book   tribal gaming
sports bookmaking   underage
team   Vicksburg, MS
token   vigorish
track   wager

ORGANIZATIONS

Bookmakers' Association
British Casino Association
Casino and Theme Party Operators Association
Center for Public Integrity
Council on Compulsive Gambling of New Jersey (CCGNJ)
Gambling Chip Collectors Association (GCCA)
Harness Tracks of America (HTA)
National Association of Bookmakers
National Association of Off-Track Betting (NAOTB)
National Council on Problem Gambling (NCPG)
National Indian Gaming Association (NIGA)
North American Gaming Regulators Association (NAGRA)
Woman's Christian Temperance Union (WCTU)

WEB SITES

American Wagering
http://www.americanwagering.com/

Atlantic City Casino Dealers Association
http://www.casino-dealers.com/atlanticcity/

Gamblers Anonymous (GA)
http://www.gamblersanonymous.org/

Las Vegas Convention and Visitors Authority
http://www.lasvegas24hours.com/

North American Training Institute
http://www.nati.org/

Gun Control

Keywords may be searched singly or in combination with other words using Boolean operators *and, or,* or *not.*

access
AK-47
ammunition
APIT (armor-piercing-incendi-
    ary-tracer)
armor-piercing ammunition
arms trade
artillery
assault rifle
assault weapon
automatic pistol
automatic weapons
ballistics
bayonet
black market
black powder
Brady Bill (1993)
bullet drop
bulletproof vest
caliber
carbine
Colt AR-15
Columbine High School massacre
    (1999)
concealed weapon
confiscation
crime
death
debate
derringer
expanding bullet
exploding bullet
firearm

freedom
gun control
Gun Control Act (1968)
gun exchange program
gun lock
gun safe
Gun-Free Schools Act (1994)
gunnery
gunpowder
guns
hand cannon
handgun
hollow-point bullet
hunting
injury
intent to commit murder
law
law enforcement
lead shot
legislation
lethal
license
machine gun
magazine
magnum
matchlock
metal detectors
metal jacket
military
military rifle
militia
murder
muzzle loader

muzzle velocity
outlaw
owner
ownership
paramilitary
permit
pistol
possession
primary market
propellant
protection
purchase
regulation
repeating weapon
responsibility
restriction
revolver
rifles
rifling
safety
sawed-off shotgun

Second Amendment, Constitution of
    the United States
secondary market
security
semiautomatic
shock
shotgun
small arms
stockpile
submachine gun
target shooting
trapshooting
trigger
trigger lock
use
UZI
velocity
violence
Violent Crime Control and Law En-
    forcement Act (1994)
waiting period
weapon

ORGANIZATIONS

American Custom Gunmakers Guild (ACGG)
Bureau of Alcohol, Tobacco, and Firearms (BATF)
Center for Studies in Criminal Justice (CSCJ)
Center to Prevent Handgun Violence (CPHV)
Citizens Committee for the Right to Keep and Bear Arms (CCRKBA)
Coalition to Stop Gun Violence (CSGV)
Educational Fund to End Handgun Violence (EFEHV)
Gun Owners Action Committee (GOAC)
Gun Owners Incorporated (GOI)
Gun Trade Association
Handgun Control, Inc. (HCI)
National Pistol Association
National Rifle Association of America (NRA)
National Shooting Sports Foundation (NSSF)
Second Amendment Foundation (SAF)
Violence Policy Center (VPC)

WEB SITES

Arms Rights and Liberty Information on the Internet
http://rkba.org/

BradyBill.com
http://www.bradybill.com/

Coalition to Stop Gun Violence
http://www.gunfree.org/

Impact Evaluation of the Public Safety and Recreational Firearms Use Protection
Act of 1994
http://www.urban.org/crime/aw/awfinal1.htm

National Rifle Association of America (NRA)
http://www.nra.org/

Second Amendment Law Library
http://www.2ndLawLib.org/

Hate Crimes

Keywords may be searched singly or in combination with other words using Boolean operators *and*, *or*, or *not*.

anti-Semitism
assault
battery
bias crimes
bigotry
black nationalism
Church Arson Prevention Act of 1996
Convention on the Elimination of All
    Forms of Racial Discrimination
    (1994)
discrimination
enforced compliance
equal rights
ethnic
gay-bashing
gender preference
harassment
Hate Crime Statistics Act of 1990
    (HCSA)
Hate Crimes Prevention Act (1999)
hatred
healing
hostility
human rights
International Covenant on Civil and
    Political Rights (1992)
intervention
intimidation
intolerance

marginalization
militia
murder
nativism
neo-Nazis
oppression
paramilitary
Patriot Movement
pluralism
prejudice
racial reconciliation
racism
rape
religion
retaliation
sexual orientation
skinheads
slander
social conscience
social structure
special rights
stereotype
subtle prejudice
supremacy
tolerance
tyranny
vandalism
verbal abuse
violence
Violence Against Women Act (1994)

ORGANIZATIONS

American Civil Liberties Union (ACLU)
American Nazi Party
Anti-Defamation League (ADL)
Center for Women Policy Studies (CWPS)
Chinese for Affirmative Action (CAA)
Citizens' Commission on Civil Rights (CCCR)
Coalition for Human Immigrants' Rights of Los Angeles
Gay Men and Lesbians Opposing Violence
Ku Klux Klan (KKK)
National Association for the Advancement of Colored People (NAACP)
National Coalition of Anti-Violence Programs
National Organization of Black Law Enforcement Executives (NOBLE)
National Task Force on Violence Against Women
Simon Wiesenthal Center
White Aryan Resistance

KEY PEOPLE

Activists & Victims
Dees, Morris
Denny, Reginald
King, Rodney
Levin, Joseph

Ly, Thien Minh
Rosenbaum, Yankel
Shepard, Matthew
VanVelkinburgh, Jeannie
Woodruff, Burrton

WEB SITES

FBI Hate Crimes Report
http://www.fbi.gov/ucr/hatecm.htm

Leadership Conference on Civil Rights/Leadership Conference Education Fund
http://civilrights.org/

Southern Poverty Law Center
http://www.splcenter.org/

SPLC: List of Hate Groups
http://www.splcenter.org/intelligenceproject/

Stop the Hate
http://www.stopthehate.org/

Homelessness

Keywords may be searched singly or in combination with other words using Boolean operators *and*, *or*, or *not*.

abandonment
abuse
Access to Community Care and Effective Services and Support (ACCESS)
addiction
Adult Education for the Homeless
affordable housing
aging
AIDS
alcoholism
anxiety
assistance
at risk
barriers
battered
chemical dependency
child care
childhood
children
chronic unemployment
chronically homeless
civil liberty
condemned housing
continuum of care
day laborer
deindustrialization
deinstitutionalization
demographic
depression
disability
dispossessed
domestic violence
drugs

economically disadvantaged
education
Education of Homeless Children and Youth
elderly
Emergency Food and Shelter Program
emergency relief
emergency shelter
emotional support
employment
encampment
episodically homeless
eviction
fair market rent (FMR)
families
farmworker
finances
financial counseling
food
foreclosure
full-time employment
gender
Great Depression
health care
health services
high rent burden
homeless
   children
   family
   individual
Homeless Persons' Survival Act (1986)
Homeless Veterans Reintegration Project

homelessness
housing
   assistance
   crisis
   needs
Housing Opportunities for Persons
    with AIDS (HOPWA)
housing shortage
HUD Homeless Assistance
human rights
hunger
immigrants
independence
inebriation
inequality
inhumanity
institutional poverty
institutionalization
invisible population
isolation
job placement
job training
Job Training for the Homeless
joblessness
jobs
learned helplessness
legislation
livelihood
living wage
low income
marginally homeless
men
mental illness
migrants
military base reuse
minimum wage
minorities
National Alliance to End Homelessness
natural disaster
nutrition
overcrowding
panhandling
pauper
permanent address
permanent housing
person with AIDS (PWA)
placement
plasma

post-traumatic stress disorder
poverty
poverty-level wages
primary health care
Projects for Assistance in Transition
    from Homelessness (PATH)
public policy
recession
recycler
redevelopment
rehabilitation
rental housing
residency
resources
runaways
rural homelessness
safe haven
safety
schooling
security
self-esteem
self-help
service agency
shelters
single
   adults
   mother
   room occupancy (SRO) housing
   women
situational poverty
skills
slums
social inequality
social order
society
solicitation
Stewart B. McKinney Homeless Assis-
    tance Act (1987)
stratification
street people
substance abuse
substandard housing
suitable housing
support services
survival sex
temporary living
temporary residence
theft

traditionally homeless
transitional housing
underemployment
unemployability
unemployment
urban homeless
veterans
vulnerability

wages
War on Poverty
welfare recipient
welfare reform
women
work experience
workforce
youth

ORGANIZATIONS

Better Boys Foundation (BBF)
Christian Relief Services
Defense for Children International—United States of America (DCI-USA)
Federal Emergency Management Agency (FEMA)
Interagency Council on the Homeless
International Child Welfare Organization (ICWO)
International Concerns for Children (ICCC)
National Association for Black Veterans (NABV)
National Law Center on Homelessness and Poverty (NLCHP)
National Network for Youth
National Resource Center on Homelessness and Mental Illness (NRCHMI)
National Student Campaign Against Hunger and Homelessness (NSCAHH)
Open Heart World Mission (OHWM)
Students Together Ending Poverty (STEP)
Travelers Aid International (TAI)

KEY PEOPLE

Activists and Legislators
Baker, Susan G.
Fuchs, Ester
Gore, Albert
Hombs, Mary Ellen
Lachenmeyer, Charles
Lachenmeyer, Nathaniel

McAllister, William
McKinney, Stewart B.
Roberts, Elizabeth Boyle
Roman, Nan
Steinbeck, John
Vila, Bob

WEB SITES

Emergency Housing Consortium (EHC)
http://www.homelessness.com/

Family Life Support Center
http://www.bcn.net/home/flsc/public_html/

Habitat for Humanity International
http://www.habitat.org/

National Coalition for the Homeless (NCH)
http://nch.ari.net/

U.S. Department of Health and Human Services (HHS): Homelessness
http://aspe.os.dhhs.gov/progsys/homeless/

U.S. Department of Housing and Urban Development (HUD)
http://www.hud.gov/

Homosexuality

Keywords may be searched singly or in combination with other words using Boolean operators *and*, *or*, or *not*.

activists
adoption
AIDS (acquired immunodeficiency
    syndrome)
AIDS Quilt
antigay bias
antihomosexual
anxiety
Aphrodite Urania
Baker v. State of Vermont (1999)
behavior
biology
bisexual
characteristics
circuit
civil rights
civil union
closet
come out
condemnation
cross-gender
culture
Defense of Marriage Act (DOMA, 1996)
discrimination
diversity
don't ask, don't tell
drag
dyke
epistemology
family
fear
freedom
gay

activists
community
men
Pride
rights
Rights movement
gender
gender identity
genetic
harassment
hermaphrodite
heterosexist
heterosexual
heterosexual privilege
HIV
homoerotic
homonegativism
homophobe
homophobia
homosexual marriage
homosexual panic
identity
intolerance
invisibility
legal protection
lesbian
lifestyle
long-term relationship
lover
marriage
military
minoritization
moral codes

morality
Names Project
oppression
outing
partner
persecution
person with AIDS (PWA)
pink triangle
prejudice
privacy
public expression
queer
   -baiting
   feminism
rainbow

rainbow flag
same sex
same-sex partner
San Francisco Gay Freedom Parade
sapphism
sexual
   orientation
   preference
   relationship
significant other
sodomy
stereotypes
Stonewall Riot (1969)
tolerance
transgender
values

ORGANIZATIONS

Center for Lesbian and Gay Studies (CLAGS)
Dignity/USA
Gay and Lesbian Parents Coalition International (GLPCI)
Gay Liberation Front (GLF)
Gaylactic Network (GN)
Homosexual Information Center (HIC)
Homosexuals Anonymous Fellowship Services (HAFS)
Johns Committee
Love in Action
Mattachine Society
National Association of Research and Therapy of Homosexuality (NARTH)
National Federation of Parents and Friends of Gays (NF/PFOG)
National Gay and Lesbian Domestic Violence Victims' Network
National Gay and Lesbian Task Force (NGLTF)
National Gay Youth Network (NGYN)
Parents, Families, and Friends of Lesbians and Gays (PFLAG)
Queer Nation

KEY PEOPLE

Activists, Researchers, & Public Figures
Bryant, Anita
DeGeneres, Ellen
Finkelstein, Arthur J.
Freud, Sigmund

John, Elton
Kinsey, Alfred Charles
Navratilova, Martina
Stryker, Jeff
Watney, Simon

WEB SITES

AIDS Coalition to Unleash Power: ACT UP/Golden Gate
http://www.actupgg.org/

Gay and Lesbian Activists Alliance
http://www.glaa.org/

Gay and Lesbian Advocates and Defenders (GLAD)
http://www.glad.org/

New York City Lesbian & Gay Community Services Center
http://www.gaycenter.org/

Out of the Past
http://www.pbs.org/outofthepast/

PlanetOut
http://www.planetout.com/

Human Rights

Keywords may be searched singly or in combination with other words using Boolean operators *and, or,* or *not.*

abolition
acculturation
adjudication
affirmative action
asylum
brotherhood
censure
children's rights
citizenship
civil
   law
   liberties
   rights
codification
commission
constitution
constitutional law
convention
country
covenant
cultural
   identity
   rights
   survival
declaration
democracy
deprivation
discrimination
dispute resolution
domestic law
domination
economic development
elections

employment discrimination
empowerment
equal
   pay
   rights
   treatment
equality
ethnic conflict
ethnicity
expression
fair and impartial trial
family
federalism
foundation
freedom
   from fear
   from religion
   of
      conscience
      expression
      information
      religion
      speech
global perspective
government
grievance procedures
health
human rights commission
Human Rights Day
human rights violations
ideology
inalienable rights
independence

individual belief
individual rights
intellectual freedom
international
    bill of rights
    community
    covenant
    crimes
    human rights law
    law
interpersonal mistreatment
intolerance
justice
labor relations
language
laws
legal pluralism
libel
liberty
litigation
mankind
media
moral suasion
national origin
nondiscrimination
oppression
parental rights
persecution
personal liberty
political
    power
    rights
    status
presumption of innocence
principle
privacy
property
protection
race

regime
relativism
religion
religious
    association
    freedom
    rights
remedy
remuneration
representation
resolution
respect
rule of law
ruling class
search and seizure
security
security of person
self-determination
separation of powers
servitude
sexual harassment
sexual orientation
slander
slavery
social
    development
    progress
    protection
sovereignty
standard of living
statutes
student rights
suffrage
telecommunications
tolerance
treaty
Universal Declaration of Human
    Rights (1948)
universalism
values

ORGANIZATIONS

Alliance for Cultural Democracy (ACD)
American Civil Liberties Union (ACLU)
Amnesty International of the U.S.A. (AIUSA)
Anne Frank Center U.S.A. (AFCUSA)
Center for Constitutional Rights (CCR)
Central American Refugee Center (CARECEN)
Congressional Human Rights Caucus (CHRC)

Council on Hemispheric Affairs (COHA)
Global Fund for Women
Human Rights Advocates International (HRAI)
Human Rights Commission (HRC)
Institute for Justice
Inter-American Commission on Human Rights (IACHR)
International League for Human Rights (ILHR)
Operation PUSH
Panamerican/PanAfrican Association (PPA)
Parents Rights Organization (PRO)
People for Life (PFL)
United Nations (UN)
Unrepresented Nations and Peoples Organization (UNPO)
Workers' Defense League (WDL)

KEY PEOPLE

Eighteenth Century
Adams, Abigail
Franklin, Benjamin
Wollstonecraft, Mary
Woolman, John

Nineteenth Century
Anthony, Susan Brownell
Bloomer, Amelia Jenks
Cartwright, Peter
Channing, William Ellery
Child, Lydia Maria Francis
Crandall, Prudence
Fuller, Margaret
Grimke Angelina
Grimke, Sarah
Howe, Julia Ward
Lovejoy, Elijah Parish
Mott, Lucretia Coffin
Parker, Theodore
Phillips, Wendell
Stanton, Elizabeth Cady
Stone, Lucy
Thoreau, Henry David
Truth, Sojourner (Isabella van
      Wagener)

Tubman, Harriet
Twentieth Century
Addams, Jane
Beard, Charles Austin
Beard, Mary Ritter
Carter, Rosalynn Smith
Catt, Carrie Chapman
Friedan, Betty Naomi
Gilman, Charlotte Perkins
Hamer, Fannie Lou
Havel, Vaclav
Menchú, Rigoberta
Neruda, Pablo
Parks, Rosa Louise
Paul, Alice
Romero, Oscar Arnulfo
Roosevelt, Eleanor
Sakharov, Andrei
Sanger, Margaret
Scott, Francis Reginald
Terrell, Mary Church
Wallenberg, Raoul
Wells-Barnett, Ida Bell
White, Walter Francis
Wiesel, Elie

WEB SITES

Amnesty International
http://www.amnesty.org/

Human Rights Net
http://www.human-rights.net/

Human Rights Watch
http://www.hrw.org/

United Nations High Commissioner for Human Rights
http://www.unhchr.ch/

University of Minnesota Human Rights Library
http://www1.umn.edu/humanrts/

Hunger

Keywords may be searched singly or in combination with other words using Boolean operators *and, or,* or *not.*

agriculture
anemia
atherosclerosis
balanced diet
beriberi
birth
breakfast programs
calories
congenital
craving
death
deficiency
disease
disorder
disposable income
eating behavior
education
emergency food supply
empowerment
epidemic
excess
famine
food
   insecurity
   intake
   production
   security
   shortage
   supply
global
growth
growth pattern
health

height
household
human development
hypertension
impairment
indicators
infant mortality
kwashiorkor
linear growth
low birth weight
lunch programs
malnourishment
malnutrition
marasmus
mental development
mental health
moral imperative
mortality
natural disaster
nutrient
nutrient intake
nutrition
nutrition-related disorder
obesity
osteoporosis
overnutrition
pellagra
physiology
population growth
poverty
pregnancy
prenatal
protein deprivation

rickets
scurvy
shortage
socioeconomic
specific deficiency
standard of living
starvation
stunting

survival
symptoms
Third World
tissue wasting
undernutrition
World Food Day
World Food Survey
xerophthalmia

ORGANIZATIONS

Alliance for Sustainability
American Institute of Nutrition
American Society for Clinical Nutrition
Bread for the World (BFW)
Committee on World Food Security (CWFS)
Food and Agriculture Organization (FAO)
Food Research and Action Center (FRAC)
Foodbanking, Inc. (FI)
Freedom from Hunger
Interfaith Hunger Appeal (IHA)
National Student Campaign Against Hunger and Homelessness (NSCAHH)
Students Together Ending Poverty (STEP)
U.S. National Committee for World Food Day (USNCWFD)
U.S.A. Harvest (USAH)

KEY PEOPLE

Brandt, Willy
de Cuéllar, Javier Pérez
Holmes, Joan

Juliá, Raúl
Kostmayer, Peter
Michaud, Jerry

WEB SITES

Forgotten Harvest
http://www.forgottenharvest.org/

The Hunger Project
http://www.thp.org/

HungerWeb
http://www.brown.edu/Departments/World_Hunger_Program/

International Food Security Treaty
http://www.treaty.org/

The State of the World's Children 2000
http://www.unicef.org/sowc00/

Immigration & Emigration

Keywords may be searched singly or in combination with other words using Boolean operators *and*, *or*, or *not*.

academic training
adjudication
adjustment of status
admission
admission number
affidavit
affidavit of support
alien
application for naturalization
arrival-departure record
asylum
authorization
Basic Naturalization Act (1906)
beneficiary
birth
border
border patrol
brain drain
business
certificate of citizenship
change of status
citizen
citizen of the United States
citizenship
client
consulate
country quota
Cuba
dependent
deportation
detainee
diplomat
disqualification

Diversity Immigrant Visa Program
Diversity Lottery
domicile
duration of status
education
Ellis Island
employee
employer
employment
entry
entry without inspection (EWI)
exclusion
exit visa
expulsion
family
female genital mutilation
fiancée visa
foreign
   birth
   national
   policy green card (INS Form I-551)
hardship
hearing
home-residence requirement
identification
identification number
illegal
illegal entry
immigrant
immigrant visa
immigration
   inspectors
   law

official
record
Immigration and Naturalization Act
   Immigration Reform and Control
      Act (1986)
inspection
intending immigrant
intent
international relations
labor certificate
land settlement
law enforcement
legal permanent resident
legal resident
mail-order bride
marriage
migrants
migration patterns
minimum income requirement
moral character
multiple-entry visa
national
national interest waiver (NIW)
native
naturalization
nonimmigrant
nonimmigrant visa
notarization
oath of allegiance
occupation
parentage
parole
passport
permanent resident
persecution
petitioner
place of residence

police
political asylum
population distribution
population trends
port of entry
poverty income level
practical training
preference
primary residence
priority date
proceeding
profession
proof of registry
quota
refugees
regulation
removal
removal proceeding
residency
seven-year rule
single-entry visa
smuggler
snakehead
sponsor
spouse
status
student
student visa
support
transfer
treaty investor visa
undocumented immigrants
U.S. citizen
visa
Visa Bulletin
visitor visa
waiver

ORGANIZATIONS

American Council on International Personnel (ACIP)
American Immigration Lawyers Association (AILA)
Center for Migration Studies of New York (CMS)
Coordinating Committee for Ellis Island (CCEI)
Council on Hemispheric Affairs (COHA)
Human Rights Campaign (HRC)
Human Rights Documentation Exchange
Immigration and Refugee Services of America (IRSA)
Immigration History Society (IHS)
Lutheran Immigration and Refugee Service (LIRS)

National Council of Agricultural Employers (NCAE)
National Immigration Project of the National Lawyers Guild (NIP/NLG)
New York Association for New Americans (NYANA)
Population Resource Center (PRC)
Research Foundation for Jewish Immigration (RFJI)
U.S. Catholic Conference/Migration and Refugee Services
U.S. Committee for Refugees (USCR)
U.S. Department of Labor
U.S. Department of State
Working Group on Refugee Resettlement (WGRR)

KEY PEOPLE

Activists & Legislators
Barton, Edmund
Burlingame, Anson
Caminetti, Anthony J.
Handlin, Oscar
Harding, Warren G.
Hoover, J. Edgar
Kenny, Elizabeth

McNary, Gene
Meissner, Doris
Owen, William D.
Ross, Edward Alsworth

Others
Castro, Fidel
Gonzalez, Elian

WEB SITES

American Immigration Center
http://www.us-immigration.com/

Immigration Home Page
http://www.lawcom.com/immigration/

U.S. Citizenship Study Pages
http://www.uscitizenship.org/

U.S. Immigration Handbook
http://www.americanlaw.com/info.html

U.S. Immigration and Naturalization Service (INS)
http://www.ins.usdoj.gov/

Juvenile Delinquency

Keywords may be searched singly or in combination with other words
using Boolean operators *and*, *or*, or *not*.

adolescents
adult crimes
alcohol
alienation
antisocial
arrests
at-risk behavior
behavioral deviant
chronic criminality
community treatment
consequences
counseling
court litigation
courts
crime
crime records
criminal
   acts
   conduct
   court
   identity
   intent
   record
criminals
delinquency
delinquency causes
delinquent
   act
   behavior
   identification
deterrent
deviance
discontent

dispute
drugs
early intervention
economy
education
etiology
expungement laws
family
family life
fighting
gang
gang activity
gang warfare
graffiti
group home
guns
hearing
House of Refuge, NY
incarceration
infancy defense
institutionalization
intervention
jurisdiction
juvenile
   boot camp
   court
   crime
   gang
   justice system
labeling theory
law enforcement
minor act
minority

misbehavior
nondelinquent
nonresidential community treatment
offense
parental control
parental disobedience
parenting
peer pressure
penalty
personal crimes
prevention
prison
probation
property
protection
public service
punitive
recidivism
reform
rehabilitation
residential treatment
restitution
rights
runaways

sentence
shoplifting
social
    gang
    psychology
    system
society
socioeconomic status (SES)
statutes
stealing
stereotypes
stigma
supervision
territory
treatment
truancy
unemployment
vandalism
violence
wages
weapon
youth
youth crime
youthful indiscretion

ORGANIZATIONS

American Correctional Association (ACA)
International Association for Community Development (AIDAC)
International Association of Juvenile and Family Court Magistrates (IAJFCM)
Minority Mothers Against Drugs and Gangs
Mothers Against Gangs
National Association of Police Athletic Leagues
Parents Against Gangs
Society for the Study of Male Psychology and Physiology (SSMPP)

WEB SITES

American Bar Association Juvenile Justice Center
http://www.abanet.org/crimjust/juvjus/home.html

Austin Gang Busters
http://www.austingangbusters.org/

Center on Juvenile and Criminal Justice
http://www.cjcj.org/

Gangs in Los Angeles County
http://www.streetgangs.com/

Juvenile Justice Magazine
http://www.juvenilejustice.com/

National Consortium on Alternatives for Youth at Risk
http://www.ncayar.org/

Office of Juvenile Justice and Delinquency Prevention (OJJDP)
http://ojjdp.ncjrs.org/

Peer Justice and Youth Empowerment
http://www.ncjrs.org/peerhome.htm

Street Soldiers/Omega Boys Club
http://www.street-soldiers.org/

Tookie's Corner
http://www.tookie.com/

An Urban Ethnography of Latino Street Gangs
http://www.csun.edu/~hcchs006/gang.html

Population

Keywords may be searched singly or in combination with other words using Boolean operators *and, or,* or *not.*

abortion
age
anthropology
baby boomers
birth
   control program
   -rate
boomtowns
census
check
cohort analysis
community size
composition
contraception
contraceptive
death
death rate
demography
development
disease
distribution
economy
education
emigration
employment
ethnic distribution
family planning
family size
famine
fertility
geographic distribution
geography
health

housing
human
   capital
   geography
immigration
incidence
indigenous
infant mortality rate
inhabitant
land settlement
life expectancy
limit
marriage
medicine
migration
   patterns
   rate
mortality
mortality rate
national population policy
native
occupational mobility
one-child family
overcrowding
overpopulation
parentage
place of residence
population
   census
   change
   control
   distribution
   growth

growth rate
trends
property
public policy
racial composition
racial distribution
relocation
replacement level
residential patterns
rural
rural population
settlement
size
social influences
Social Security

society
socioeconomics
standard of living
structural unemployment
survey
total fertility rate (TFR)
trend analysis
unchecked population growth
urban
urban population
urbanization
world life expectancy
world population
zero population growth

ORGANIZATIONS

Environment and Population Centre
Human Biology Association (HBA)
United Nations Statistical Office
World Service Authority (WSA)

KEY PEOPLE

Authors & Researchers
Berelson, Bernard
Carr-Saunders, Alexander Morris
East, Edward Murray

Huxley, Aldous Leonard
Malthus, Thomas Robert
Ricardo, David
Sanger, Margaret

WEB SITES

6 Billion Human Beings
http://www.popexpo.net/

Population Index
http://popindex.princeton.edu/

Population Reference Bureau
http://www.prb.org/

Sustainability of Human Progress
http://www-formal.stanford.edu/jmc/progress/index.html

U.S. Census Bureau Population Topics
http://www.census.gov/ftp/pub/population/www/

Poverty

Keywords may be searched singly or in combination with other words using Boolean operators *and*, *or*, or *not*.

Aid to Families with Dependent
    Children (AFDC)
alcoholism
annual income
assistance
benefits
child care
children
clothing
dependent
developing nations
disability
disadvantaged environment
disease
drug abuse
earned income
economic
    condition
    deprivation
    development
    disadvantaged
    insecurity
    plight
economically depressed areas
education
educational opportunity
family
feminization of poverty
food
food stamps
Great Society
group home
health services

homelessness
housing
hunger
impoverish
income
infant mortality
inflation
life expectancy
low
    income
    income group
    wages
lower class
malnutrition
mental illness
minimal level
minority
poor
population
poverty
    level
    rate
    -stricken
    threshold
programs
public assistance
public housing
recession
research
single mother
single parent
slums
social

position
Security Act (1935)
services
welfare
socioeconomic status (SES)
special needs
standard of living
starvation

Supplemental Security Income
support
underemployment
unemployment
War on Poverty
welfare
welfare recipients
women

ORGANIZATIONS

Center for Community Action of B'Nai B'rith International
Center for Urban and Regional Studies (CURS)
Child and Family Policy Center (CFPC)
Children's Defense Fund (CDF)
Concerned Care International (CCI)
End Poverty in America Society (EPIA Society)
Food for the Poor
Food Research and Action Center (FRAC)
Free Store/Food Bank (FS/FB)
Friends Outside (FO)
International Voluntary Services (IVS)
National Center for Children in Poverty (NCCP)
National Law Center on Homelessness and Poverty (NLCHP)
National Organization to Insure Survival Economics (NOISE)
National Student Campaign Against Hunger and Homelessness (NSCAHH)
Overseas Development Network (ODN)
Social Responsibilities Round Table (SRRT)
Society for the Study of Social Problems (SSSP)
U.S. Department of Health and Human Services
U.S. Department of Housing and Urban Development
Welfare Law Center
Western Center on Law and Poverty (WCLP)

KEY PEOPLE

Activists & Lawmakers
Becker, Dorothy
Clinton, Bill
Dugdale, Richard Louis

Hartley, Robert M.
Johnson, Lyndon Baines
Lowell, Josephine Shaw
Roosevelt, Franklin Delano

WEB SITES

American Bar Association Commission on Homelessness and Poverty
http://www.abanet.org/homeless/home.html

National Community Building Network
http://www.ncbn.org/

Programme for Research on Poverty Alleviation
http://www.citechco.net/grameen/poverty_research/

Salvation Army International Headquarters
http://www.salvationarmy.org/

Race Relations

Keywords may be searched singly or in combination with other words using Boolean operators *and, or,* or *not*.

achievement
affirmative action
anthropology
apartheid
biology
biracial
black
   history
   power
   -white relations
busing
civil rights
civil rights legislation
cultural
   differences
   influences
   pluralism
   traits
culture
de facto segregation
de jure segregation
desegregation
   effects
   litigation
   plan
discrimination
equal
   educational opportunity
   facilities
   opportunities
ethnic
   bias
   discrimination

   distribution
   groups
   relations
   stereotypes
ethnicity
ethnocentrism
geographic distribution
ghetto
housing
human geography
identification
incidence
indigenous populations
individual differences
integration
intermarriage
interracial relations
minority group influences
minority groups
nature-nurture controversy
neighborhood integration
physical characteristics
population distribution
population trends
racial
   attitudes
   balance
   bias
   composition
   differences
   discrimination
   distribution
   factors

identification
integration
interaction
residential patterns
reverse discrimination
school
    desegregation
    resegregation
    segregation
segregation
segregationist

selective admission
separate but equal
separatist
slavery
social differences
stereotype
tenants' rights
tokenism
transracial adoption
voluntary desegregation
whites

ORGANIZATIONS

Black Silent Majority Committee of the U.S.A. (BSMC)
Boston Theological Institute (BTI)
Coalition for Harmony of Races in the U.S. (CHORUS)
Common Destiny Alliance (CODA)
Consortium on Peace Research, Education and Development (COPRED)
Friends Peace Committee (FPC)
Human Rights and Race Relations Centre (HRRRC)
Institute of Race Relations (IRR)
National Center for Urban Ethnic Affairs (NCUEA)
South African Institute of Race Relations

WEB SITES

Anti-Defamation League
http://www.adl.org/

HateWatch
http://www.hatewatch.org/

National Association for the Advancement of Colored People (NAACP)
http://www.naacp.org/

Race Relations: Background Reports
http://www.pbs.org/newshour/bb/race_relations/race_relations.html

South African Institute of Race Relations
http://www.sairr.org.za/

Resistance Movements

Keywords may be searched singly or in combination with other words using Boolean operators *and, or,* or *not.*

absolute pacifism
aggression
arbitration
Boston Tea Party (1773)
boycott
civic strike
Civil Disobedience
civil rights movement
civilian insurrection
collective security
coup d'état
defense capacity
demonstration
disarmament
economic noncooperation
economic sanctions
embargo
general strike
guerrilla warfare
human dignity
ideology
invasion
just war
justice
mediation
military

moral
  objectives
  persuasion
  protest
morality
mutiny
nonviolence
nonviolent action
nonviolent resistance
pacifism
passive resistance
protests
relative pacifism
repudiation
restriction
sanctions
satyagraha
sit-in
social responsibility
social structure
strike
subversion
suspension
transarmament
uprising
violence
work stoppage

ORGANIZATIONS

Association of Antifascists and Victims of Nazism in Israel
Federal Austrian Organisation of Resistance Fighters and Victims of Fascism
    (FAORFVF)
Free French

Free the Eagle (FTE)
Front de l'Independance (FI)
Groundwork for a Just World (GW)
Hungarian Federation of Resisters and Antifascists (HFRAF)
Movement Against Racism and for Friendship Between Peoples
Permanent Court of Arbitration
Sons of Liberty
United Nations (UN)
War Resisters' International (WRI)

KEY PEOPLE

Eighteenth Century
Adams, Samuel
Dickinson, John

Nineteenth Century
Crazy Horse
Douglass, Frederick
Garrison, William Lloyd
Hofer, Andreas
Phillips, Wendell
Red Cloud
Sitting Bull (Tatanka Yotanka)
Thoreau, Henry David
Tubman, Harriet

Twentieth Century
Aragon, Louis
Bonhoeffer, Dietrich
Calvino, Italo
Cartier-Bresson, Henri
de Gasperi, Alcide

de Gaulle, Charles
Dimitrov, Georgi M.
Doisneau, Robert
Gandhi, Mohandas K.
King, Martin Luther, Jr.
Levi, Primo
Malraux, André
Mandela, Nelson R.
Mandela, Winnie
Mannerheim, Carl Gustaf Emil
Mitterrand, François Maurice
Nehru, Jawaharlal
Pavese, Cesare
Pompidou, Georges
Sartre, Jean-Paul
Tito, Josip Broz
Weil, Simone
Zhivkov, Todor

WEB SITES

Afrikaner Weerstandsbeweging
http://www.lantic.co.za/~awb/

Kosovo and Metohia Web Site
http://www.kosovo.com/

National Movement of Iranian Resistance
http://www.netlink.co.uk/users/impact/namir/namirm.html

National Resistance Movements
http://www.webcom.com/hrin/resist.html

Tibet Online
http://www.tibet.org/

Sexual Harassment

Keywords may be searched singly or in combination with other words using Boolean operators *and*, *or*, or *not*.

age
Antioch code
antisocial behavior
appearance
assault
awareness
complaint
conduct
education
emotional abuse
employment
environment
favoritism
fear
Gebser v. Lago Vista Independent School District (1998)
gestures
graffiti
grievance procedure
hostile environment
intimidation
job
physical contact
prevention
promotion

quid pro quo
raise
rape
resolution
same-sex harrassment
sex
sex discrimination
sexual
   abuse
   activity
   advance
   conduct
   favors
   harassment policy
   innuendo
sexuality
sexually explicit materials
suggestive comments
Title VII of the Civil Rights Act of 1964
Title IX of the Education Amendments of 1972
touching
unwanted sexual conduct
verbal abuse
warning signals
workplace

ORGANIZATIONS

Canadian Association Against Sexual Harassment in Higher Education (CAASHHE)
Greek League for Women's Rights
Labor Education and Research Project (LERP)
National Coalition of Free Men (NCFM)

National Council for Research on Women (NCRW)
New Zealand Educational Institute (NZEI)—Women's Network
Society's League Against Molestation (SLAM)
Women's Alliance for Job Equity (WAJE)

WEB SITES

Harassment Hotline
http://www.end-harassment.com/

Sexual Harassment in the Workplace
http://www.employer-employee.com/sexhar1.htm

Sexual Harassment: It's Not Academic
http://www.ed.gov/offices/OCR/ocrshpam.html

Sexual Harassment Resources
http://www.feminist.org/911/harass.html

Women's Rights at Work
http://www.citizenactionny.org/wrw_dir/index.html

Sociology

Keywords may be searched singly or in combination with other words using Boolean operators *and, or,* or *not*.

aging
alienation
anomie
anthropology
archaeology
area studies
authoritarianism
bureaucracy
caregiver
caseworker
Chicago School of Thought
child caregiver
collective conscience
collective forgetting
collective remembering
community development
community health
counseling
counselor
crime
criminology
critical theory
cross-cultural study
cult
culture and social structure
customs
data
data analysis
death
demography
determinism
deviance
donor

dramaturgy
dying
economics
education
education research
educational sociology
egocentrism
elitism
employment
environmental interactions
equality
estrangement
ethics
ethnic group
ethnicity
ethnography
ethnology
ethnomethodology
ethnopicture
evaluation research
evolution
family
fieldwork
folkways
functionalism
geist
gender
generation
geography
gerontology
globalization
group interaction
Hegelian philosophy

ORGANIZATIONS

American Society for the Defense of Tradition, Family and Property (TFP)
American Studies Association (ASA)
Association for Humanist Sociology (AHS)
Association for the Sociology of Religion (ASR)
Association of Social and Behavioral Scientists (ASBS)
British Sociological Association (BSA)
Committee on the Status of Women in Sociology (CSWS)
European Sociological Association
International Association for Cross-Cultural Communication
International Association of Buddhist Studies (IABS)
International Association of Family Sociology (IAFS)
International Association of French Language Sociologists (AISLF)
International Organization for the Study of Group Tensions (IOSGT)
International Political Science Association (IPSA)
International Rural Sociology Association (IRSA)
International Sociological Association (ISA)
National Council for the Social Studies (NCSS)
National Opinion Research Center
Society for Social Studies of Science (4S)
Sociological Practice Association (SPA)
Sociological Research Association (SRA)
Sociologists for Women in Society (SWS)
The Independent Institute (TII)
Western Social Science Association (WSSA)

KEY PEOPLE

Seventeenth Century
Hobbes, Thomas
Locke, John

Eighteenth Century
Hume, David
Kant, Immanuel
Paine, Thomas
Rousseau, Jean Jacques
Smith, Adam
Wollstonecraft, Mary

Nineteenth Century
Bentham, Jeremy
Darwin, Charles Robert
Hegel, Georg Wilhelm Friedrich
Malthus, Thomas Robert
Mandeville, Bernard
Saint-Simon, Claude

Twentieth Century
Addams, Jane
Benedict, Ruth Fulton
Boas, Franz
Bourdieu, Pierre
Bryson, Gladys
Buber, Martin
Coleman, James Samuel
Collins, Patricia Hill
Coontz, Stephanie
Fonseca, Isabel
Freud, Sigmund
Fromm, Erich
Gallup, George Horace
Marx, Karl
Mead, George Herbert
Mead, Margaret
Merton, Robert King
Mills, C. Wright
Pavlov, Ivan Petrovich
Weber, Max

historical sociological perspective
history
human
   biology
   relationships
   rights
   services
humanitarianism
idealism
ideology
individualism
inequality
information literacy
interactionism
international relations
labeling
law
linguistics
marketing
marriage
Marxism
Marxist analysis
mass media
mass phenomena
mechanical solidarity
mental health
methodology
morality
parole officer
penology
personal autonomy
political science
politics
polls
pragmatism
probation officer
psychology
public agency
public opinion
race
radical sociology
reference group
rehabilitation
relationships
religion
religious movements
research

research methodology
rural sociology
sect
social
   action
   biology
   change
   characteristic
   clock
   condition
   data
   development
   differentiation
   gerontology
   history
   institution
   network
   order
   problem
   psychology
   research
   service agency
   stratification
   theory
   welfare
   work
society
sociocultural pattern
sociocultural system
sociolinguistics
sociology
solidarity
statistics
support groups
surveys
symbolic interactionism
thanatology
urban
   development
   social research
   sociology
values
violence
voluntary agency
welfare agency
welfare services
women's studies
work

ORGANIZATIONS

American Society for the Defense of Tradition, Family and Property (TFP)
American Studies Association (ASA)
Association for Humanist Sociology (AHS)
Association for the Sociology of Religion (ASR)
Association of Social and Behavioral Scientists (ASBS)
British Sociological Association (BSA)
Committee on the Status of Women in Sociology (CSWS)
European Sociological Association
International Association for Cross-Cultural Communication
International Association of Buddhist Studies (IABS)
International Association of Family Sociology (IAFS)
International Association of French Language Sociologists (AISLF)
International Organization for the Study of Group Tensions (IOSGT)
International Political Science Association (IPSA)
International Rural Sociology Association (IRSA)
International Sociological Association (ISA)
National Council for the Social Studies (NCSS)
National Opinion Research Center
Society for Social Studies of Science (4S)
Sociological Practice Association (SPA)
Sociological Research Association (SRA)
Sociologists for Women in Society (SWS)
The Independent Institute (TII)
Western Social Science Association (WSSA)

KEY PEOPLE

Seventeenth Century
Hobbes, Thomas
Locke, John

Eighteenth Century
Hume, David
Kant, Immanuel
Paine, Thomas
Rousseau, Jean Jacques
Smith, Adam
Wollstonecraft, Mary

Nineteenth Century
Bentham, Jeremy
Darwin, Charles Robert
Hegel, Georg Wilhelm Friedrich
Malthus, Thomas Robert
Mandeville, Bernard
Saint-Simon, Claude

Twentieth Century
Addams, Jane
Benedict, Ruth Fulton
Boas, Franz
Bourdieu, Pierre
Bryson, Gladys
Buber, Martin
Coleman, James Samuel
Collins, Patricia Hill
Coontz, Stephanie
Fonseca, Isabel
Freud, Sigmund
Fromm, Erich
Gallup, George Horace
Marx, Karl
Mead, George Herbert
Mead, Margaret
Merton, Robert King
Mills, C. Wright
Pavlov, Ivan Petrovich
Weber, Max

WEB SITES

American Sociological Association (ASA)
http://www.asanet.org/

Social Psychology Network
http://www.socialpsychology.org/

Society for Applied Sociology
http://www.appliedsoc.org/

SocioWeb
http://www.socioweb.com/~markbl/socioweb/

Sprawl Resource Guide
http://www.plannersweb.com/sprawl.html

Terrorism

Keywords may be searched singly or in combination with other words
using Boolean operators *and*, *or*, or *not*.

Act for the Prevention and Punishment
of the Crime of Hostage-Taking
(1984)
airlines
Alfred P. Murrah Federal Building,
Oklahoma City, OK
ambassadors
anarchy
antiterrorism
Antiterrorism and Effective Death
Penalty Act (1996)
assassination
attack
attorney general
bilateral agreement
biochemical
biological terrorism
biological warfare
bioterrorism
bomb
bombing
chemical warfare
civilian aircraft
consulate
counterintelligence
counterterrorism
defense
deportation
diplomacy
diplomatic personnel
diplomats
domestic terrorism
ecoterrorism

embassy
emergency programs
emergency response
evidence
explosives
extradition
extremists
fear
foreign policy
freedom fighter
funding
germ warfare
global terrorism
government
government-sponsored terrorism
guerrilla warfare
Gunpowder Plot (1605)
host government
hostage-taker
hostages
ideology
imprisonment
intelligence community
international
    Convention Against the Taking of
        Hostages (1979)
    cooperation
    crime
    terrorism
    Terrorism Information Rewards Pro-
        gram
investigation
jihad

jurisdiction
law enforcement
legislation
Middle East
Middle East peace process
military
military installation
murder
national border
nationalist
noncombatant
Olympic Park Bombing, Atlanta, GA
    (1996)
Pan American Flight 103 (1988)
paramilitary
patriot movement
peacekeeping
penalty
plot
political party
politics
premeditation
prevention
prisoner exchange
prosecution

protection
rescue
resistance
revolution
risk
rule of law
safety
sanctions
sarin gas attacks
Secretary of State
smallpox warfare
state-sponsored terrorism
subnational group
suicide bombing
terrorist
travel advisory
treaty
U.S. national
Unabomber
violence
war
water supply
weapons
World Trade Center bombing (1993)
zealot

ORGANIZATIONS

1st Special Forces Operational Detachment—Delta
Abu Nidal
Al Fatah
al-Jihad
al-Qaida
Anti-Defamation League (ADL)
Aum Supreme Truth (Aum)
Baader-Meinhoff Gang
Black September
Bureau of Diplomatic Security
Delta Force
Democratic Front for the Liberation of Palestine (DFLP)
Federal Bureau of Investigation (FBI)
Hamas
Hizballah (Party of God)
Institute for Victims of Trauma (IVT)
Institute of Strategic Studies on Terrorism
International Organization for the Study of Group Tensions (IOSGT)
International Security Council (ISC)
International Society of Political Psychology (ISPP)
Irgun

Irish Republican Army (IRA)
Islamic Jihad
Khmer Rouge
Kurdistan Workers' Party
Legions of the Underground (LoU)
Liberation Tigers of Tamil Eelam
Mujahedin-e Khalq Organization
No Greater Love (NGL)
Office of Terrorism, Narcotics and International Crime
People Against Telephone Terrorism and Harassment (PATTH)
Popular Front for the Liberation of Palestine
Red Brigades
Sendero Luminoso (Shining Path)
Sicilian Mafia
Stern Gang
United Nations (UN)
Weather Underground
Youth Institute for Peace in the Middle East (YIPME)

KEY PEOPLE

Cambodia
Pol Pot (Saloth Sar)

Cuba
Guevara, Che

France
Robespierre, Maximilien Marie Isidore

Middle East
Abdel-Rahman, Omar
bin Laden, Osama

Yousef, Ramzi Ahmed

United Kingdom
Fawkes, Guy

United States
Kaczynski, Theodore
McVeigh, Timothy J.
Nichols, Terry L.
Nordeen, William
Wilcox, Philip C., Jr.

WEB SITES

The Counter-Terrorism Page
http://www.terrorism.net/

Terrorism Research Center
http://www.terrorism.com/

Terrorists, Freedom Fighters, Propagandists, and Mercenaries on the Net
http://RVL4.ecn.purdue.edu/~cromwell/lt/terror.html

U.S. Information Agency: Response to Terrorism
http://usinfo.state.gov/topical/pol/terror/

U.S. Intelligence Community
http://www.odci.gov/ic/

U.S. State Department: Counterterrorism
http://www.state.gov/www/global/terrorism/index.html

Vegetarianism

Keywords may be searched singly or in combination with other words using Boolean operators *and*, *or*, or *not*.

allergies
amino acids
animal
    exploitation
    fat
    flesh
    food
    rights
beef
benefits
bovine growth hormone (bgh)
Buddhist
calcium
calories
cancer
cattle
cholesterol
cholesterol-free
cooking
cruelty-free
dairy
dairy products
degenerative diseases
diabetes
diet
dining
disease prevention
eggs
environmental science
ethics
factory farming
fat
fish

food
    additives
    groups
    resources
    source
    service
fortification
fortified
Frankenfoods
fruitarians
fruits
grains
health
health food
heart disease
high blood pressure
Hindu
horticulture
internal ecology
lacto-ovo-vegetarian
lacto-vegetarian
land use
leather
lifestyle
low fat
macrobiotic
meal planning
meat
meat substitute
meat-eater
menu
milk
minerals

miso
morality
nonhuman animal life
nutrients
nutrition
nutritional supplement
obesity
organic
phyoestrogen
plant
poultry
processed foods
protein
raw food
recipes
reincarnation
religion
restaurants
rice
salmonella

salt
saturated fat
semivegetarian
sodium
soy
  milk
  protein
soybeans
sprouts
stroke
supplements
tempeh
tofu
veal
vegan
veganism
vegetables
vitamin supplements
vitamins
whole grains
wool

ORGANIZATIONS

American Dietetic Association (ADA)
American Vegan Society (AVS)
Animal Alternatives
Animal Liberation (AL)
Animal Rights International (ARI)
Association of Vegetarian Dietitians and Nutrition Educators (VEGEDINE)
Beyond Beef
Coalition for Non-Violent Food (CONF)
Culture and Animals Foundation (CAF)
Farm Animal Reform Movement (FARM)
International Non-Violence and Vegetarian Society
International Vegetarian Union (IVU)
North American Vegetarian Society (NAVS)
People for the Ethical Treatment of Animals (PETA)
Student Action Corps for Animals (SACA)
United Poultry Concerns (UPC)
Vegan Action
Vegetarian Awareness Network (VEGANET)
Vegetarian Education Network (VENet)
Vegetarian Resource Group (VRG)

KEY PEOPLE

Vegetarians
Aaron, Henry Louis, "Hank"
Anthony, Susan B.
Baldwin, Alec

Bardot, Brigitte
Basinger, Kim
Bergen, Candice
Cameron, Kirk

Chavez, Cesar
Clinton, Chelsea
Dalai Lama
Darwin, Charles Robert
Gandhi, Mohandas
Fox, Michael J.
Gillespie, Dizzy
Lake, Ricki
Lang, K. D.

LaRussa, Tony
McCartney, Linda
McCartney, Paul
Pitt, Brad
Rogers, Fred
Sinclair, Upton
Singer, Isaac Bashevis
Tyler, Liv
Walker, Alice

WEB SITES

Animal Rights Resource Site
http://animalconcerns.org/

I Am a Vegetarian: Here's Why
http://arts.ucsc.edu/Derek/Home/Veg.html

EatVeg
http://www.newveg.av.org/

Veggies Unite!
http://www.vegweb.com/

World Guide to Vegetarianism
http://www.veg.org/veg/Guide/index.html

Welfare Reform

Keywords may be searched singly or in combination with other words using Boolean operators *and*, *or*, or *not*.

abandonment
absent parent
agency role
Aid to Families with Dependent
    Children (AFDC)
applicant
assistance
Balanced Budget Act
basic needs
benefits
block grant
cash
cash assistance
child
   poverty
   protection
   support
children
citizen
citizenship
Civilian Conservation Corps (CCC)
clothing
custody
cycle of dependence
dependence
dependent
derivative eligibility
disability
disability insurance
disadvantaged
earned income tax credit (EITC)
economically disadvantaged
education

elderly
eligibility
eligibility criteria
emergency housing
employment
enforcement
entitlement
family
   cap
   income
   Support Act (1988)
federal funds
Federal Welfare Reform Law (1996)
FICA taxes
financial management
food
Food Stamp Program
foster care
general welfare
government
government assistance
grant
Great Society
hardship exemption
health
health insurance
hire
homelessness
housing management
humanitarianism
illegitimacy provisions
immigrant
implementation

ORGANIZATIONS

Center for Law and Social Policy (CLASP)
Center on Budget and Policy Priorities
Congressional Black Caucus (CBC)
Economic Policy Institute
Family Resource Coalition of America (FRC)
Homes for the Homeless
Institute for Women's Policy Research
Milken Institute for Job and Capital Formation
National Association of Community Action Agencies (NACAA)
National Black Caucus of State Legislators (NBCSL)
National Coalition for the Homeless
National Council of Women's Organizations
National Immigration Law Center
Public Agenda
Rockefeller Foundation
Russell Sage Foundation
Twentieth Century Fund
Urban Institute
Women in Community Service (WICS)

WEB SITES

The Basics: Welfare Reform
http://www.tcf.org/Publications/Basics/welfare/

Idea Central: Welfare and Families
http://epn.org/ideacentral/welfare/

National Senior Citizens Law Center
http://www.nsclc.org

Social Security Administration
http://www.ssa.gov/welfare/welfare.html

Welfare Information Network
http://www.welfareinfo.org/

Welfare Reform Academy, University of Maryland
http://www.welfare-reform-academy.org/

Women's Rights

Keywords may be searched singly or in combination with other words using Boolean operators *and*, *or*, or *not*.

abolitionists
Adkins v. Children's Hospital (1923)
advancement
child custody
childbearing
civil rights
Civil Rights Act (1964)
coeducation
consciousness-raising
constitutional equality
coverture
Decade for Women (1975–1985)
decision making
Declaration of Sentiments and Resolutions
denial
disadvantage
discrimination
disenfranchise
disparity
divorce
due process
economic
   class
   parity
   status
education
employment
employment rights
empowerment
enfranchise
equal
   employment

Employment Opportunity Act (1972)
   pay
   Pay Act (1963)
   protection
   rights
   Rights Amendment (ERA)
equality
equity
females
feminism
fertility regulation
Fifteenth Amendement, Constitution of the United States (1870)
Fourteenth Amendment, Constitution of the United States (1868)
freedom
glass ceiling
health
higher education
Higher Education Act (1972)
homemaking
housewife
identity
independence
Industrial Revolution
inequity
intellect
labor
legal identity
legal rights
legislation
lifestyle

Lochner v. New York (1905)
marriage
Married Women's Property Act (1848)
ministry
Muller v. Oregon (1908)
natural rights
Nineteenth Amendment, Constitution
    of the United States (1920)
opportunity
political power
power
professional
property
property rights
protective legislation
protest
reform
religion
remuneration
representation
reproductive rights
restriction
rightful place
Ritchie v. People (1895)
Roe v. Wade (1973)
role
second wave

Seneca Falls Convention (1848)
sex
    discrimination
    fairness
social
    order
    reform
society
status
stereotypes
subordinate
suffragist
temperance
tradition
voluntary motherhood
voting rights
Voting Rights Act (1965)
wage gap
woman suffrage
women's
    education
    Equality Day (1981)
    liberation
    Strike for Equality (1970)
    studies
work hours
working women
workplace

ORGANIZATIONS

American Birth Control League
American Equal Rights Association
American Woman Suffrage Association (AWSA)
Boston Theological Institute (BTI)
Center for Women Policy Studies (CWPS)
Centre for Women's Studies and Development
Commission on the Status of Women
Committee on Women in Asian Studies (CWAS)
Equal Employment Opportunity Commission (EEOC)
Equal Rights International
International Ladies' Garment Workers' Union (ILGWU)
League of Women Voters
National American Woman Suffrage Association (NAWSA)
National Council of Women's Organizations
National Woman Suffrage Association (NWSA)
National Women's Conference Center
National Women's History Project (NWHP)
National Women's Party
National Women's Studies Association (NWSA)

Planned Parenthood Federation of America
United Nations Commission on the Status of Women (CSW)
Western Social Science Association (WSSA)
Women's Bureau of the Department of Labor
Women's Christian Temperance Union (WCTU)
Women's Equity Action League (WEAL)
Women's History Network (WHN)
Women's Studies Center (WSC)
Women's Trade Union League of New York

KEY PEOPLE

Eighteenth Century
Wollstonecraft, Mary

Nineteenth Century
Anthony, Susan B.
Blackwell, Elizabeth
Bloomer, Amelia
Gage, Matilda Joslyn
Grimké, Angelina
Grimké, Sarah
Howe, Julia Ward
Livermore, Mary A.
Miller, Elizabeth Smith
Mott, Lucretia
Rose, Ernestine
Stanton, Elizabeth Cady
Stone, Lucy
Truth, Sojourner (Isabella van
    Wagener)
Willard, Emma Hart
Wright, Fanny
Wright, Martha Coffin Pelham

Twentieth Century
Allen, Florence Ellinwood
Beard, Mary Ritter
Blackwell, Alice Stone
Blatch, Harriet Eaton Stanton
Burns, Lucy
Catt, Carrie Chapman
Friedan, Betty Naomi
Gilman, Charlotte Anna Perkins
Goldman, Emma
Griffiths, Martha Wright
Kelley, Florence
Lockwood, Belva Ann
O'Connor, Sandra Day
Paul, Alice
Peterson, Esther
Sanger, Margaret
Schlafly, Phyllis
Shaw, Anna Howard
Smeal, Eleanor
Smith, Margaret Chase
Steinem, Gloria
Wilson, Woodrow
Woodhull, Victoria

WEB SITES

Gifts of Speech: Women's Speeches from Around the World
http://gos.sbc.edu/

Guerrilla Girls
http://www.guerrillagirls.com/

The History of Women's Suffrage in America
http://www.historychannel.com/exhibits/woman/main.html

Living the Legacy: The Women's Rights Movement 1848–1998
http://www.Legacy98.org/

National Museum of Women's History
http://www.nmwh.org/

The National Organization for Women (NOW)
http://www.now.org/

National Women's Hall of Fame
http://www.greatwomen.org/index.html

National Women's History Project
http://www.nwhp.org/

United Nations Division for the Advancement of Women
http://www.un.org/womenwatch/daw/

Votes for Women: 1850–1920
http://lcweb2.loc.gov/ammem/vfwhtml/vfwhome.html

Women Leaders Online/Women Organizing for Change
http://wlo.org/

SPORTS & RECREATIONAL INTERESTS

Recreation

Keywords may be searched singly or in combination with other words using Boolean operators *and*, *or*, or *not*.

adventure sports
amusement park
aquarium
art activities
athletic field
athletics
auditorium
bicycling
billiards
boating
camping
canoeing
collecting
community recreation programs
community resources
computer games
computers
cooking
dancing
dating
day camp programs
diving
drinking
extracurricular activities
field house
fishing
gambling
games
gardening
gliding
gymnasium
hobbies
horseback riding

hospitality
hunting
leisure
leisure time
lifetime sports
mountain climbing
movies
museum
music activities
outdoor activities
outdoor recreation
outreach programs
park design
parks
parties
party
physical activities
physical recreation
planetarium
play
playground activities
playgrounds
pleasure boating
popular culture
puzzles
reading
recreation finances
recreation legislation
recreational facilities
recreational programs
recreationists
resident camp programs
reunions

road trip
rowing
sailing
school recreational programs
shopping
singing
skateboarding
skin diving
skydiving
Special Olympics
spectator sports
student unions
summer camp
surfing
swimming

television
theater
theme park
therapeutic recreation
tourism
trails
travel
trivia
underwater diving
vacation
video games
waterskiing
wilderness pursuits
wildlife management
women's athletics
zoos

ORGANIZATIONS

America Outdoors (AO)
Association of Directors of Recreation, Leisure and Tourism
International Family Recreation Association (IFRA)
International Touring Alliance (ITA)
Recreation Vehicle Industry Association (RVIA)
Society of Recreation Executives (SRE)
Special Recreation for Disabled

WEB SITES

American Hiking Society
http://www.americanhiking.org/

American Numismatic Association
http://www.money.org

American Scouting Traders Association
http://asta.scouter.org/

Concrete Canoe Project
http://www.sea.ucla.edu/asce/canoe.html

ESPN.com
http://espn.go.com/

GardenNet
http://gardennet.com/

Kinder Crafts
http://www.enchantedlearning.com/crafts/

MSN Computing Central: Computer Games Forum
http://computingcentral.msn.com/topics/computergames/

National Model Railroad Association
http://www.nmra.org/

RootsWeb Genealogical Data Cooperative
http://www.rootsweb.com/

Surflink
http://www.surflink.com/

Ultimate Rollercoaster
http://www.ultimaterollercoaster.com/

Yahooligans!
http://www.yahooligans.com/

Sports

Keywords may be searched singly or in combination with other words using Boolean operators *and, or,* or *not.*

adventure racing
amateur athletics
aquatic sports
archery
arthroscopic surgery
athlete
athletic equipment
athletic fields
athletics
Australian rules football
auto racing
badminton
baseball
basketball
baton twirling
biathlon
bicycling
billiards
biomechanics
boat racing
bobsledding
boomerang
bowling
boxing
cheerleading
clinical diagnosis
club sports
coaches
coaching
college athletics
contests
courts
cricket

croquet
cross-country
cross-country skiing
curling
cycling
diving
dog racing
dogsledding
eligibility
equestrian
exercise
exercise physiology
extracurricular activities
extramural athletics
extreme sports
fencing
field house
fields
figure skating
fishing
football
game
golf
gymnasium
gymnastics
handball
hiking
hockey
horse racing
horseback riding
injuries
inline skating
intercollegiate athletics

intramural athletics
intramural sports
jai alai
jogging
judo
karate
lacrosse
leisure
lifetime sports
locker room
luge
managers
marathon
marksmanship
martial arts
matches
medical services
motor learning
motor reaction
motorcycle racing
officiating
Olympic Games
orienteering
paddleball
paintball
parks
physical
    education
    fitness
    therapy
pitch
playground
polo
preventive medicine
professional sports
racewalking
racquet sports
racquetball
recreation
referee
rehabilitation
rodeo
roller skating

rowing
rugby
running
sailing
scuba diving
sandboarding
skateboarding
skating
skydiving
snowboarding
snowmobiling
snowskiing
soccer
softball
Special Olympics
sport history
sport psychology
sports
    medicine
    news reporting
    physiology
sportsmanship
squash
stadium
surfing
swimming
table tennis
teams
team sports
tennis
track and field
triathlon
umpire
venue
volleyball
wakeboarding
walking
water polo
waterskiing
weightlifting
windsurfing
winter sports
women's athletics
wrestling

ORGANIZATIONS

American College of Sports Medicine (ACSM)
American Council on Exercise (ACE)
American Fitness Association (AFA)

Association for the Advancement of Applied Sport Psychology
Center for Sports Sponsorship (CSS)
International Council for Health, Physical Education, Recreation, Sport, and
    Dance (ICHPERSD)
International Facility Management Association (IFMA)
International Society of Sports Psychology (ISSP)
National Association for Girls and Women in Sport (NAGWS)
National Association for Sport and Physical Education (NASPE)
National Association of Governor's Councils on Physical Fitness and Sports
National Sportscasters and Sportswriters Association (NSSA)
National Youth Sports Safety Foundation (NYSSF)
Pro Athletes Outreach (PAO)
U.S. Organization for Disabled Athletes (USODA)
U.S. Soccer Federation (USSF)

KEY PEOPLE

Baseball
Aaron, Henry Louis, "Hank"
Canseco, Jose
Clemens, Roger
Cobb, Tyrus Raymond, "Ty"
DiMaggio, Joe
Garciaparra, Nomar
Glavine, Tom
Griffey, Ken, Jr.
Guerrero, Vladimir
Henderson, Rickey
Jenkins, Geoff
Johnson, Randy
Larkin, Barry
Maddux, Greg
Mantle, Mickey
Martinez, Pedro
Mays, Willie
McGwire, Mark
Paige, Satchel
Piazza, Mike
Ripkin, Cal, Jr.
Robinson, Jackie
Rose, Pete
Ruth, George Herman, "Babe"
Ryan, Nolan
Sosa, Sammy
Thome, Jim

Basketball
Barkley, Charles
Bird, Larry
Bryant, Kobe

Carter, Vince
Chamberlain, Wilt
Duncan, Tim
Edwards, Teresa
Elliott, Sean
Erving, Julius Winfield, "Dr. J"
Ewing, Patrick
Garnett, Kevin
Hill, Grant
Holdsclaw, Chamique
Hornacek, Jeff
Iverson, Allen
Jabbar, Kareen Abdul (Lew Alcindor)
Jordan, Michael
Leslie, Lisa
Lobo, Rebecca
Majerle, Dan
Mills, Tausha
Mourning, Alonzo
O'Neal, Shaquille
Payton, Gary
Pippen, Scottie
Robinson, David
Sprewell, Latrell
Swoopes, Sheryl
Wallace, Rasheed
Williams, Jason

Boxing
Ali, Muhammad (Cassius Clay)
De La Hoya, Oscar
Duva, Lou
Futch, Eddie

Holyfield, Evander
Jones, Roy, Jr.
Lewis, Lennox
Marciano, Rocky
Tyson, Mike

Football
Brooks, Derrick
Brown, Jim
Bruce, Isaac
Bryant, Paul W., "Bear"
Carter, Cris
Elway, John
Favre, Brett
Lombardi, Vince
Manning, Peyton
McNair, Steve
Montana, Joe
Moss, Randy
Payton, Walter
Rice, Jerry
Smith, Emmitt
Warner, Kurt
Williams, Ricky
Young, Steve

Golf
Azinger, Paul
Davis, Laura
Janzen, Lee
Lopez, Nancy
Love, Davis, III
Nicklaus, Jack
Norman, Greg
O'Meara, Mark
Palmer, Arnold
Singh, Vijay
Sorenstam, Annika
Woods, Tiger

Gymnastics
Atler, Vanessa
Bondarenko, Alexei
Comaneci, Nadia
Dawes, Dominique
Ivankov, Ivan
Karolyi, Bela
Lan, Sang
McNamara, Julianne
Miller, Shannon
Moceanu, Dominique

Nemov, Aleksei
Retton, Mary Lou
Strug, Kerri
Zmeskal, Kim

Hockey
Andreychuk, Dave
Bondra, Peter
Bourque, Ray
Bure, Pavel
Fedorov, Sergei
Forsberg, Peter
Gilmour, Doug
Gretzky, Wayne
Howe, Gordie
Hull, Brett
Jagr, Jaromir
LeClair, John
Lindros, Eric
Messier, Mark
Roy, Patrick
Selanne, Teemu
Turgeon, Pierre
Yzerman, Steve

Ice Skating
Blair, Bonnie
Henie, Sonja
Kwan, Michelle
Lipinski, Tara
Slutskaya, Irina
Stojko, Elvis
Uagudin, Alexei
Yamaguchi, Kristi Tsuya

Soccer
Akers, Michelle
Beckenbauer, Franz
Diaz Arce, Raul
Hamm, Mia
Kreis, Jason
Lassiter, Roy
Pelé
Van Nistelrooy, Ruud

Swimming
Bennett, Brooke
Biondi, Matt
Caulkins, Tracy
Dolan, Tom
Evans, Janet

Gaines, Rowdy
Haislett, Nicole
Hall, Gary
Jager, Tom
Meagher, Mary T.
Moses, Ed
Munz, Diana
Otto, Kristen
Sanders, Summer
Spitz, Mark
Thompson, Jenny
Walker, Neil

Tennis
Agassi, Andre
Ashe, Arthur
Davenport, Lindsay
Evert, Chris
Gibson, Althea
Graf, Steffi
Hingis, Martina
Kafelnikov, Yevgeny
King, Billie Jean
Kournikova, Anna
McEnroe, John
Navratilova, Martina
Novotna, Jana
Pierce, Mary

Sabatini, Gabriela
Sampras, Pete
Sanchez-Vicario, Arantxa
Seles, Monica
Williams, Serena
Williams, Venus

Track and Field
Bannister, Roger
Beamon, Bob
Decker, Mary
Devers, Gail
Dwight, Tim
Johnson, Michael
Jones, Marion
Joyner, Florence Griffith
Joyner-Kersee, Jackie
Lewis, Carl
Mills, Billy
Moses, Edwin
Oerter, Al
Owens, Jesse
Powell, Mike
Prefontaine, Steve
Redmond, Derek
Rudolph, Wilma
Thorpe, Jim
Zaharias, Mildred "Babe" Didrickson

WEB SITES

Amateur Athletic Union (AAU)
http://www.aausports.org/

ESPN.com
http://espn.go.com/

Fellowship of Christian Athletes (FCA)
http://www.gospelcom.net/fca/

National Association of Sports Officials (NASO)
http://www.naso.org/

National Collegiate Athletic Association (NCAA)
http://www.ncaa.org/

National Federation of State High School Associations
http://www.nfhs.org/

United States Olympic Committee
http://www.olympic-usa.org/

Womens Sports Foundation
http://www.wsf.org.uk/

UFOs (Unidentified Flying Objects)

Keywords may be searched singly or in combination with other words using Boolean operators *and*, *or*, or *not*.

abductees
abduction
alien artifacts
alien life form (ALF)
aliens
android
Area 51
astronomical unit (AU)
black project
Blues
Carswell Air Force Base, TX
cattle mutilations
CE3 reports
close encounter of the
    first kind (CE1)
    second kind (CE2)
    third kind (CE3)
Condon Report (1969)
contact
contactee
cover-up
craft
crop circles
dark side hypothesis
daylight disk
Draconian
Drake equation
Dreamland
Durant Report
electromagnetic disturbance
ET Exposure Law (1969)
extraterrestrial
    biological entity (EBE)

hypothesis (ETH)
Fermi paradox
fireball
flying disc
flying saucer
Freedom of Information Act (FOIA)
galaxy
genetic experimentation
genetic manipulation
ghost rocket
green fireballs
Grey
hoax
hollow earth
humanoid
Hynek Classification System
identified alien craft (IAC)
identified flying object (IFO)
invasion
landing
little green men (LGM)
Los Alamos, NM
Lyran
Majestic Twelve (MJ-12)
Martians
men in black (MIB)
metaphysics
meteorite
missing time experience (MTE)
mutilation
national defense
near-death experience (NDE)
nocturnal light

observation
observatory
occult
out-of-body experience (OBE)
paranormal
parallel universe
past life recall
phenomena
Philadelphia Experiment
physical abduction
Pleiadian
Project
   Aquarius
   Blue Book
   Redlight
   Twinkle
propulsion
Psi/Bio Energy Field Extraction
radar-visuals
retrieval
Roswell Incident (1947)

sighting
Sirian
Socorro, NM
space alien
space brothers
spacecraft
space-time continuum
star warriors
Taos hum
techno/telepathic lucid dream
telepathic
time travel
travel
Tunguska Event (1908)
UFO phenomenon
ufologist
ufology
unidentified flying object (UFO)
unusual ground markings (UGM)
von Neumann machine
witness
zoo hypothesis

ORGANIZATIONS

Aerial Phenomena Research Organization (APRO)
Aetherius Society
Ancient Astronaut Society
Borderland Sciences Research Foundation (BSRF)
British UFO Research Association (BUFORA)
Center for UFO Studies (CUFOS)
Central Intelligence Agency (CIA)
Citizens Against UFO Secrecy (CAUS)
Collectors of Unusual Data—International (COUD-I)
Committee for the Scientific Investigation of Claims of the Paranormal (CSICOP)
Federal Aviation Administration (FAA)
Federal Bureau of Investigation (FBI)
The Federation
Fund for UFO Research (FUFOR)
Ground Saucer Watch (GSW)
Heaven's Gate
Institute for UFO Contactee Studies (IFUFOCS)
Inter-Galactic Spacecraft UFO Intercontinental Research and Analytic Network
International Committee for UFO Research (ICUR)
J. Allen Hynek Center for UFO Studies (CUFOS)
Jason Society
Mutual UFO Network (MUFON)
National Aeronautics and Space Administration (NASA)
National Investigations Committee on Unidentified Flying Object (NICUFO)
National Security Agency (NSA)

Project Starlight International (PSI)
Robertson Panel
Society for the Investigation of the Unexplained (SITU)
Society of Earthbound Extraterrestrials (SEE)
Stargate International
UFO Contact Center International (UFOCCI)
UFO Information Retrieval Center (UFOIRC)

KEY PEOPLE

Authors, Researchers, & Witnesses
Adamski, George
Arnold, Kenneth
Bell, Art
Bronk, Detlev
Brown, Thomas Townsend
Bullard, Thomas E.
Bush, Vannevar
Fawcett, Lawrence
Fermi, Enrico
Fort, Charles
Fowler, Raymond
Fry, Philip
Garoutté, Aileen
Greenwood, Barry
Hynek, J. Allen

Keyhoe, Donald
Klass, Philip
Lazar, Robert
Lear, John
Luca, Betty Andreasson
Newman, William
Oberg, James
Randle, Kevin
Sagan, Carl
Scully, Frank
Todd, Richard
Uvarov, Valery
Vallee, Jacques
Von Daniken, Eric
Zamora, Lonnie

WEB SITES

Alien Website
http://www.holodeck.f9.co.uk/

AREA51.NET
http://www.area51.net/

Gulf Breeze UFOs
http://www.gulfbreezeufos.com/

International Society for UFO Research
http://www.isur.com/

SETI Institute (Search for Extraterrestrial Intelligence)
http://www.seti-inst.edu/

UFOINFO
http://ufoinfo.com/

About the Authors

RANDALL M. MACDONALD is currently Collection Development Librarian for the Florida Southern College faculty and a doctoral candidate in the Instructional Technology Ph.D. program at the University of South Florida in Tampa. He is also the author of *The Internet and the School Library Media Specialist* (Greenwood, 1997).

SUSAN PRIEST MACDONALD is currently Media Specialist at Lawton Chiles Middle Academy in Lakeland, Florida, and a former media specialist at Jesse Keen Elementary School. She has worked for over twenty years in public and school libraries, specializing in on-line catalog and Internet research.